CONNECT with WORDS

GRADE 2

School Specialty Publishing

Send all inquiries to:
School Specialty Publishing
8720 Orion Place
Columbus, OH 43240-2111

ISBN 0-7696-7432-1

1 2 3 4 5 6 7 8 9 10 POH 12 11 10 09 08 07

AMERICAN
EDUCATION
PUBLISHING™

Columbus, Ohio

Table of Contents

Unit 1 5
Week 01 6
Week 02 14
Week 03 22
Review 29

Unit 2 30
Week 04 31
Week 05 39
Week 06 47
Review 54

Unit 3 55
Week 07 56
Week 08 64
Week 09 72
Review 79

Unit 4 80
Week 10 81
Week 11 89
Week 12 97
Review 104

Unit 5 105
Week 13 106
Week 14 114
Week 15 122
Review 129

Unit 6 130
Week 16 131
Week 17 139
Week 18 147
Review 154

Story Words

Directions: Read about fiction and nonfiction books. Then, look at each different type of book listed. Write **F** if the book is fiction. Write **NF** if the book is nonfiction.

There are many kinds of books. Some books have make-believe stories about princesses and dragons. Some books contain nursery rhymes, like Mother Goose. These are fiction.

Some books contain facts about space and plants. And still other books have stories about famous people in history like Abraham Lincoln. These are nonfiction.

__F__ 1. nursery rhyme

__F__ 2. fairy tale

__NF__ 3. true life story of a famous athlete

__F__ 4. Aesop's fables

__NF__ 5. dictionary entry about foxes

__NF__ 6. book about national monuments

__F__ 7. story about a talking tree

__NF__ 8. story about how a tadpole becomes a frog

__NF__ 9. story about animal habitats

__F__ 10. riddles and jokes

282

Story Words

The **main idea** tells about the whole picture.

Directions: Fill in the circle beside the sentence that tells the main idea of each picture.

1. ● She saw a shooting star.
   ○ She likes to climb hills.
   ○ She likes to stay up late.

2. ○ Skateboarding can be done anywhere.
   ○ Skateboarding is easy.
   ● Skateboarders should wear helmets.

3. ● Grandpa is a great storyteller.
   ○ Grandpa is boring.
   ○ Grandpa is funny.

4. ● Mom made me a birthday cake.
   ○ We ate ice cream.
   ○ I opened presents.

283

Clothing Words

Word Bank			
glasses	jacket	mittens	pants
skirt	slippers	sneakers	socks

Directions: Use the words in the Word Bank to complete the sentences.

1. Be sure to tie the laces of your __sneakers__ so you won't trip and fall.

2. I put on my __socks__ before I put on my shoes.

3. On a cool day, my __jacket__ keeps me warm.

4. In the winter, I wear long __pants__ to keep my legs warm.

5. A bathrobe and __slippers__ are comfortable to wear at night.

6. Mr. Jesse wears __glasses__ to read the newspaper.

7. My sister wore a pleated __skirt__ and a sweater.

8. In the winter, __mittens__ keep my hands warm.

284

Words About Landforms

Directions: Use the words in the Word Bank to solve the riddles. Then, color the pictures.

Word Bank					
lake	island	plain	river	mountain	peninsula

Color the pictures.

1. I have water on three sides. I am a __peninsula__

3. I have water all around me. I am an __island__

5. I am wet and have land all around me. I am a __lake__

2. I am long and narrow and flow through the land. I am a __river__

4. I am raised land, larger than a hill. I am a __mountain__

6. I am low and flat. I am a __plain__

285

Words About the Ocean Floor

Directions: Have you ever wondered what is under the sand on a beach? Some beaches are really layers of rocks, pebbles, shells, and sand. Follow the instructions to create your own ocean floor.

You will need:
sand
rocks
shells
pebbles
a glass jar
water

1. Put the sand, rocks, shells, and pebbles in the glass jar. Add the same amount of each material.

2. Fill the jar to the top with water.

3. Close the lid tightly!

4. Shake the jar 10 times.

5. Set the jar aside for one day.

6. Draw a picture of the jar and its contents.

Pictures will vary.

286

Words About Rocks

Directions: Go outside and gather a pile of rocks. Follow the instructions below.

Medium

Large   Small

Size
Arrange your rocks in three piles by size. Count the rocks in each pile.
Number of large rocks __Answers will vary.__
Number of medium rocks _____
Number of small rocks _____

Color
Arrange your rocks in three piles by color. Count the rocks in each pile.
Number of dark-colored rocks _____
Number of medium-colored rocks _____
Number of light-colored rocks _____
List every color you see on these rocks. _____

Feel
Arrange your rocks in three piles by feel. Count the rocks in each pile.
Number of smooth rocks _____
Number of rough rocks _____
Number of rough and smooth rocks _____

287

Shape Words

Directions: A class goes to the sandbox on the playground. They take a cylinder, a cone, a cube, and a prism.

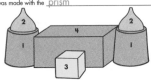

cylinder   cone   cube   prism

They pack sand in the shapes and then build structures. Look at the picture below. Use the picture to write the name of the shape the children used to make each part.

Part 1 was made with the _cylinder_

Part 2 was made with the _cone_

Part 3 was made with the _cube_

Part 4 was made with the _prism_

Create a structure of your own using the shapes at the top of the page.

288

Story Words

A story has a **setting** that tells where and when the story takes place.

Directions: Read the story. Then, answer the questions about the setting.

The Amazon jungle is a huge rain forest in South America. It is full of gigantic green trees, thick jungle vines, and many species of dangerous animals. It is very humid in the jungle.

1. What is the weather like in the Amazon jungle?
   It is humid in the jungle.

2. Where is the Amazon jungle located?
   The Amazon jungle is in South America.

3. Would it be easy to travel in the Amazon jungle? Why or why not?
   Answers will vary – suggested answer: No, it would not be easy to travel in the jungle because there are giant trees, thick vines, and dangerous animals.

4. Does it rain a lot in the Amazon jungle?
   Yes. The Amazon jungle is a rain forest.

289

Story Words

A **main idea** tells what the story is about. The **supporting details** tell more about the main idea.

A **character** is the person, animal, or object that a story is about. You cannot have a story without a character.

Directions: Read the story below. Then, answer the questions.

The cake is done. Dad takes it from the oven. Dylan and Dana want to frost the cake. "I want to use white frosting," says Dylan. "I want to use red frosting," says Dana. "We will use both your ideas," says Dad. "We will have pink frosting!"

1. Which sentence tells the main idea?

   The cake will have red frosting.

   (Pink frosting is made of red and white frosting.)

2. What is one supporting detail? _Answers will vary-suggested answer: Dad offered to use both the red and white frosting._

3. Who are two characters in the story? _Answers will vary-can include Dad, Dylan, or Dana._

290

Words About Books

A **book** has many parts. The **title** is the name of the book. The **author** is the person who wrote the book. The **illustrator** is the person who drew the pictures. The **table of contents** is located at the beginning of the book. It lists what is in the book. The **glossary** is a little dictionary in the back to help you with unfamiliar words. Books are often divided into smaller sections of information called **chapters**.

Directions: Look at one of your books. Write the parts you see below.

1. The title of my book is _Answers will vary._

2. The author is _____

3. The illustrator is _____

4. My book has a table of contents.   Yes or No

5. My book has a glossary.   Yes or No

6. My book is divided into chapters.   Yes or No

291

Clothing Words

Directions: Circle the pictures that are articles of clothing.

hat   coat   mittens   bike

duck   bird   lion   cat

ball   gloves   cap   shirt

tree   grass   bush   leaf

dress   skirt

292

Words About Animal Habitats

Directions: Read the story. Then, write each animal's name under **water** or **land** to tell where it lives.

Animals live in different **habitats**. A habitat is the place of an animal's natural home. Many animals live on land and others live in water. Most animals that live in water breathe with gills. Animals that live on land breathe with lungs.

fish	shrimp	giraffe	dog
cat	eel	whale	horse
bear	deer	shark	jellyfish

WATER
1. _fish_   4. _whale_
2. _shrimp_   5. _shark_
3. _eel_   6. _jellyfish_

LAND
1. _cat_   4. _giraffe_
2. _bear_   5. _dog_
3. _deer_   6. _horse_

293

Words About Animal Habitats

Directions: Read the story. Then, read the bird names in the Word Bank. Write each bird name under **land** or **water** to tell where it lives.

land? water?

Carlos and Joshua learned that some birds like living near land and others like living near the water. They decided to write a book about land birds and water birds, but they needed some help. They looked in the library to find out which birds live near water and which birds live near land.

Word Bank			
blue jay	cardinal	duck	goose
hummingbird	parrot	pelican	puffin
roadrunner	swan	eagle	penguin

LAND
1. blue jay
2. hummingbird
3. roadrunner
4. cardinal
5. parrot
6. eagle

WATER
1. swan
2. duck
3. pelican
4. goose
5. puffin
6. penguin

294

Words About Sand

Directions: Read about sand. Use the bold words to find and circle the words about sand in the puzzle. Look across and down. Then, color the picture.

Have you ever felt warm **sand** on a **beach**? Sand is made of weathered **rocks**. The **weathering** is caused by **rain** and wind. The rocks are broken into **fragments** and carried to the sea. **Waves** deposit the particles on the beach. Heavier rocks sink to the bottom **layer**. Lighter particles stay on top. This is what you feel under your feet!

Color the picture.

295

Shape Words

Directions: Draw a line from each word to the correct shapes.

Use a red line for circles.
Use a blue line for squares.
Use a yellow line for rectangles.
Use a green line for triangles.

Circle   Square   Triangle   Rectangle

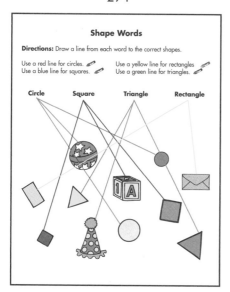

296

Story Words

A **fact** is something that can be proven. An **opinion** is a belief about something that cannot be proven.

Directions: Read about recycling. Then, follow the instructions.

What do you throw away every day? What could you do with these things? You could change an old greeting card into a new card. You could make a puppet with an old paper bag. Old buttons make great refrigerator magnets. You can plant seeds in plastic cups. Cardboard tubes make perfect rockets. So, use your imagination!

1. Write **F** next to each fact and **O** next to each opinion.

   O   Cardboard tubes are ugly.

   F   Buttons can be made into refrigerator magnets.

   F   An old greeting card can be changed into a new card.

   O   Paper-bag puppets are cute.

   F   Seeds can be planted in plastic cups.

   F   Rockets can be made from cardboard tubes.

2. What could you do with a cardboard tube?   Answers will vary.

297

Story Words

In some paragraphs, the order of the sentences is very important. **Transition words**, such as **first**, **then**, **now**, and **finally**, offer clues to help show the sequence of the sentences.

Directions: Read about how to make a snowman. Circle the transition words. Then, write the numbers 1, 2, 3, or 4 in each box to show the correct sequence.

It is fun to make a snowman. (First) find things for the snowman's eyes and nose. Dress warmly. (Then) go outdoors. Roll a big snowball. (Now) roll another to put on top of it. Roll a small snowball for the head. (Finally) put on the snowman's face.

1   2
3   4

298

Story Words

Something that is **real** could actually happen. Something that is **fantasy** is not real. It could not happen.

Examples:
   Real: Dogs can bark.
   Fantasy: Dogs can fly.

Directions: Look at the sentences. Write **real** or **fantasy** next to each one.

1. My cat can talk to me.   fantasy
2. Witches ride brooms and cast spells.   fantasy
3. Dad can mow the lawn.   real
4. I ride a magic carpet to school.   fantasy
5. I have a man-eating tree.   fantasy
6. My sandbox has toys in it.   real
7. Mom can bake chocolate chip cookies.   real
8. Mark has tomatoes and corn in his garden.   real
9. Jack grows candy and ice cream in his garden.   fantasy
10. I make my bed every day.   real
11. Write your own real sentence.   Sentences will vary.

12. Write your own fantasy sentence.   Sentences will vary.

299

Clothing Words

Directions: Read the story. Use context clues to figure out the missing words. Write a word from the Word Bank to complete each sentence. Then, answer the questions.

Word Bank

socks   scarf   sweaters   mittens

Maria bundles up. She sticks her arms through

two ___sweaters___ . She tugs three pairs

of ___socks___ over her feet. She wraps a ___scarf___

around her neck. At last, she pulls her ___mittens___ onto

her hands. Maria goes outside to play. Nobody is warmer than Maria.

1. What clue words helped you figure out sweaters?

___sticks, through, arms___

2. What clue words helped you figure out mittens?

___pulls, hands___

300

Words About Soil

Most soil is made of particles of sand, clay, rocks, or organic matter. **Organic matter** is made of dead plants and leaves.

Directions: This truck is moving loads of soil. Follow the trail. Circle the words that name things that help make soil.

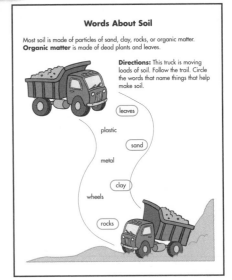

leaves
plastic
sand
metal
clay
wheels
rocks

301

Words About Soil

Directions: Read about soil and earthworms. Use the bold words to find and circle the words in the puzzle. Look across and down.

Soil that has earthworms will be rich and healthy with lots of **organic** matter. The **earthworm** is not a picky eater. It will eat anything organic, from dead leaves to banana peels. Its waste is called **compost**. Earthworms **dig**, **mix**, and **fertilize** the soil. **Plants** love this kind of soil.

```
d i m j f d u d d g
s d i g e c d c d h
g h x d r b f c o j
e e a r t h w o r m
c r y d i u n m g d
y s d v l d d p a j
s f f u i l a o n k
u n k m z b h s i f
i m l q e h l t c n
p l a n t s y j c s
```

302

Words About Gardening

Directions: Read about garden soil. Then, read each sentence. If it is a fact, write **F**. If it is an opinion, write **O**.

Before you start a garden, make sure you have good soil. It should be easy to turn. To do this, break it up with a shovel. This will allow the water to move through it. You can add old grass clippings and dead leaves to the soil to give it nutrients. If you take the time to create good soil, you will have a beautiful garden!

1. Soil smells wonderful.   O

2. Grass clippings and dead leaves are good for soil.   F

3. Good soil makes a beautiful garden.   F

4. A shovel is hard to use.   O

5. Breaking up the soil allows the water to move through it. F

303

Unit 12 Review

Directions: Write a story about an animal. Answer the questions to help you get started.

Is your story fiction or nonfiction? ___Answers will vary.___
What is the main idea of your story? _____
Where does your story take place? _____
What is the animal's habitat? _____
Does the character in your story have a name? _____

_____
Title

_____
Author

___Stories will vary.___
_____
_____
_____
_____
_____
_____
_____

304

Unit 7 155
Week 19 156
Week 20 164
Week 21 172
Review 179

Unit 8 180
Week 22 181
Week 23 189
Week 24 197
Review 204

Unit 9 205
Week 25 206
Week 26 214
Week 27 222
Review 229

Unit 10 230
Week 28 231
Week 29 239
Week 30 247
Review 254

Unit 11 255
Week 31 256
Week 32 264
Week 33 272
Review 279

Unit 12 280
Week 34 281
Week 35 289
Week 36 297
Review 304

Answer Key 305

About The Book

Connect With Words is designed to help students increase their vocabulary skills with cross-curricular, grade-appropriate words and activities.

Activity Pages
Connect With Words is divided into 36 weeks, which is the average length of the school year. Each book is broken down into three-week units with a review lesson at the conclusion of each unit. The activity pages in the book focus on important words from different subject areas.

Keywords
A keyword is listed at the bottom of each activity page. This keyword is the link that connects students to the online activities via the CD, providing extra practice.

How to Use the CD
After inserting the CD into your computer, first follow the directions to register for the online activities database. Your registration is free and good for one year. After you have registered, click on the unit that your student is currently working on. Then, click on the appropriate keyword. This will take you to an online database of activities related to that keyword. You may choose to download up to 200 activities, which you may then print. Also included on the CD is a printable progress chart so your student can keep track of his or her progress through the workbook.

For further explanation of the online database, CD, or for technical help, refer to the help me file located on the CD.

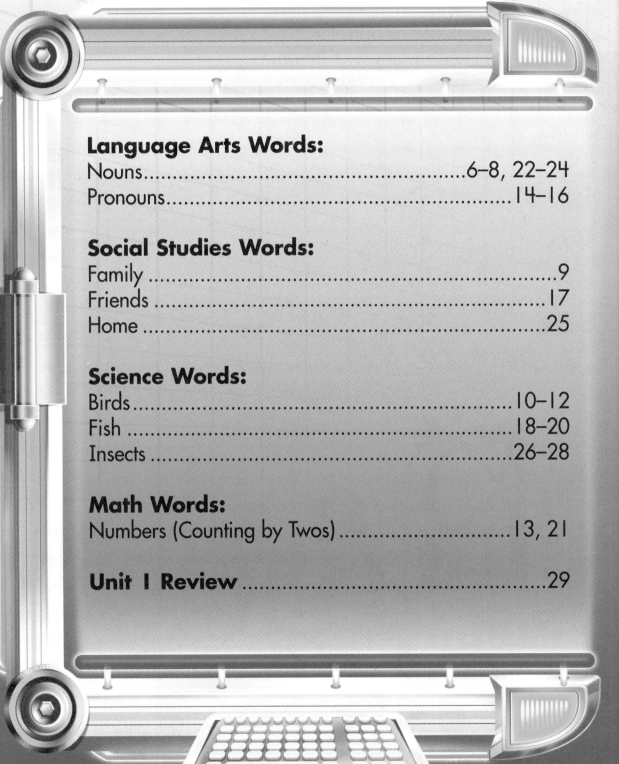

Language Arts Words:
Nouns..6–8, 22–24
Pronouns..14–16

Social Studies Words:
Family 9
Friends 17
Home 25

Science Words:
Birds...10–12
Fish 18–20
Insects 26–28

Math Words:
Numbers (Counting by Twos)...........................13, 21

Unit 1 Review 29

Name:_____

Words That Are Nouns

A **noun** names a person, place, or thing.

Directions: The boy found many things in the old trunk. Circle the nouns in each row.

1. look	sit	kite	photo
2. block	hammer	letter	kneel
3. cry	hat	dress	smile
4. basket	doll	eat	run
5. fiddle	book	sing	blanket

Name:_____

Words That Are Nouns

Directions: Read the sentences. Circle the nouns. Then, write the nouns next to the pictures.

1. Our family likes to go to the park.   _____

_____

2. We play on the swings.

_____

3. We eat cake.

_____

4. We drink lemonade.

_____

_____

5. We throw the ball to our dog.

_____

6. Then we go home.

_____

Name:_____

Words That Are Nouns

Directions: Read the sentences. Fill in the circle below each noun.

1. First, the boy had to feed his puppy.
   ○　○　○　○

2. He got fresh water for his pet.
   ○　○　○○　○

3. Next, the boy poured some dry food into a bowl.
   ○　○　○　○

4. He set the dish on the floor in the kitchen.
   ○　○　○　○

5. Then, he called his dog to come to dinner.
   ○　○　○

6. The boy and his dad worked in the garden.
   ○　○　○　○

7. The father turned the dirt with a shovel.
   ○　○　○　○

8. The boy carefully dropped seeds into little holes.
   ○　○　○　○

9. Soon, tiny plants would sprout from the soil.
   ○　○　○　○

10. Sunshine and showers would help the radishes grow.
    ○　○　○　○

Name:_____

Words About Family

Directions: Use the Word Bank to find the words that name family members. Circle the words in the puzzle. Look across and down.

Word Bank			
mother	father	grandpa	grandma
sister	brother	baby	puppy

```
G L S I S T E R
R Y T B P N X F
A G R A N D P A
N Q L B H B G T
D N T Y Z M Y H
M P U P P Y G E
A N M O T H E R
B R O T H E R X
```

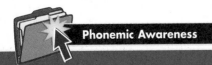

Name:_____

Words About Birds

Directions: Use the words in the Word Bank to complete the puzzle about birds.

Across

2. Birds are _____ -blooded animals.

3. Birds lay _____ from which baby birds are hatched.

5. Like human beings, birds use _____ to breathe.

Down

1. Birds are covered with _____ to keep them warm and dry.

4. A bird's mouth is called a _____ .

Word Bank				
feathers	bill	lungs	eggs	warm

Name:_____

Words About Birds

Directions: The eggs in the nest contain the names of different birds. Fill in the names in the puzzle. The last letter of one name becomes the first letter of the next name. For example, the last letter of **parrot** is **t**, so that is the first letter of the next word, **turkey**.

Start at the outside edge and spiral in toward the center. The first three are done for you.

EAGLE THRUSH DOVE
IBIS KIWI
HUMMINGBIRD PARROT ROBIN
YELLOWHAMMER NIGHTHAWK SWIFT TURKEY

P	A	R	R	O	T	U	R	K	E	Y
										E
										L
										L
										O
			R	E	M	M	A	H		

UNIT 1

Name:_____

Words About Birds

A **fact** is a statement that is true. It can be proven. Here is a fact: Birds have wings. An **opinion** is a statement based on feeling or belief. It cannot be proven. Here is an opinion: My canary is pretty.

Directions: Read the statements about birds. Write **F** next to each fact. Write **O** next to each opinion.

_____ 1. Birds have two feet.

_____ 2. All birds lay eggs.

_____ 3. Parrots are too noisy.

_____ 4. All birds have feathers and wings.

_____ 5. It would be great to be a bird and fly south for the winter.

_____ 6. Birds have hard beaks or bills instead of teeth.

_____ 7. Pigeons are fun to watch.

_____ 8. Some birds cannot fly.

_____ 9. Parakeets make good pets.

_____ 10. A penguin is a bird.

Words About Counting

Directions: Each basket a player makes is worth two points. Help your home team win by counting by twos to beat the other team's score.

Home	two	Visitor

two
_____
_____
eight
_____
_____
_____
_____
sixteen
_____
twenty
_____
_____
_____
twenty-eight
_____
thirty-two

Winner!

Final Score	
Home	
Visitor	**thirty**

Name:_____

Words That Are Pronouns

Pronouns are words that can be used instead of nouns. **She**, **he**, **it**, and **they** are pronouns.

Directions: Read each sentence. Then, write **she**, **he**, **it**, or **they** on the line to replace the underlined word or words.

1. <u>Dan</u> likes funny jokes. _____ likes funny jokes.

2. <u>Peg and Sam</u> went to the zoo. _____ went to the zoo.

3. <u>My dog</u> likes to dig in the yard. _____ likes to dig in the yard.

4. <u>Sara</u> is a very good dancer. _____ is a very good dancer.

5. <u>Fred and Ted</u> are twins. _____ are twins.

Words That Are Pronouns

Directions: Read each sentence. Then, write each sentence again using the correct pronoun to replace the underlined word or words.

1. <u>Tommy</u> packed sandwiches and apples.

_____

2. Tommy hiked along <u>the trail</u>.

_____

3. <u>Ed and Larry</u> caught up with Tommy.

_____

4. <u>Rita</u> met the boys at the trail's end.

_____

5. <u>Tommy</u> sent Bill one of his photos later.

_____

6. <u>The boys</u> ate their lunches under a tree.

_____

7. After lunch, <u>Rita</u> gave the boys a cookie.

_____

Name:_____

Words That Are Pronouns

Use the pronouns **I** and **we** when talking about the person or people doing an action.

Example: I can roller skate. **We** can roller skate.

Use **me** and **us** when talking about something that is happening to a person or people.

Example: They gave **me** the roller skates.
They gave **us** the roller skates.

Directions: Circle the correct pronoun that completes each sentence. Then, write it on the line.

Example: _____We_____ are going to the picnic together.   **We**, **Us**

1. _____ am finished with my science project.   **I, Me**

2. Eric passed the football to _____.   **me, I**

3. They ate dinner with _____ last night   **we, us**

4. _____ like spinach better than ice cream.   **I, Me**

5. Mom came in the room to tell _____ good night.   **me, I**

6. _____ had a pizza party in our backyard.   **Us, We**

7. They told _____ the good news.   **us, we**

8. Tom and _____ went to the store.   **me, I**

9. She is taking _____ with her to the movies.   **I, me**

10. Katie and _____ are good friends.   **I, me**

Name:_____

Words About Friends

Directions: Friends are great! Use the Word Bank to find the words that describe a good friend. Circle them in the puzzle. Look across, down, diagonally, and backward.

Word Bank			
smart	funny	gentle	nice
helpful	honest	polite	kind

```
H G S H W Q J P
K O E L P C N O
M I N N Z R I L
R J N E T N C I
V M T D S L E T
F U N N Y T E E
L U F P L E H F
K S M A R T R K
```

Name:_____

Words About Fish

Fish live almost anywhere there is water. Although fish come in many different shapes, colors, and sizes, they are alike in many ways.

- All fish have backbones.
- Fish breathe with gills.
- Most fish are cold-blooded.

- Most fish have fins.
- Many fish have scales.
- Some fish have funny names.

Directions: The letters in each fish name are mixed up. Unscramble the letters and write each name correctly on the line. Use the clues to help you. Then, use your imagination to draw each fish.

_____ rparto fish (a talking bird)	_____ oinlfish (king of the beasts)	_____ gknifish (opposite of queen)
_____ tbturelfy fish (an insect with colorful wings)	_____ ogatfish (a nanny- or a billy-)	_____ opprucneifish (animal with quills)

Name:_____

Words About Fish

Most fish have ways to protect themselves from danger. Two of these fish are the **trigger fish** and the **porcupinefish**. The trigger fish lives on the ocean reef. When it sees danger, it swims into its private hole, puts its top fin up and squeezes itself in tight. Then, a predator cannot take it from its hiding place. The porcupinefish also lives on the ocean reef. When it senses danger, it puffs up like a balloon by swallowing air or water. When it puffs up, poisonous spikes stand out on its body. After the danger is gone, it deflates its body.

Directions: Complete the sentences about trigger fish and porcupinefish.

1. Trigger fish and porcupinefish live on the _____.

2. The trigger fish swims into its private _____.

3. The porcupinefish puffs up like a _____.

UNIT 1

Name:_____

Words About Fish

Directions: Read about sea horses. Then, answer the questions.

Sea horses are fish, not horses. A sea horse's head looks like a horse's head. It has a tail like a monkey's tail. A sea horse looks very strange.

1. (Circle the correct answer.)
   A sea horse is a kind of

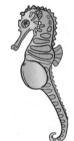

horse.

monkey.

fish.

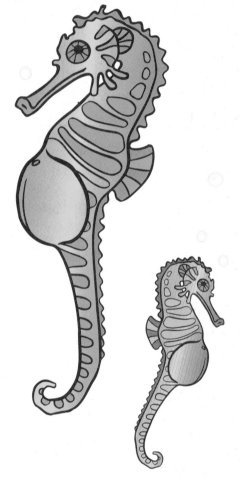

2. What does a sea horse's head look like?

   _____

   _____

3. What makes a sea horse look strange?

   a. _____

   b. _____

Name:_____

Words About Counting

Directions: Trace a path following the even numbers (two, four, six, etc.) to get through the maze.

Start

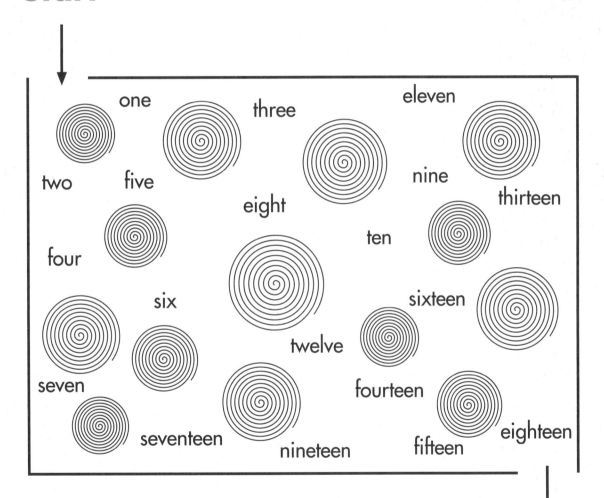

one
three
eleven
two   five
nine
thirteen
eight
four
ten
six
sixteen
seven
twelve
fourteen
seventeen
nineteen
fifteen
eighteen

Finish

Name:_____

Words That Are Nouns

Word Bank

books	bus	chalkboard	classroom	crayons
desk	pencil	playground	school	teacher

Directions: Use the words in the Word Bank to complete each sentence. Write the correct noun on the line.

1. There are many kinds of _____ to read in school.

2. Miss Lopez is my second-grade _____ .

3. You can color pictures with _____ .

4. Children sit in a _____ to learn.

5. I ride to school on the _____ .

6. There are swings and slides on our school _____ .

7. There is a _____ building next to the park.

8. The teacher writes sentences on the _____ .

9. I write a story with a _____ .

10. My _____ is in the front of the classroom.

Name:_____

Words That Are Nouns

A **noun** names a person, place, or thing.

Directions: Circle the two nouns in each sentence.

Example: (Mom) reads a (book).

1. The bird flew to its nest.

2. The kite was high in the air.

3. The children played a game.

4. The books fell on the ground.

5. The monkey climbed a tree.

UNIT 1

Name:_____

Words That Are Nouns

Directions: The cookie jars hold different kinds of nouns. Read the nouns on the cookies. Decide if they are people, places, or things. Then, write each noun on the correct jar.

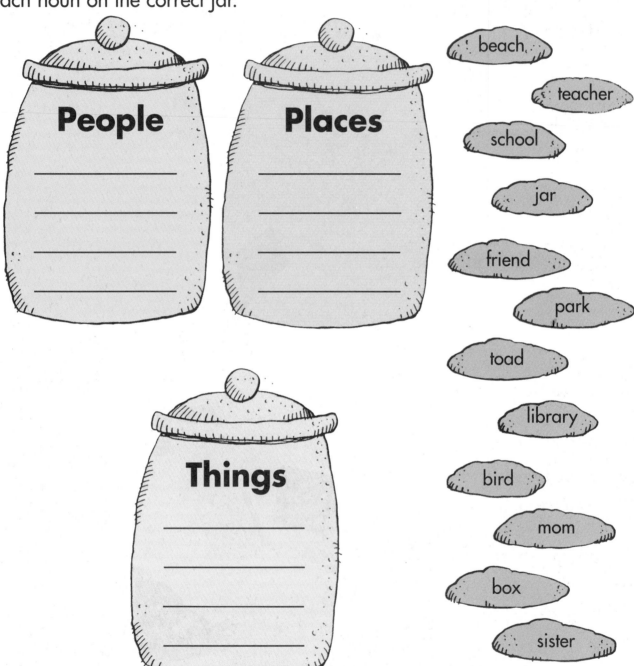

People

_____
_____
_____
_____

Places

_____
_____
_____
_____

Things

_____
_____
_____
_____

beach

teacher

school

jar

friend

park

toad

library

bird

mom

box

sister

Name:_____

UNIT 1

Words About Home

Word Bank				
bedroom	blanket	bathroom	dishes	house
kitchen	sink	stove	table	yard

Directions: Write the correct word from the Word Bank beside each picture.

1.  _____

4.  _____

2.  _____

5.  _____

3.  _____

6.  _____

Directions: Use the words in the Word Bank to complete each sentence.

7. Mark has a swing set in his back _____ .

8. I use a _____ to keep warm when it is cold.

9. Mother cooks dinner on the _____ .

10. You can wash your hands in the _____ .

UNIT 1

Name:_____

Words About Insects

Sometimes, two small words can be put together to make one new word. The new word is called a **compound word**.

Some insect names are compound words:

fire + **fly** = **firefly**
water + **bug** = **waterbug**

Directions: Find the two words that make up each insect's name. Write the two words on the lines. Then, color the insects.

1.  butterfly

_____ _____

2.  grasshopper

_____ _____

3.   ladybug

_____ _____

UNIT 1

Name:_____

Words About Insects

All insects have these body parts:

Head at the front

Thorax in the middle

Abdomen at the back

Six **legs**—three on each side of the thorax

Two **eyes** on the head

Two **antennae** attached to the head

Some insects also have **wings**.

Directions: Draw your favorite insect. Include all the body parts listed above.

UNIT 1

Name:_____

Words About Insects

Directions: Read about ladybugs. Then, answer the questions.

A ladybug is a kind of beetle. Ladybugs can be found all over the world. There are more than 4,500 kinds of ladybugs! Ladybugs are small insects. They are usually yellow, orange, or red and have small black spots on their backs. Their bright colors help protect them from predators.

Ladybugs are very good for gardens. They are considered good luck because they eat other insects that damage plants.

1. Where can ladybugs be found? _____

2. What color are ladybugs? _____

3. Why are ladybugs brightly colored? _____

   _____

4. What do ladybugs eat? _____

5. Why are ladybugs good for gardens? _____

Name:_____

Unit 1 Review

Directions: Read each sentence. Write **F** next to each fact. Write **O** next to each opinion. Then, underline the nouns.

_____ 1. Lemonade is a drink made from lemons.

_____ 2. My grandma is a very nice woman.

_____ 3. A porcupinefish can puff up like a balloon.

_____ 4. The children like to play on the playground.

_____ 5. An ibis is a pretty bird.

_____ 6. My house has two bathrooms.

_____ 7. Some insects have wings.

_____ 8. A bird uses its bill to pick up food.

_____ 9. Planting seeds with my dad is fun.

_____ 10. A sea horse is a kind of strange fish.

Language Arts Words:
Verbs 31–33, 39–41, 47–49

Social Studies Words:
Community Places 34, 42, 50

Science Words—Animals:
Reptiles 35–37
Mammals...43–44
Zoo Animals 45
Animal Young 51–53

Math Words:
Numbers (Counting) 38
Numbers (Counting by Twos, Fives, and Tens) 46

Unit 2 Review 54

Name:_____

Words That Are Verbs

A **verb** is the action word in a sentence. A verb tells what someone or something does. **Run**, **sleep**, and **jump** are verbs.

Directions: Circle the verb in each sentence.

1. We play baseball every day.

2. Susan pitches the ball very well.

3. Mike swings the bat harder than anyone.

4. Chris slides into home base.

5. Laura hits a home run.

Name:_____

Words That Are Verbs

A **verb** can tell when something happens. Sometimes, **-ed** is added at the end of a verb to tell that something has already happened.

Example: Let's **play** at my house today. We **played** at your house yesterday.

Directions: Circle the correct verb that completes each sentence. Then, write it on the line.

1. Today, I will _____ my dog, Fritz.
   wash   washed

2. Last week, Fritz _____ when we said, "Bath time, Fritz."
   cry   cried

3. My sister likes to _____ wash Fritz.
   help   helped

4. One time she _____ Fritz by herself.
   clean   cleaned

5. Fritz will _____ a lot better after his bath.
   look   looked

Verbs   **32**

Name:_____

Words That Are Verbs

Some verbs do not show action. Instead, they link the subject with the second part of the sentence. These types of verbs are **linking verbs**. **Am**, **is**, **are**, **was**, and **were** are linking verbs.

Examples: Many people **are** collectors.
His collection **is** large.

Directions: Underline the linking verb in each sentence.

1. I am happy.

2. Toy collecting is a nice hobby.

3. Mom and dad are helpful.

4. The rabbit is beautiful.

5. Itsy and Bitsy are stuffed mice.

6. Monday was special.

7. I was excited.

8. The class was impressed.

9. The elephants were gray.

10. My friends were a good audience.

Name:_____

UNIT 2

Words About Community Places

Word Bank

bakery   bank   library   post office   school   hospital

Directions: Read each clue. Write the word from the Word Bank that names the place being described. Write the word on the line.

1.  Save your cash. Bring it here.
It will grow year to year. _____

2.  French bread, muffins, chocolate cake.
Here's the place where people bake. _____

3.  Here's the place to learn to read.
Our teacher will help us succeed. _____

4.  Come inside and take a look.
When you leave, check out a book. _____

5.  Buy some stamps. Mail a letter.
To do these things, there's no place better. _____

6.  Come here if you need health care.
A doctor will be waiting there. _____

Name:_____

Words About Reptiles

A **reptile** is a cold-blooded animal with scaly skin and a backbone.
A **snake** is a reptile.

Directions: Read about snakes. Then, write the correct answers to complete each sentence.

There are many facts about snakes that might surprise someone. A snake's skin is dry. Most snakes are shy. They will hide from people. Snakes eat mice and rats. They do not chew them up. Snakes' jaws drop open to swallow their food whole.

1. A snake's skin feels_____.

2. Most snakes are _____.

3. Snakes eat

   a. _____.

   b. _____.

Name:_____

Words About Reptiles

There are about 6,000 kinds of reptiles. They range in length from 2 inches to almost 30 feet. Even though reptiles seem quite different, they all breathe with lungs, are cold-blooded, have scaly skin, and have a backbone.

Directions: In the Reptile House at the zoo, each animal needs to be placed in the correct area. Read the information about each reptile. Then, read the clues to write the name of each reptile in its area.

| **Giant Tortoise** can live over 100 years. It can hide under its shell for protection. | **Reticulated Python** is the longest snake. One was almost 33 feet long. | **Saltwater Crocodile** is one of the largest reptiles. It can weigh 1,000 pounds. | **Komodo Dragon** is a dragon-like reptile. It is the largest living lizard. |

Clues:
- The snake is between the largest lizard and the largest member of the turtle family.
- A relative of the alligator is on the far right side.

Name:_____

Words About Reptiles

Directions: Circle each word along the trail that names a reptile.

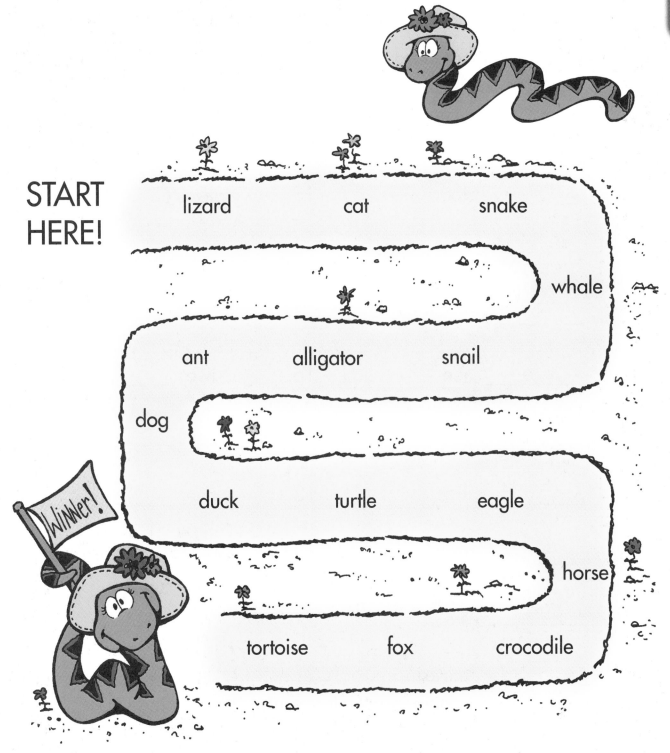

START HERE!

lizard   cat   snake

whale

ant   alligator   snail

dog

duck   turtle   eagle

horse

tortoise   fox   crocodile

Name:_____

Words About Counting

Directions: Follow the directions in each column to write the missing number words.

Write the number word
that is one less.

Write the number word
that is one greater.

1. _____ , sixteen

2. _____ , four

3. _____ , two

4. _____ , three

5. _____ , ten

6. _____ , eleven

7. _____ , five

8. _____ , fourteen

9. _____ , six

10. _____ , thirteen

11. _____ , seven

12. six, _____

13. five, _____

14. nine, _____

15. eleven, _____

16. two, _____

17. four, _____

18. one, _____

19. twelve, _____

20. nineteen, _____

21. ten, _____

22. three, _____

Name:_____

Words That Are Verbs

A **verb** is a word that can show action.

Examples: I **jump**.   He **kicks**.   He **walks**.

Directions: Underline the verb in each sentence. Then, write it on the line.

1. Our school plays games on Field Day.   _____

2. Juan runs 50 yards.   _____

3. Carmen hops in a sack race.   _____

4. Paula tosses a ball through a hoop.   _____

5. One girl carries a jellybean on a spoon.   _____

6. Lola bounces the ball.   _____

7. Some boys chase after balloons.   _____

8. The children cheer for the winners.   _____

Name:_____

Words That Are Verbs

Directions: Circle the verb in each sentence.

1. The woman paints a picture.

2. The puppy chases its ball.

3. The students go to school.

4. Butterflies fly in the air.

5. The baby drinks from a cup.

UNIT 2

Name:_____

Words That Are Verbs

Directions: Fill in the bubble beside the verb that best matches each picture.

Example:

- (A) drop
- (B) help
- (C) climb
- (D) slide

1.

- (A) mix
- (B) fix
- (C) eat
- (D) chew

3.

- (A) drink
- (B) glass
- (C) milk
- (D) spill

2.

- (A) lake
- (B) boil
- (C) bake
- (D) lick

4.

- (A) hug
- (B) laugh
- (C) tug
- (D) cook

Name:_____

Words About Libraries

Directions: Read the paragraph below. Then, find and circle the bold words in the puzzle. Look across, down, and diagonally.

A **library** is a great place to visit in the **summer**. It provides **books** and other items for **education** and **fun**. The **librarian** is helpful and friendly. Most libraries have summer programs, such as **reading** contests, summer **movies**, and **story** times. It is hard to believe this great place is **free**!

r	c	m	s	n	r	h	i	s	j
e	s	o	m	t	q	v	f	k	h
a	d	v	c	s	o	w	v	u	o
d	l	i	b	r	a	r	i	a	n
i	b	e	o	x	z	e	y	r	e
n	i	s	o	h	d	f	g	u	t
g	o	r	k	l	a	b	r	b	e
s	u	n	s	s	u	m	m	e	r
l	i	b	r	a	r	y	r	e	e
e	d	u	c	a	t	i	o	n	l

UNIT 2

Name:_____

Words About Mammals

Directions: A **mammal** is a warm-blooded animal with hair or fur. Write the mammal name from the Word Bank beside the correct picture. The first one is done for you.

Word Bank					
fox	rabbit	bear	squirrel	mouse	deer

1. _____squirrel_____

2. _____

3. _____

4. _____

5. _____

6. _____

Name: _____

UNIT 2

Words About Mammals

Directions: Use the words in the Word Bank to find and circle orange the names of three animals that would make good pets. Circle blue the names of three wild animals. Circle green the two animals that live on a farm. Also, find and circle the animal sounds.

Word Bank

BEAR CAT LION SHEEP BIRD DOG COW TIGER

A	M	E	O	W	W	N	L	I	O	N
B	M	D	O	G	G	X	I	I	S	O
A	B	E	A	R	R	V	L	M	H	R
R	M	R	M	O	O	U	S	E	E	K
K	C	A	B	B	I	R	D	S	E	M
I	O	T	T	I	G	E	R	M	P	Q
B	W	N	O	W	W	R	Q	N	E	N
D	N	C	P	H	H	I	D	U	D	N
F	K	C	A	T	T	R	O	A	R	M

Name:_____

Words About Zoo Animals

Directions: Write the name of the animal that answers each riddle on the line. Use the pictures and animal names to help you.

bear   zebra   monkey   kangaroo

camel   lion   elephant

1. I am big and brown. I sleep all winter.
   What am I?   _____

2. I look like a horse with black and white
   stripes? What am I?   _____

3. I have one or two humps on my back.
   Sometimes, people ride me. What am I?   _____

4. I am a very big animal. I have a long
   nose called a trunk. What am I?   _____

5. I have sharp teeth and claws. I am a
   great big cat. What am I?   _____

6. I have a huge, strong tail. My baby
   rides in my pouch. What am I?   _____

7. I like to climb. I eat bananas. I make
   people laugh. What am I?   _____

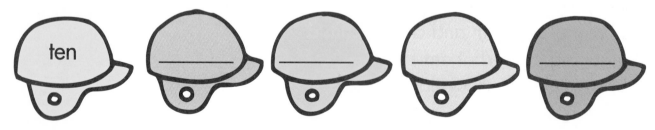
Name:_____

UNIT 2

Words About Counting

Directions: Write the missing number words on the lines.

1. Count by twos:

two   four   _____   _____   _____

2. Count by fives:

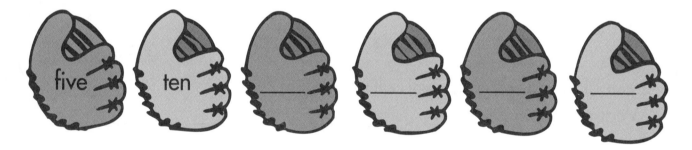

five   ten   _____   _____   _____   _____

3. Count by tens:

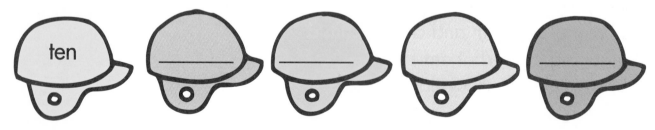

ten   _____   _____   _____   _____

Name:_____

Words That Are Verbs

Directions: Write a sentence that tells what happens in each picture. Use the **verb** under the picture. The first one is done for you.

1.

falls

breaks

cleans

A glass falls off the table.

_____

_____

2.

fixes

cuts

lifts

_____

_____

_____

UNIT 2

Name:_____

Words That Are Verbs

Directions: Underline the verb in each sentence.

1. The tigers slept in the hot sun.

2. The lion cubs played by the fence.

3. The elephant ate the salty peanuts.

4. The ducks swam in the deep lake.

48

UNIT 2

Name:_____

Words That Are Verbs

Directions: Read the two sentences in each story. Then, use the verb under the last picture to write one more sentence to tell what happens next.

1.

Today is Mike's birthday.

Mike asked four friends to come.

cut _____

2.

Edith's dog walked in the mud.

He got mud in the house.

_____

cleaned

Name:_____

Words About Community Places

Directions: Look at the pictures. Circle the word that names each community place.

1.

pet store

bakery

florist

2.

bakery

library

post office

3.

florist

post office

school

Name:_____

Words For Animal Young

UNIT 2

Directions: Use the story about baby animals to complete the chart below. Write the kind of animal that belongs with each special baby name.

Many animals are called special names when they are young. A baby deer is called a **fawn**. A baby cat is called a **kitten**.

Some young animals have the same name as other kinds of baby animals. A baby elephant is a **calf**. A baby whale is a **calf**. A baby giraffe is a **calf**.

A baby cow is a **calf**.

Some baby animals are called **cubs**. A baby lion, a baby bear, a baby tiger, and a baby fox are all called **cubs**.

Some baby animals are called **colts**. A young horse is a **colt**. A baby zebra is a **colt**. A baby donkey is a **colt**.

calf	cub	colt
_____	_____	_____
_____	_____	_____
_____	_____	_____
_____	_____	

UNIT 2

Words For Animal Young

Directions: Look at the pictures of the mother animals and their babies.
Write **calf**, **cub**, or **colt** on the line to name each baby.

1.

_____

4.

_____

2.

_____

5.

_____

3.

_____

6.

_____

Name:_____

Words For Animal Young

Directions: Read the story about baby animals. Then, write the word from the story that completes each sentence.

Baby cats are called **kittens**. They love to play. A baby dog is a **puppy**. Puppies chew on old shoes. They run and bark. A baby sheep is a **lamb**. Lambs eat grass. A baby duck is a **duckling**. Ducklings swim with their wide, webbed feet. Baby horses are **foals**. A foal can walk the day it is born! A baby goat is a **kid**. Some people call children **kids**, too!

1. A baby cat is called a _____ .

2. A baby dog is called a _____ .

3. A baby sheep is a _____ .

4. _____ swim with webbed feet.

5. A _____ can walk the day it is born.

6. A baby goat is a _____ .

Name:_____

Unit 2 Review

Directions: Circle the verb in each sentence. Underline the community place.

1. There are hundreds of books at the library.

2. We eat delicious desserts from the bakery.

3. We buy our fish at the pet store.

4. He visits the reptile house at the zoo.

5. Children learn lots of new things at school.

Directions: Write a sentence to tell what you know about each topic below.

1. reptiles _____

_____

2. mammals _____

_____

3. animal young _____

_____

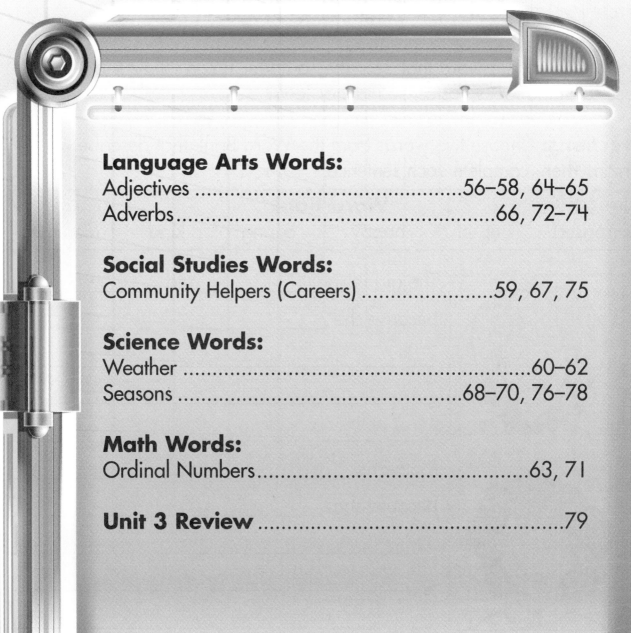

Language Arts Words:
Adjectives 56–58, 64–65
Adverbs...66, 72–74

Social Studies Words:
Community Helpers (Careers) 59, 67, 75

Science Words:
Weather 60–62
Seasons 68–70, 76–78

Math Words:
Ordinal Numbers...63, 71

Unit 3 Review 79

Name:_____

Words That Are Adjectives

An **adjective** is a word that describes a noun. It can tell how a person, place, or thing looks, tastes, sounds, or feels.

Directions: Choose two words from the Word Bank that describe each person. Then, complete each sentence.

Word Bank					
surprised	upset	happy	caring	kind	confused

1. The girl is _____ and _____

   because she _____

   _____

   _____

   _____

2. Mother is _____ and _____

   because she _____

   _____

   _____

   _____

3. Father is _____ and _____

   because he _____

   _____

   _____

   _____

Adjectives   56   © 2007 School Specialty Publishing

Words That Are Adjectives

Use an **adjective** that best describes a noun or pronoun. Be specific.

Example: David had a nice birthday.
David had a **fun** birthday.

Directions: Read each sentence. Write the sentence again, replacing **nice** or **good** with a better adjective from the Word Bank.

Word Bank					
sturdy	new	great	chocolate	delicious	special

1. David bought a nice pair of in-line skates.

_____

2. He received a nice helmet.

_____

3. He got nice kneepads.

_____

4. Dad baked a good cake.

_____

5. David made a good wish.

_____

6. Mom served good ice cream.

_____

Name:_____

Words That Are Adjectives

An **adjective** is a word that describes a noun.

Example: Yolanda has a **tasty** lunch.

Directions: Color each space that has an adjective. Do not color the other spaces.

again

juicy

thick   big   tasty

with

orange

smooth

eat

sour

white

crunchy

red

long

fresh

cold

hard

drink

Name:_____

Words About Community Helpers

Directions: Use the words in the Word Bank to answer each clue. Write the answer on the line.

Word Bank			
captain	dentist	fireman	doctor
plumber	police	teacher	baker

1. I think I have a cavity in my tooth.
   Who can help me?

   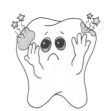

   _____

2. My mom needs to order a wedding cake
   for my uncle. Who can help her?

   _____

3. I hurt my ankle during gym class.
   Who can help me?

   _____

4. My pipes are leaking.
   Who can help me?

   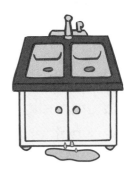

   _____

Name:_____

Weather Words

Directions: Use the words in the Word Bank to complete the puzzle about weather.

UNIT 3

Word Bank
clouds
lightning
outside
rainy
snow
storm
sunny
thunder
weather

Across

2. The conditions outside, like sunshine or rain

4. Flash of light seen during a storm

5. Wind and rain make a _____.

6. An umbrella is needed when the weather is _____.

7. There are no clouds on a bright, _____ day.

8. The opposite of inside

Down

1. A loud noise heard during a rainstorm

3. White, puffy objects that float in the sky

9. Frozen rain that falls in the winter

Name:_____

Weather Words

Directions: Write a sentence about each picture. Use weather words from the Word Bank.

Word Bank					
windy	cool	cold	rainy	wet	cloudy

UNIT 3

1. _____

2. _____

3. _____

4. _____

Name:_____

Weather Words

Directions: Use the Word Bank to write the weather word that completes each sentence. Put a period at the end of the telling sentences and a question mark at the end of the asking sentences.

Word Bank		
rainbow	wind	blizzard
rain	hot	sun

Example:

Do flowers grow in the ____sun____ ?

1. The _____ almost blew me away ☐

2. This huge umbrella protects me from the _____ ☐

3. During the _____ , the snow was blowing hard ☐

4. Did you see the beautiful _____ after it rained ☐

UNIT 3

Name:_____

Ordinal Number Words

Ordinal numbers tell the order in a series. **First**, **second**, and **third** are ordinal numbers.

Directions: Follow the instructions to color the train cars. The first car is the engine.

- Color the third car blue.
- Color the eighth car green.
- Color the fifth car orange.
- Color the sixth car yellow.
- Color the fourth car brown.
- Color the second car purple.
- Color the first car red.
- Color the seventh car black.

UNIT 3

Name:_____

Words That Are Adjectives

Directions: Adjectives can make a sentence more interesting. Write a word from the Word Bank on each line to improve the sentence.

Word Bank				
fast	huge	expensive	brave	smart
wide	terrible	sturdy	beautiful	empty

1. The skater won a medal.

   The _____ skater won a _____ medal.

2. The jewels were in the safe.

   The _____ jewels were in the _____ safe.

3. The airplane flew through the storm.

   The _____ airplane flew through the _____ storm.

4. A fireman rushed into the house.

   A _____ fireman rushed into the _____ house.

5. The detective hid behind the tree.

   The _____ detective hid behind the _____ tree.

Name:_____

Words That Are Adjectives

Directions: Write an adjective on each line. Draw a picture to match each sentence.

1. The _____ flag waved over the _____ building.

4. A _____ lion searched for food in the _____ jungle.

2. We saw _____ fish in the _____ aquarium.

5. Her _____ car was parked by the _____ van.

3. The _____ dog barked and chased the _____ truck.

6. The _____ building was filled with _____ packages.

Adjectives

65

Name:_____

Words That Are Adverbs

Describing words can also tell about an action. These words are called **adverbs**.

Examples: The turtle moved **slowly**.
The rabbit moved **quickly**.

The word **slowly** describes how the turtle moved. The word **quickly** describes how the rabbit moved.

Directions: Write a word from the Word Bank on the line to describe each action.

1. Sidney played the piano_____ .

2. The child sang _____ .

3. The horse ran _____ .

4. The snow fell _____ .

5. The man drove _____ .

6. The teacher talked _____ .

Word Bank

loudly

softly

quickly

slowly

wildly

happily

UNIT 3

Name:_____

Words About Community Helpers

The people who work in your community do important jobs.

Directions: Write a sentence to show what you know about each community helper.

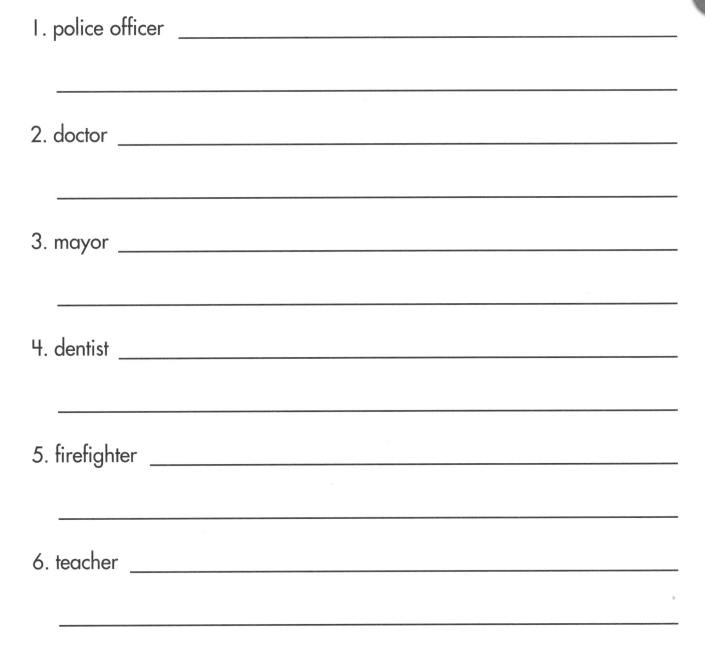

1. police officer _____

_____

2. doctor _____

_____

3. mayor _____

_____

4. dentist _____

_____

5. firefighter _____

_____

6. teacher _____

_____

Name:_____

UNIT 3

Winter Words

Directions: Fill in the circle beside the word that best completes each sentence.

It was a _____ winter day. Alicia
$\qquad$ 1

and her brother Randy hurried out

in their warm _____ . They played
$\qquad$ 2

in the _____ . They made a
$\qquad$ 3

big _____ .
$\qquad$ 4

1. (A) sandy

   (B) hot

   (C) cold

2. (A) snowsuits

   (B) shorts

   (C) swimsuits

3. (A) snow

   (B) rain

   (C) sun

4. (A) house

   (B) snowman

   (C) kite

Name:_____

Spring Words

Directions: Fill in the circle beside the word that best completes each sentence. Then, write the word on the line.

UNIT 3

1. In the spring, _____ poke out of the snow.

- (A) flowers
- (B) birds
- (C) kids
- (D) rocks

3. The _____ make nests and lay eggs.

- (A) flowers
- (B) birds
- (C) kids
- (D) rocks

2. The weather gets warmer, so _____ melts.

- (A) mud
- (B) snow
- (C) water
- (D) ice cream

4. Trees get new _____ and blossoms.

- (A) leaves
- (B) birds
- (C) kids
- (D) rocks

Name:_____

UNIT 3

Summer Words

Directions: Fill in the circle beside the word that best completes each sentence.

It is a _____ summer day. The
$\quad\quad\quad$ 1

children are out of _____ . It is
$\quad\quad\quad\quad\quad\quad$ 2

time to have _____ . The _____
$\quad\quad\quad\quad$ 3 $\quad\quad\quad\quad$ 4

is the best place to be!

1. (A) rainy

   (B) hot

   (C) cold

3. (A) run

   (B) fun

   (C) sun

2. (A) time

   (B) line

   (C) school

4. (A) pal

   (B) pool

   (C) pole

Name:_____

Ordinal Number Words

Directions: Look at the treats in the box. Circle the ordinal number for each treat.

1.

2.

3.

4.

16.

5.

15.

6.

14.

7.

13.

8.

12.

11.

10.

9.

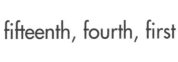 third, sixteenth, fifth

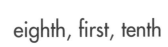 fifteenth, fourth, first

 twelfth, second, seventh

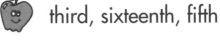 third, eleventh, fifteenth

 eighth, first, tenth

 sixteenth, thirteenth, third

 ninth, second, thirteenth

 sixth, seventh, ninth

Name:_____

UNIT 3

Words That Are Adverbs

Directions: Read the sentences about the picture. Circle the words that are adverbs. Then, color the picture.

1. On Saturday, we finally did some work on the house.

2. Bill hammered loudly on the wall.

3. Jan carefully painted the door.

4. Scott was tired, so he worked slowly.

5. We hoped to finish the work quickly.

Name:_____

Words That Are Adverbs

An **adverb** describes a verb. It tells how, when, or where an action takes place.

Examples: The space shuttle blasted off **yesterday**. (when)
It rose **quickly** into the sky. (how)
We watched **outdoors**. (where)

Directions: Write **how**, **when**, or **where** on the line to explain what each adverb tells.

1. I run today. _____

2. I run outside. _____

3. I run tomorrow. _____

4. I run around. _____

5. I run nearby. _____

6. I run sometimes. _____

7. I run there. _____

8. I run far. _____

9. I run happily. _____

10. I run weekly. _____

11. I run swiftly. _____

12. I run first. _____

13. I run next. _____

14. I run gracefully. _____

Directions: Circle the adverb in each pair of words.

1. soon, supper

2. neatly, nine

3. proudly, prove

4. help, easily

5. warmly, wonder

6. quilt, quickly

7. finally, feather

8. quietly, quacks

9. sail, safely

Adverbs

73

Name: _____

Words That Are Adverbs

Directions: Complete each sentence with an adverb from the Word Bank.

Word Bank			
quietly	loudly	quickly	suddenly

1. The rain came down _____ .

2. The raindrops hit the tent _____ .

3. The bird flew _____ into the tent.

4. He waited _____ for the rain to stop.

UNIT 3

Name:_____

Words for Community Helpers

Directions: Use the words in the Word Bank to write the names of two community helpers that fit each description.

UNIT 3

Word Bank			
mathematician	veterinarian	teacher	chef
police officer	nurse	doctor	accountant
mail carrier	seamstress	librarian	tailor
delivery person	farmer	umpire	zookeeper

1. Place importance on books   _____ _____

2. Work with needle and thread   _____ _____

3. Work with food   _____ _____

4. Make sure people follow rules   _____ _____

5. Deliver mail and packages   _____ _____

6. Take care of medical needs   _____ _____

7. Work with animals   _____ _____

8. Use numbers often   _____ _____

Autumn Words

Directions: Fill in the circle beside the word that best completes each sentence. Then, write the word on the line.

UNIT 3

1. In the autumn, _____ fall from the trees.

   Ⓐ flowers

   Ⓑ birds

   Ⓒ leaves

   Ⓓ branches

2. The weather gets _____, so you need a sweater.

   Ⓐ rainy

   Ⓑ cool

   Ⓒ hot

   Ⓓ snowy

3. In the autumn, children go back to _____ .

   Ⓐ school

   Ⓑ town

   Ⓒ sleep

   Ⓓ read

4. Another word for autumn is _____ .

   Ⓐ cool

   Ⓑ fall

   Ⓒ winter

   Ⓓ harvest

Name:_____

Words About Seasons

Directions: Write three words on the lines to tell about each season.

Spring

_____

_____

_____

Summer

_____

_____

_____

Fall

_____

_____

_____

Winter

_____

_____

_____

Seasons

77

Name:_____

Words About Seasons

Directions: Use the words in the Word Bank to complete the puzzle about the seasons.

Across

2. In the winter, I _____ in the snow.
3. In the spring, birds lay their _____ .
5. In the autumn, leaves fall from the _____ .

Down

1. In the spring, _____ start to bloom.
4. I swim on a _____ summer day.

Word Bank		
flowers	eggs	hot
trees		play

Name:_____

Unit 3 Review

Directions: Use the Word Bank to write the job word that completes each sentence. Then, circle the two adjectives in each sentence.

Word Bank				
zookeeper	plumber	mathematician	nurse	seamstress

1. The smart _____ solves the difficult problems.

2. The talented _____ sews a beautiful dress.

3. The caring _____ takes care of her sick patient.

4. The busy _____ feeds the hungry animals.

5. The handy _____ fixes the leaky sink.

Directions: Use the Word Bank to write the weather word that completes each sentence.

Word Bank			
clouds	weather	lightning	sunny

1. I saw _____ flash outside my window.

2. A _____ day is perfect for a picnic.

3. The rain _____ were thick and dark.

4. When the _____ is cold, you should dress warmly.

79

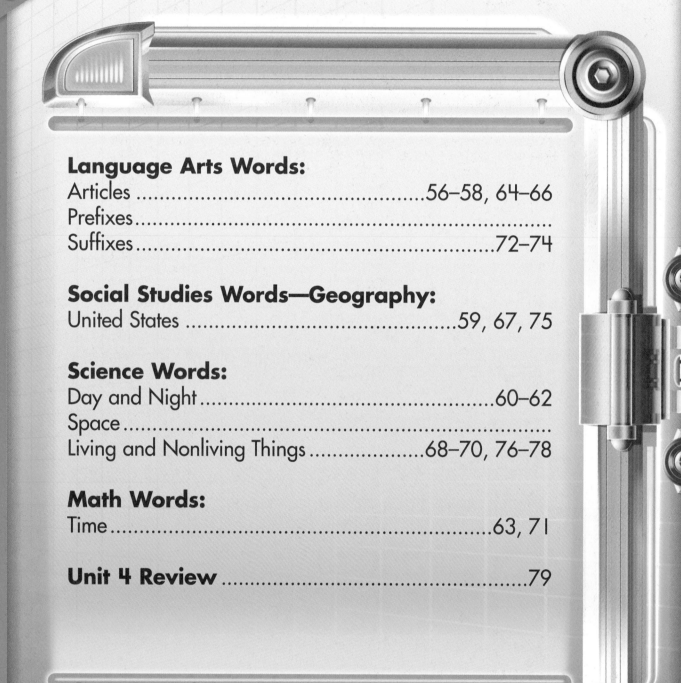

UNIT 4

Language Arts Words:
Articles 56–58, 64–66
Prefixes...
Suffixes 72–74

Social Studies Words—Geography:
United States 59, 67, 75

Science Words:
Day and Night...60–62
Space ....
Living and Nonliving Things 68–70, 76–78

Math Words:
Time...63, 71

Unit 4 Review 79

Name:_____

Words That Are Articles

Articles are words that come before nouns. **A** and **an** are articles. Use **a** before a word that begins with a consonant. Use **an** before a word that begins with a vowel.

Example: A man ran fast. He was **an** energetic man.

Directions: Circle the correct article that completes each sentence.

1. Our class had **a** / **an** picnic in the park.

2. Miss Lee passed **an** / **a** ball to me.

3. We saw **a** / **an** anthill by the trees.

4. **A** / **An** woman fished by the pond.

5. Today was **a** / **an** fun day.

UNIT 4

Name:_____

Words That Are Articles

Directions: Read each sentence. Write **a** or **an** on the line to complete the sentence.

UNIT 4

1. My family went to _____ zoo to see some wild animals.

2. We saw _____ elephant that was really big.

3. _____ lion waved its tail at us as we walked by.

4. There was _____ alligator that showed us its large teeth.

5. There were monkeys swinging playfully from the branches of _____ tree.

6. My family had _____ great day!

Name:_____

Words That Are Articles

Directions: Write **a** or **an** beside each word.

Examples: **a** turtle
　　　　　　an owl

1. _____ kangaroo

2. _____ ostrich

3. _____ frog

4. _____ goat

5. _____ lion

6. _____ elephant

7. _____ snail

8. _____ bat

9. _____ tiger

10. _____ cat

11. _____ ant

12. _____ zebra

13. _____ pig

14. _____ dog

15. _____ whale

16. _____ skunk

Name:_____

Words About the United States

Directions: Study the map of the United States. Follow the instructions.

1. Draw a star on the state where you live.

2. Draw a line from your state to the Atlantic Ocean.

3. Draw a triangle in the Gulf of Mexico.

4. Draw a circle in the Pacific Ocean.

5. Color each state that borders your state a different color.

Name:_____

Words That Are Articles

Directions: Write **a** or **an** beside each word.

Examples: a turtle
an owl

1. _____ kangaroo

2. _____ ostrich

3. _____ frog

4. _____ goat

5. _____ lion

6. _____ elephant

7. _____ snail

8. _____ bat

9. _____ tiger

10. _____ cat

11. _____ ant

12. _____ zebra

13. _____ pig

14. _____ dog

15. _____ whale

16. _____ skunk

 Articles

83

© 2007 School Specialty Publishing

Name:_____

Words About the United States

Directions: Study the map of the United States. Follow the instructions.

1. Draw a star on the state where you live.

2. Draw a line from your state to the Atlantic Ocean.

3. Draw a triangle in the Gulf of Mexico.

4. Draw a circle in the Pacific Ocean.

5. Color each state that borders your state a different color.

UNIT 4

Name:_____

Words About Day and Night

Directions: Read the words in the Word Bank. If they relate to day, write them under the sun. If they relate to night, write them under the moon.

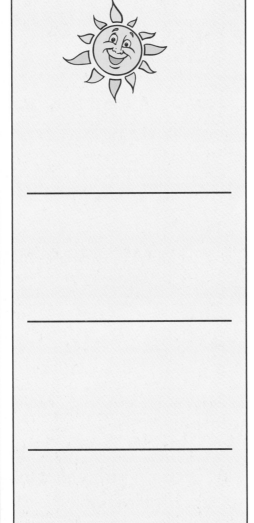

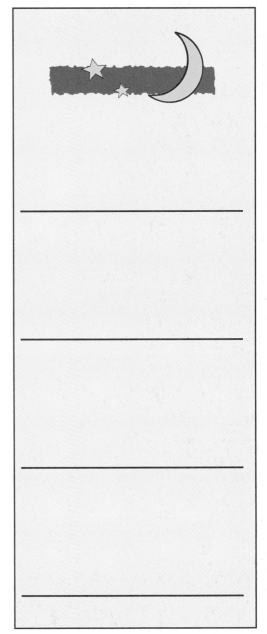

Word Bank

sun

light

moon

awake

asleep

dark

stars

heat

Name:_____

Time of Day Words

Directions: Fill in the circle beside the word that answers each question.

1. Which word means "not light"?

   (A) dark

   (B) hot

   (C) cool

2. Which word means "full of sun"?

   (A) sunshine

   (B) dark

   (C) sunny

3. Which word means "the early hours of night"?

   (A) morning

   (B) dawn

   (C) evening

4. Which word is "the time when the sun comes up"?

   (A) sunrise

   (B) sunset

   (C) sunshine

5. Which word means "middle of the day"?

   (A) dawn

   (B) dusk

   (C) noon

6. Which word means "middle of the night"?

   (A) midnight

   (B) midday

   (C) night

UNIT 4

Day and Night

86

Name:_____

Space Words

Directions: Read each clue. Find the matching word in the puzzle and write it on the line. Connect the puzzle dots in the same order as your answers. Then, color the picture.

Clues

1. The planet we live on _____

2. The closest star _____

3. They shine in the sky at night. _____

4. Earth is a _____ .

5. Planets, stars, and moons are in

_____ .

6. Time when the sun shines

_____

7. A group of stars

_____

8. A person who travels in space

_____

9. The path a planet follows to travel

around the sun _____

10. It gives us light at night.

_____

11. People who study the

stars _____

12. You use this to see the

stars. _____

13. Time when the sun does not

shine _____

14. We feel this from the sun.

_____

Earth

sun

night

heat

stars

telescope

planet

space

astronomers

moon

day

constellation

orbit

astronaut

87

UNIT 4

Name:_____

Time Words

Directions: Circle each mouse if it has a time word.

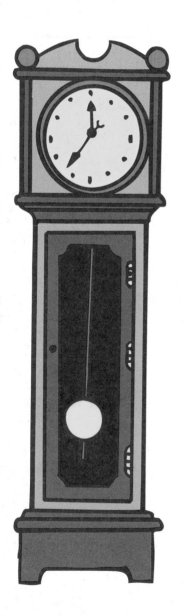

minute

week

flower

month

hour

day

catch

second

patch

year

Words With Prefixes

A **prefix** is a word part that goes at the beginning of a base word to change the word's meaning. The prefix **re-** means "again."

Example:    **Refill** means "to fill again."

Directions: Look at the pictures. Read the base words. Add the prefix **re** to the base word to show that the action is being repeated. Write the new word on the line.

read

1. _____

paint

2. _____

build

3. _____

write

4. _____

use

5. _____

pay

6. _____

Name:_____

Words With Prefixes

The prefixes **un-** and **dis-** mean "not" or "the opposite of."

Unlocked means "not locked."

Dismount is the opposite of "mount."

Directions: Look at the pictures. Circle the word that tells about each picture. Then, write the word on the line.

tied

untied

1. _____

like

dislike

4. _____

happy

unhappy

2. _____

obey

disobey

5. _____

safe

unsafe

3. _____

honest

dishonest

6. _____

Name:_____

Words With Prefixes

The prefix **un-** means "not." The prefix **mis-** means "bad or wrong."

Directions: Change the meaning of the sentences by adding the prefixes to the bold words. Write the new word on the line to complete each sentence.

1. The boy was **lucky** because he **read** the directions.

   The boy was (un) _____ because he

   (mis) _____ the directions.

2. When Mary **behaved**, she felt **happy**.

   When Mary (mis) _____ ,

   she felt (un) _____ .

3. Mike **understood** because he was **familiar** with the book.

   Mike (mis) _____ because he was

   (un) _____ with the book.

UNIT 4

Name:_____

Words About Your State

Directions: The United States of America has 50 states. Think about your own state. Answer the questions.

1. What is the name of your state?

_____

2. What is your state capital?

_____

3. What is the name of your city or town?

_____

4. What is special about your state?

_____

_____

_____

THANK YOU FOR VISITING OUR GREAT STATE!

UNIT 4

Name:_____

Space Words

Directions: Read the paragraph. Then, use the bold words to answer the questions.

There are eight planets that move around the sun. Our planet is **Earth**. Earth is closest to **Mars** and **Venus**. **Jupiter** is the largest planet. It is many times larger than Earth. **Saturn** is the planet with seven rings around it. The smallest planet is called **Mercury**!

1. How many planets are there?   three   eight   seven

2. I am your planet. _____

3. We are closest to Earth. _____   _____

4. I am the largest planet. _____

5. I am the planet with seven rings. _____

6. I am the smallest planet. _____

7. Draw three red rings around Saturn.

UNIT 4

Name:_____

Words About Planets

In our solar system, eight planets circle the sun. **Mercury** is the planet closest to the sun, followed by the planets **Venus**, **Earth**, and **Mars**. These four planets are called the **inner solar system**. The **outer solar system** is made up of **Jupiter**, **Saturn**, **Uranus**, and **Neptune**.

Directions: Write the names of the planets on the lines according to their distances from the sun. Then, color the picture.

Neptune	Jupiter	Earth	Mercury
Venus	Uranus	Saturn	Mars

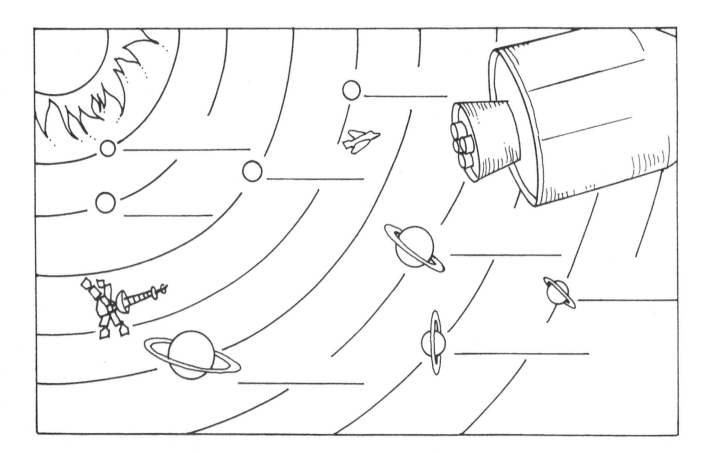

Name:_____

Space Words

Directions: Read each sentence. Write the correct word on the line from the Word Bank.

Word Bank
Mercury
Earth
Jupiter
planets
sun
star

1. Our solar system has eight of these. _____

2. This is a planet with land and water. _____

3. This is a huge star you see during the day. _____

4. This is the beginning of a popular lullaby, "Twinkle, twinkle,

   little _____ ."

5. This is the smallest planet. _____

6. This is the largest planet. _____

Name:_____

Time Words

A clock has two hands to tell us the time.
The big hand is called the **minute hand**.
The little hand is called the **hour hand**.

Directions: Color the minute hand purple.
Color the hour hand yellow. Then, write **minute
hand** or **hour hand** on the line to complete
each sentence correctly.

On this clock, the
_____ is
pointing to the
number 9.

The _____
is pointing to the
number 12.

That is how a clock tells us it is 9 o'clock.

On this clock, the _____ is pointing to the
number 12.
The _____ is pointing to the number 3.
That is how a clock tells us it is 3 o'clock.

Name:_____

Words With Suffixes

A **suffix** is a word part that is added to the end of a word to change its meaning.

The suffix **-ful** means "full of." **Wonderful** means "full of wonder."
The suffix **-less** means "without." **Comfortless** means "without comfort."
The suffix **-ness** means "a state of being." **Sadness** means "being sad."
The suffix **-ly** means "in this way." **Carefully** means "in a careful way."

Directions: Add the suffixes to the base words to make new words. Write the new words on the lines.

1. color + ful = _____

2. help + less = _____

3. quiet + ly = _____

4. nice + ly = _____

5. fit + ness = _____

Suffixes

97

Name:_____

Words With Suffixes

A **suffix** is a word part that goes at the end of a word to change its meaning.

UNIT 4

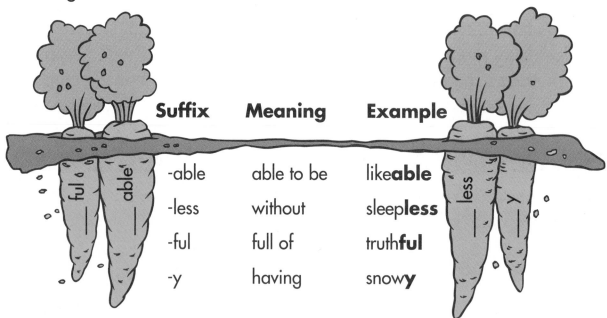

Suffix	Meaning	Example
-able	able to be	like**able**
-less	without	sleep**less**
-ful	full of	truth**ful**
-y	having	snow**y**

Directions: Circle the suffix in each word.

Example: fluff(y)

1. rainy
2. blameless
3. peaceful

4. thoughtful
5. enjoyable
6. careless

7. likeable
8. helpful
9. silky

Directions: Write a word on the line for each meaning.

1. full of hope _____
2. without hope _____
3. without power_____

4. having rain _____
5. able to break _____
6. full of cheer _____

Name:_____

Words With Suffixes

Directions: Add the suffixes to the base words to make new words. Write the words on the lines.

1. help + ful = _____

2. care + less = _____

3. clean + ness = _____

4. wind + y = _____

5. love + ly = _____

6. break + able = _____

Directions: Use the new words from above to complete the sentences.

1. Flying a kite works best on a _____ day.

2. My mother never lets my brother near _____ things in the store.

3. Sally is always _____ to her mother.

4. I earned an allowance for the _____ of my room.

5. The flowers are _____ .

6. It is _____ to cross the street without looking both ways.

Suffixes

99

UNIT 4

Name:_____

Words About the United States

UNIT 4

Directions: Read the state facts. Use the map to locate each state. Then, follow the directions to color the map.

1. The Liberty Bell rang at the first reading of the Declaration of Independence. It is in Philadelphia, Pennsylvania. Color Pennsylvania red.

2. The Statue of Liberty is in New York Harbor. Color New York blue.

3. Rhode Island is the smallest state. Color Rhode Island yellow.

4. Florida is called "The Sunshine State." Color Florida orange.

5. Idaho is famous for its potatoes. Color Idaho brown.

6. Hawaii was the 50th state to join the United States. This state is made of eight main islands. Color Hawaii green.

7. Montana means "mountain" in Spanish. Color Montana purple.

Name:_____

Space Words

Word Bank		
astronomer	Earth	moon
sun	planets	stars	space

Directions: Use the words in the Word Bank to complete the sentences.

1. A constellation is a group of _____ .

2. You can see the _____ in the night sky.

3. Mars is one of the eight _____ .

4. An _____ studies the stars.

5. We live on the planet _____ .

6. You cannot see the _____ shine at night.

7. Rockets can fly into _____ .

UNIT 4

Name:_____

Space Words

If you look in the sky on a clear night, you may see groups of stars. People draw imaginary lines between those stars to form pictures of animals, people, or things. Each picture is called a **constellation**. One constellation is called **The Big Dipper**. It looks like a cup with a long handle.

Directions: Connect the stars from 1 to 7 to make The Big Dipper.

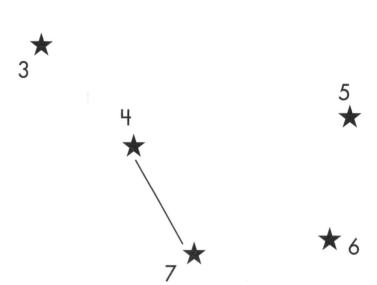

UNIT 4

Name:_____

Space Words

Directions: Read about Kim the astronomer. Then, fill in the circle beside the word that correctly completes each sentence.

Kim loves to look at the night sky. She is interested in astronomy. Her dad got her a telescope. Things that are far away, like the moon, stars, and planets, look bigger through her telescope. Kim and her family camp at a state park, away from city lights. Kim always brings her telescope. On these clear nights, she can enjoy the wonders of the night sky.

1. The study of stars and planets is called _____ .

   Ⓐ   astronomy

   Ⓑ   geology

   Ⓒ   math

3. Kim enjoys clear nights in a _____ .

   Ⓐ   city

   Ⓑ   state park

   Ⓒ   small town

2. Things in the sky look bigger with a _____ .

   Ⓐ   microscope

   Ⓑ   telescope

   Ⓒ   magnifying glass

Name:_____

Unit 4 Review

Directions: Write the letter of each description on the right that matches the words on the left.

1. ____ a

2. ____ minute hand

3. ____ sunrise

4. ____ Hawaii

5. ____ Gulf of Mexico

6. ____ ness

7. ____ second, minute, hour

8. ____ The Big Dipper

9. ____ stars

10. ____ astronomer

11. ____ unsafe, disobey, reread

12. ____ Jupiter

a. The largest planet

b. Things you see in the night sky

c. Time words

d. Words with prefixes

e. Use this article before a word that begins with a consonant.

f. State made up of eight main islands

g. A person who studies the stars

h. A constellation

i. The big hand on a clock

j. The body of water near Texas

k. A suffix that means "a state of being"

l. The time when the sun comes up

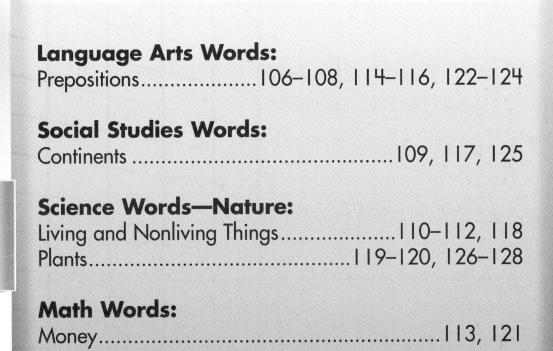

Language Arts Words:
Prepositions....................106–108, 114–116, 122–124

Social Studies Words:
Continents 109, 117, 125

Science Words—Nature:
Living and Nonliving Things...................110–112, 118
Plants...119–120, 126–128

Math Words:
Money..113, 121

Unit 5 Review 129

Name:_____

Words That Are Prepositions

Prepositions are words that show a connection between a noun or pronoun and another word. **Across** and **between** are prepositions.

Directions: Follow the directions to complete the picture.

- Draw a matching black circle across from the black circle.
- Draw a triangle between the circles.
- Draw a big circle around all the shapes.
- Color funny hair on the outside of the big circle.
- Write your clown's name beside him.
- Color your clown.

Name:_____

Words That Are Prepositions

Directions: Use a preposition from the first box and words from the second box to complete each sentence. The first one is done for you.

between	around	inside	outside	behind	across

the yard	the house	the table	the school	the box
the hill	the picture	the field	the puddle	the park

1. Our garden grows <u>behind the house</u> .

2. We like to play _____ .

3. The street is _____ .

4. Can you run _____ ?

5. Let's ride bikes _____ .

UNIT 5

Name:_____

Words That Are Prepositions

Directions: Draw a line from each sentence to its picture. Then, complete each sentence with the word under the picture. Write the word on the line.

Example:

He is walking __behind__ the tree.

outside

1. We stay _____ when it rains.

behind

between

2. She drew a dog _____ his house.

3. She stands _____ her friends.

across

4. They walked _____ the bridge.

around

5. Let the cat go _____ .

beside

6. Draw a circle _____ the fish.

inside

UNIT 5

Name:_____

Words About Continents

Continents are huge landmasses on the earth. The map shows the seven continents.

Directions: Complete each sentence by writing the correct continent on the line. Use the map to help you. Then, color the map.

1. The continent east of Antarctica is _____ .

2. The continent east of South America is _____ .

3. The continent farthest south is _____ .

4. We live on the continent of _____ .

5. There are _____ continents.

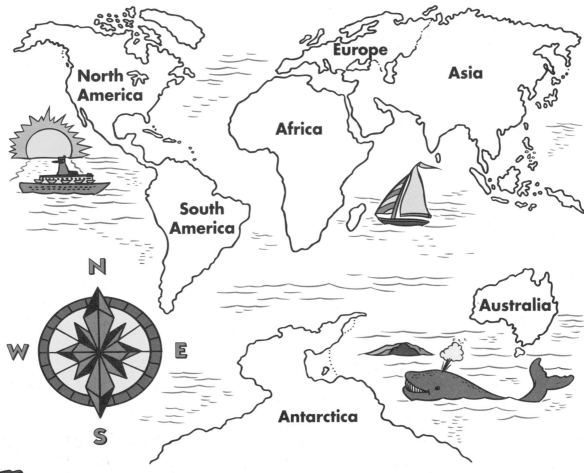

UNIT 5

Name:_____

Words About Living and Nonliving Things

Living things need air, food, and water to live. **Nonliving** things are not alive.

Directions: Write each word from the Word Bank in the correct category.

Living	Nonliving
1. _____	1. _____
2. _____	2. _____
3. _____	3. _____
4. _____	4. _____
5. _____	5. _____
6. _____	6. _____

Word Bank

car	kitten	cow
truck	nest	plane
hen	boat	dog
bird	rock	tree

Name:_____

Words About Living and Nonliving Things

Directions: Write each word from the Word Bank in the correct category.

Living	Nonliving
1. _____	1. _____
2. _____	2. _____
3. _____	3. _____
4. _____	4. _____
5. _____	5. _____
6. _____	6. _____

UNIT 5

Word Bank

flower	book	boy	dog	chair	bread
tree	camera	car	horse	ant	shoe

Name:_____

Words About Living and Nonliving Things

Directions: Use yellow to color the spaces that have words about living things. Use blue to color the spaces that have words about nonliving things.

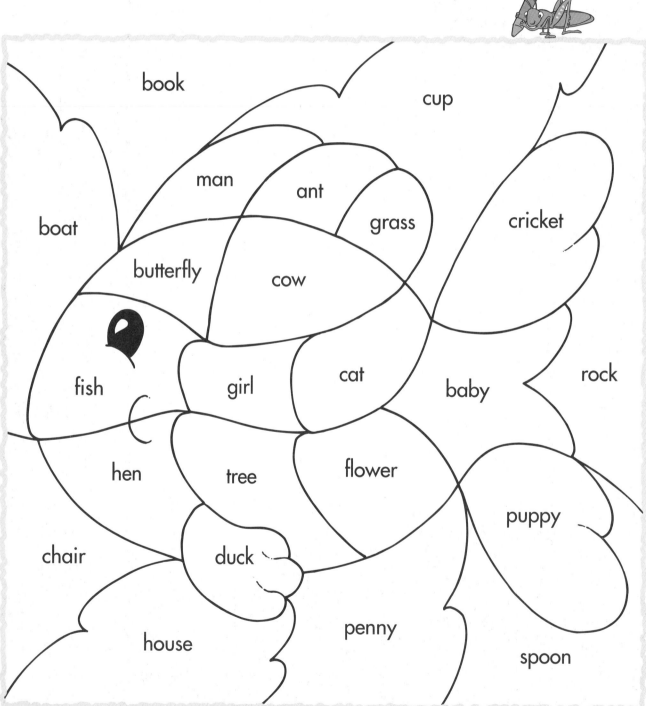

UNIT 5

Name:_____

Money Words

"One dollar" can be written as $1.00.

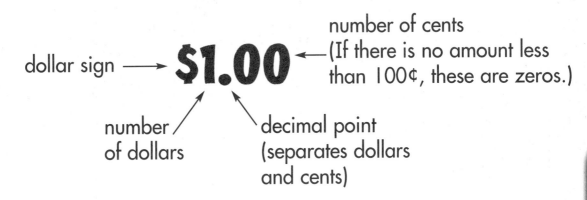

dollar sign →

number of cents (If there is no amount less than 100¢, these are zeros.)

$1.00

number of dollars

decimal point (separates dollars and cents)

This is the most common way to write **one dollar**.

Written this way, the number of dollars stays to the left of the decimal point and the cents stay to the right.

Directions: Circle the best answer that completes each sentence.

1. A **decimal point / dot** separates dollars and cents.

2. The symbol $ is called a **dollar bill / dollar sign**.

3. The numbers to the left of the decimal point are the **cents / dollars**.

4. The numbers to the right of the decimal point are the **cents / dollars**.

Name:_____

Words That Are Prepositions

Directions: Use the words in the Word Bank to answer each question.

1. Where is the slice of pizza? _____

    _____

2. Where is the boy sitting? _____

    _____

3. Where is the trash can? _____

    _____

4. Where is the silverware? _____

    _____

Word Bank

next to

near

by

beside

in front of

behind

Name:_____

Words That Are Prepositions

Directions: Draw a ball where it belongs in each picture.

1. under the table

2. in front of the box

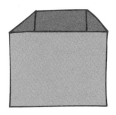

3. next to the chair

4. on the table

5. beside the box

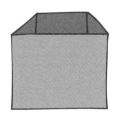

6. to the right of the chair

Directions: Write a preposition on the line to tell where the ball is in each drawing.

1.

2.

_____   _____

UNIT 5

Name:_____

Words That Are Prepositions

Directions: Follow the instructions to complete the picture. The prepositions will tell you where to draw things in the room.

Draw a between the two . Color it red.

Draw a 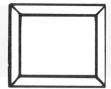 under the window. Color it green.

Draw three big  on the wall. Color them orange.

Name:_____

Words About Continents

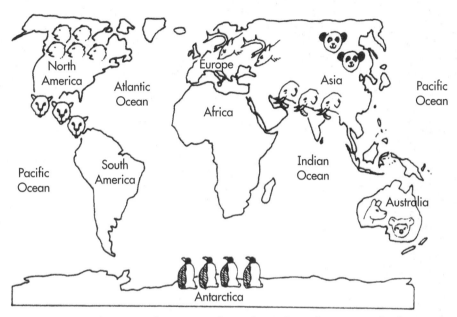

Directions: The map above shows what kinds of animals live on each continent. Color one square for each animal on the map. Use a different color for each animal. Then, color the map.

kangaroo					
elephant					
panda					
koala					
polar bear					
reindeer					
penguin					
jaguar					
	1	2	3	4	5

Name:_____

Words About Living and Nonliving Things

Directions: Look at each picture. Fill in the correct circle beside the word to show whether each thing is living or nonliving.

UNIT 5

1. ○ Living ○ Nonliving

2. ○ Living ○ Nonliving

3. ○ Living ○ Nonliving

4. ○ Living ○ Nonliving

5. ○ Living ○ Nonliving

6. ○ Living ○ Nonliving

7. ○ Living ○ Nonliving

8. ○ Living ○ Nonliving

9. ○ Living ○ Nonliving

10. ○ Living ○ Nonliving

11. ○ Living ○ Nonliving

12. ○ Living ○ Nonliving

Living and Nonliving Things

Name:_____

Words About Plants

Directions: Read the instructions and use the words in the Word Bank to complete the chart. Start at the arrow.

Word Bank

flower

root

leaf

stem

seed

1. Go right 5 spaces. Then go down 3 spaces and left 5 spaces. Write the word that names what grows into a new plant here.
2. Now go up 2 spaces. Then go right 6 spaces and down 3 spaces. Write the word that names the part of the plant that is underground here.
3. Now go up 3 spaces. Then go left 3 spaces and down 1 space. Write the word that names the part of the plant that makes the food here.
4. Now go right 2 spaces. Then go up 1 space and left 4 spaces. Write the word that names the part of the plant that carries food and water to the rest of the plant here.
5. Now go down 2 spaces. Then go right 5 spaces and up 3 spaces. Write the word that names the part of the plant that makes the seeds here.

Plants

© 2007 School Specialty Publishing

Name:_____

Words About Plants

Directions: Read the story. Then, complete the sentences.

Weed is the word used for any plant that grows where it is not wanted. Grasses that grow in your flower or vegetable garden are weeds. An unwanted flower growing in your lawn is also a weed. Dandelions are this kind of weed.

People do not plant weeds. They grow very fast. If you do not pull them out or kill them, weeds will crowd out the plants that you want to grow. The seeds of many kinds of weeds are spread by the wind. Birds and other animals also carry weed seeds.

1. A weed is any plant that grows _____

_____ .

2. One kind of flowering weed is the _____

_____ .

3. Two things that spread the seeds of weeds are

_____ and _____ .

UNIT 5

Name:_____

Money Words

Directions: Read the words on the coins. To fill the piggy bank, find the words and circle them. Look across, down, and diagonally.

money
bank

earn
count

quarter
dime

nickel
penny

dollar
savings

coins
cents

```
Q U A M S B R I D P L
T U D S O A M B S E C
A S A V I N G S P N O
B A S R O K E C E A I
A C E N T S I Y N T N
L O T L R E H S N O S
N I C K E L R D Y R Q
P F K E N Q U I L D U
D O L L A R Q V E I E
O M G A M R S G J M D
P E R C O U N T O E R
```

Name:_____

Words That Are Prepositions

Directions: Use a preposition to tell where the cat is in each sentence. The first one is done for you.

1.  The cat is behind the box.

2.  _____
_____

3.  _____
_____

4.  _____
_____

5.  _____
_____

Name:_____

Words That Are Prepositions

Prepositions show a connection between a noun and another word. Some prepositions are **on**, **in**, **to**, **toward**, **over**, and **behind**.

Directions: Read the story. Then, circle the prepositions.

Molly had the bat in her hands. The catcher had his mask on his face. He crouched behind home plate. Everyone had their eyes on the pitcher. Roy yelled, "Hit it toward second base!" Molly listened. She hit the ball so hard that it went over the fence. Molly raced to first base.

Name:_____

Words That Are Prepositions

Directions: Use one of the prepositions from the Word Bank to complete each sentence.

Word Bank					
between	around	inside	outside	beside	across

Example:

She will hide ___under___ the basket.

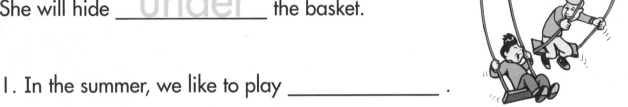

1. In the summer, we like to play _____ .

2. She can swim _____ the lake.

3. Put the bird _____ its cage so it won't fly away.

4. Sit _____ Bill and me so we can all work together.

5. Your picture is right _____ mine on the wall.

6. The fence goes _____ the house.

UNIT 5

Name:_____

Words About Continents

Directions: Use the words in the Word Bank to write the name of each continent below its picture.

1. _____

3. _____

5. _____

2. _____

4. _____

6. _____

7. _____

Word Bank			
Africa	Asia	Europe	South America
Antarctica	Australia	North America	

Name:_____

Words About Plants

Directions: Read about the Venus flytrap. Then, read each sentence below. If it is true, circle the sentence. If it is not true, put an **X** on the sentence.

Many insects eat plants. There is one kind of plant that eats insects. It is the Venus flytrap. The Venus flytrap works like a trap. Each leaf is shaped like a circle. The circle is in two parts. When the leaf closes, the two parts fold together. The leaf has little spikes all the way around it. Inside the leaf, there are little hairs. If an insect touches the little hairs, the two sides of the Venus flytrap leaf will clap together. The spikes will trap the insect inside. The Venus flytrap will then eat the insect.

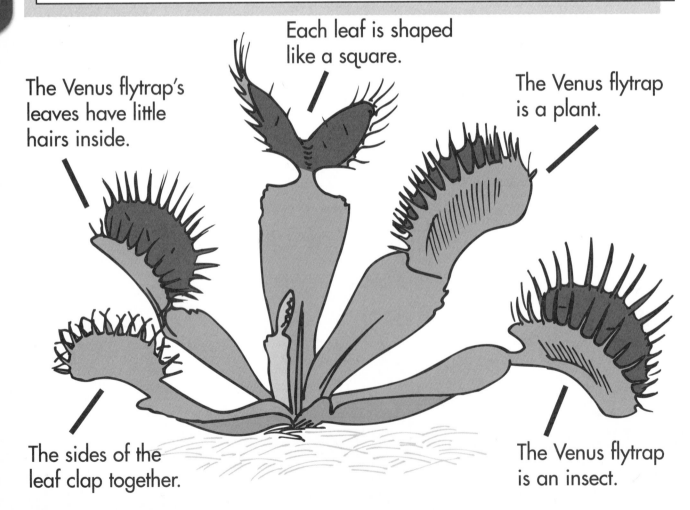

Each leaf is shaped like a square.

The Venus flytrap's leaves have little hairs inside.

The Venus flytrap is a plant.

The sides of the leaf clap together.

The Venus flytrap is an insect.

Name:_____

Words About Plants

Directions: Use the words in the Word Bank to label the parts of the plant.

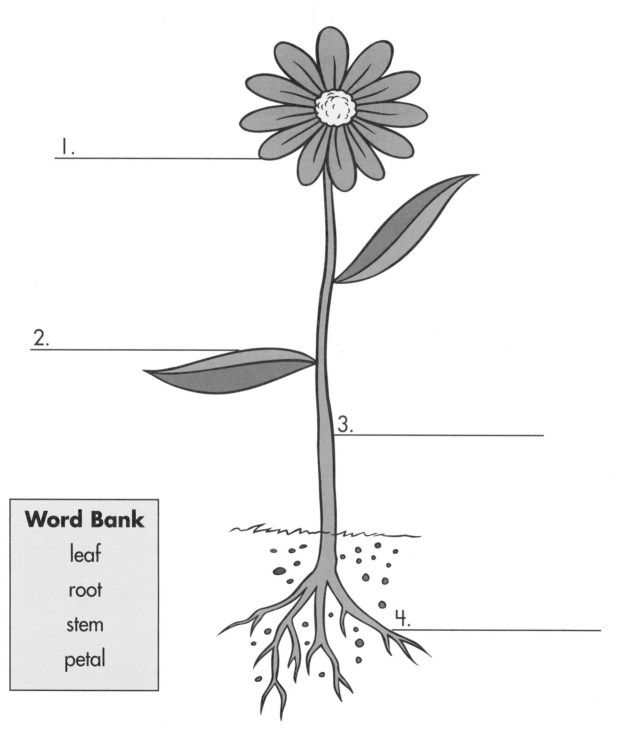

1._____

2._____

3._____

4._____

Word Bank

leaf

root

stem

petal

UNIT 5

Name:_____

Words About Plants

Directions: Use a word from the Word Bank to complete each sentence. Then, color the picture.

Max and Gina spent the morning at the park. They planted a _____ . First, they dug a hole. They took the tree out of the container. They loosened the _____ gently so that they had room to grow in the ground. Max and Gina put the tree in the hole. The _____ of the tree was slim and weak, so they staked it. Soon, the top _____ would be strong and full of leaves.

Word Bank

trunk

branches

tree

roots

© 2007 School Specialty Publishing

Name:_____

Unit 5 Review

Directions: Circle the correct word that completes each sentence. Then, write the word on the line.

1. A plant grows from a _____ .
   petal   seed

2. Elephants and _____ live in Asia.
   pandas   koalas

3. Trees, people, and animals are _____ things.
   living   nonliving

4. We stay _____ to keep dry when it rains.
   outside   inside

5. Four _____ equal $1.00.
   dimes   quarters

6. A car, a book, and a _____ are examples of nonliving things.
   cat   chair

7. The children ran _____ the school to return to class.
   toward   behind

8. There are _____ continents.
   eleven   seven

9. My baby sister sits _____ an umbrella to protect herself from the sun.
   under   next to

10. The _____ of a plant lives underground.
    root   leaf

UNIT 5

UNIT 6

Language Arts Words:
Synonyms 131–133, 139–141, 147–149

Social Studies Words:
Early America 134, 142
Native Americans 150

Science Words—Plants:
Trees 135–137, 151
Plants (General Information) 143, 153
Seeds 144–145
Flowers 152

Math Words:
Fractions 138, 146

Unit 6 Review 154

Name:_____

Words That Are Synonyms

Synonyms are words with nearly the same meaning.

Directions: Draw a line to match each word on the left with its synonym on the right.

infant	hello
forest	coat
bucket	grin
hi	baby
bunny	woods
cheerful	fall
jacket	repair
alike	small
smile	same
autumn	hop
little	skinny
thin	top
jump	rabbit
shirt	pail
fix	happy

Synonyms

131

© 2007 School Specialty Publishing

Name:_____

Words That Are Synonyms

Directions: Read the story. Then, write a synonym from the Word Bank to complete each sentence.

Word Bank

| funny | unhappy |
| windy | little |

A New Balloon

It was a breezy day. The wind blew the small child's balloon away. The child was sad. A silly clown gave him a new balloon.

1. It was a _____ day.

2. The wind blew the _____ child's balloon away.

3. The child was _____ .

4. A _____ clown gave him a new balloon.

UNIT 6

Name:_____

Words That Are Synonyms

Directions: Read the sentences that tell about each picture. Draw a circle around the word that means the same as the bold word.

1.

The child is **unhappy**.

hungry   sad

2.

The baby was very **tired**.

sleepy   hurt

3.

The ladybug is so **tiny**.

small   red

4.

The flowers are **lovely**.

pretty   green

5.

The **funny** clown made us laugh.

glad   silly

6.

We saw a **scary** tiger.

frightening   ugly

UNIT 6

Name:_____

Words About Early America

Although the lives of the colonists were different than ours today, many of their needs were the same.

Directions: Unscramble the names of objects we use today. The first letter of each word is underlined. Then, draw a line to match similar objects of the past and present. Color the pictures.

UNIT 6

Present

c<u>e</u>telrci   nka<u>b</u>lte

_____   _____

ma<u>pl</u>

_____

sat<u>em</u>hc

_____

tl<u>p</u>ea

_____

e<u>p</u>n

_____

Past

candles

bed warmer

quill and ink well

wooden trencher

tinder box

Name:_____

Words About Trees

Directions: Read the words in the Word Bank. These things all come from trees! Circle the words in the puzzle. Look across and down. Then, color the picture.

Word Bank

syrup   lumber   medicine
fruit   furniture   shelter
nuts   paper   rubber

P	S	H	E	L	T	E	R	F
A	R	U	B	B	E	R	L	R
P	K	N	U	T	S	L	U	U
E	S	Y	R	U	P	W	M	I
R	N	M	M	V	J	B	T	T
M	E	D	I	C	I	N	E	D
F	U	R	N	I	T	U	R	E

Words About Leaves

This tricky tree has four different kinds of leaves: ash, poison ivy, silver maple, and white oak.

Directions: Follow the instructions. Then, answer the questions.

1. Underline the white oak leaves. 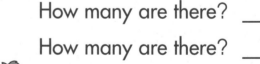 How many are there? _____

2. Circle the ash leaves. How many are there? _____

3. Draw an **X** on the poison ivy leaves. How many are there? _____

4. Draw a box around the silver maple leaves. How many are there? _____

Name:_____

Words About Leaves

Directions: Gather some leaves. Put your leaves into groups by type. Then, answer the questions.

white oak   red oak   pine   ash

elm   silver maple   red maple

1. How many white oak leaves did you find? _____

2. How many red oak leaves did you find? _____

3. How many pine needles did you find? _____

4. How many ash leaves did you find? _____

5. How many elm leaves did you find? _____

6. How many silver maple leaves did you find? _____

7. How many red maple leaves did you find? _____

8. What other kinds of leaves did you find? Use a book to help you name them. Write their names here. _____

_____

_____

_____

UNIT 6

Name:_____

Fraction Words

Directions: Read each fraction. Draw a line from the fraction to the shape with that amount shaded.

1. one-fourth

2. two-fourths

3. one-half

4. one-third

5. two-thirds

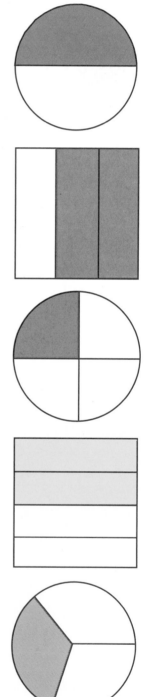

Name:_____

Words That Are Synonyms

Directions: Circle the two words in each line that have almost the same meaning.

1. gooey   sticky   hard

2. slow   hurry   rush

3. slope   hill   sled

4. stop   green   end

5. treat   pledge   promise

6. piece   bit   pie

7. excuse   easy   simple

8. complete   whole   pile

Name:_____

Words That Are Synonyms

Synonyms are words that have almost the same meaning. **Tired** and **sleepy** are synonyms. **Talk** and **speak** are synonyms.

Directions: Draw a line from each word on the left to its synonym on the right.

1. drink   ill

2. open   stare

3. shy   kind

4. stand   sip

5. sick   rise

6. good   told

7. said   unlock

8. look   timid

Name:_____

Words That Are Synonyms

Directions: Circle the synonym of the bold word in each sentence.

1. I am **happy** to write you a letter.

   glad   sad

2. I hope my grandma will like this **gift**.

   present   toaster

3. I always **laugh** when I watch my silly kitten.

   chuckle   worry

4. My friend loves to **talk** on the telephone.

   draw   chat

5. The little boy was **charming** to his grandmother.

   delightful   naughty

6. Can you please **sew** this fabric together?

   hitch   stitch

Name:_____

Words About Early America

Directions: Read the story. Circle the correct word that completes each sentence. Then, color the map.

From about 1760 to 1850, pioneers moved westward across the United States. They traveled in big covered wagons along several trails. Some started in a swampy area in Nauvoo, Illinois. Others started in Independence, Missouri. Some trails are marked on the map below.

1. In the 1800s, pioneers moved toward the **eastern / western** part of the United States.
2. They traveled by **train / wagon**.
3. The city of Independence is in **Illinois / Missouri**.

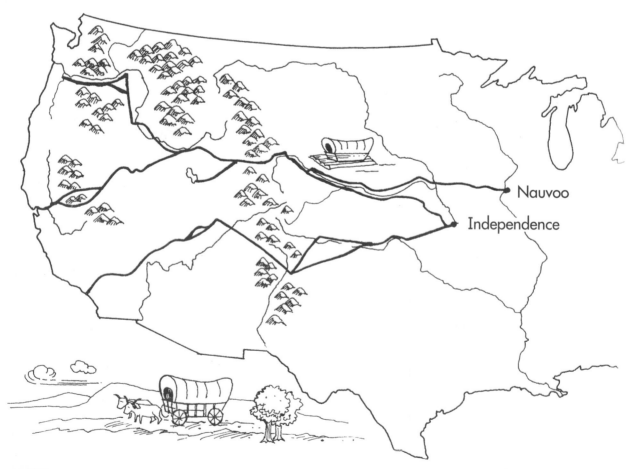

UNIT 6

Name:_____

Words About Plants

Directions: Use the pictures to complete the puzzle about plants. Write the missing letters in the puzzle.

Name:_____

Words About Seeds and Plants

Seeds are found in different parts of the plant. Some seeds are found in the flower. Some seeds are found in the fruit or the nut.

Directions: Color the part of the plant that has the seed. Use the words in the Word Bank to name the seeds.

Word Bank	
pine	maple
apple	acorn
corn	dandelion

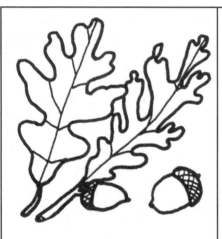

_____

_____

_____

_____

_____

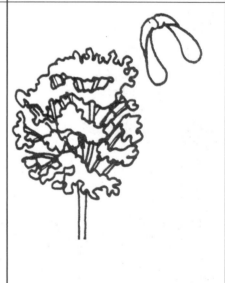

_____

UNIT 6

Name:_____

Words About Seeds

Directions: Read about seeds. Then, answer the questions.

The outer covering of a seed is called the seed coat. The seed coat protects the embryo, which is the tiny plant that lives in the seed. With sunlight, water, and oxygen, the tiny plant will explode out of the seed. This process is called germination.

The plant's roots, stem, and leaves will begin to grow. The plant will produce flowers, which will make a new batch of seeds.

1. What is the outer covering of a seed called? _____

   _____

2. What does the outer covering do? _____

   _____

3. What does a seed need to grow into a plant? _____

   _____

4. What is it called when a tiny plant explodes out of a seed? _____

   _____

5. What three parts of the plant begin to grow after germination? _____

   _____

UNIT 6

Name:_____

Fraction Words

Directions: Color each shape that is divided into equal parts.

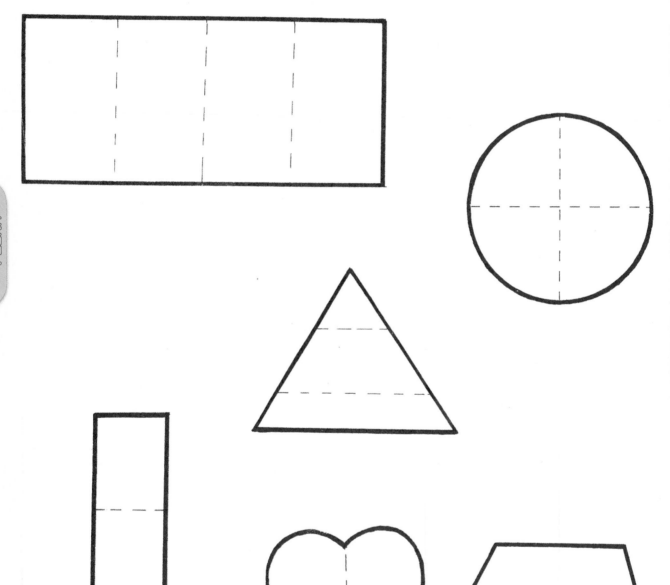

Words That Are Synonyms

Word Bank				
small	sofa	speak	woman	yell

Directions: Rewrite each sentence. Replace the underlined word with a synonym from the Word Bank.

1. My mother is the <u>lady</u> sitting on the bench.

_____

_____

2. Mrs. Roberts told the dog to get off the <u>couch</u>.

_____

_____

3. Jane has a <u>little</u> box of hair ribbons.

_____

_____

4. Don't <u>shout</u> so loudly.

_____

_____

5. You should <u>talk</u> softly when you are in the library.

_____

_____

Name:_____

Words That Are Synonyms

Directions: Use the Word Bank to write a word that has almost the same meaning as the bold word in each sentence.

Hey, you're *large*!

And you're *big*!

Word Bank		
itchy	fortress	phantom
instructor	job	difficult

1. My **teacher** is very smart! _____

2. I don't like that sweater. It is too **scratchy**. _____

3. My teacher gave a very **hard** test in math. _____

4. The prince lived in a **castle**. _____

5. Everyone has a **task** to do in my house. _____

6. The **ghost** at the fun house was so scary! _____

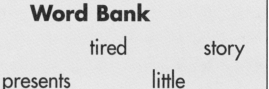

Name:_____

Words That Are Synonyms

Directions: Read the sentences. Use the Word Bank to write the synonym of each underlined word.

Word Bank		
friend	tired	story
presents	little	

1. I want to go to bed because I am very <u>sleepy</u>. _____

2. On my birthday, I like to open my <u>gifts</u>. _____

3. My <u>pal</u> and I like to play ball. _____

4. My favorite <u>tale</u> is *Cinderella*. _____

5. The mouse was so <u>tiny</u> that it was hard to catch. _____

Name:_____

Words About Native Americans

Directions: Use the pictures of the Native American houses to answer each riddle. Then, color the pictures.

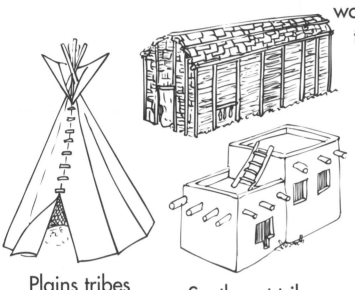

Eastern woodland tribes

Plains tribes

Southwest tribes

Northwest coastal tribes

1. This house has no beds. Many families live in it. It is made of adobe brick. It has no doors, only windows. Whose house is it? _____	3. This is called a plank house. Many families live in it. It is made of large beams and trees. It has a totem pole in front. Whose house is it? _____
2. This is called a long house. It has bunk beds. It is made of branches and bark. Fire burns in the center of it. Whose house is it? _____	4. This house can be set up in 10 minutes. One family lives in it. It is made of poles and animal skins. A fire burns inside. Whose house is it? _____

Name:_____

Words About Trees

Many different foods come from trees. People and animals eat this food.

Directions: Color the pictures of foods that come from trees.

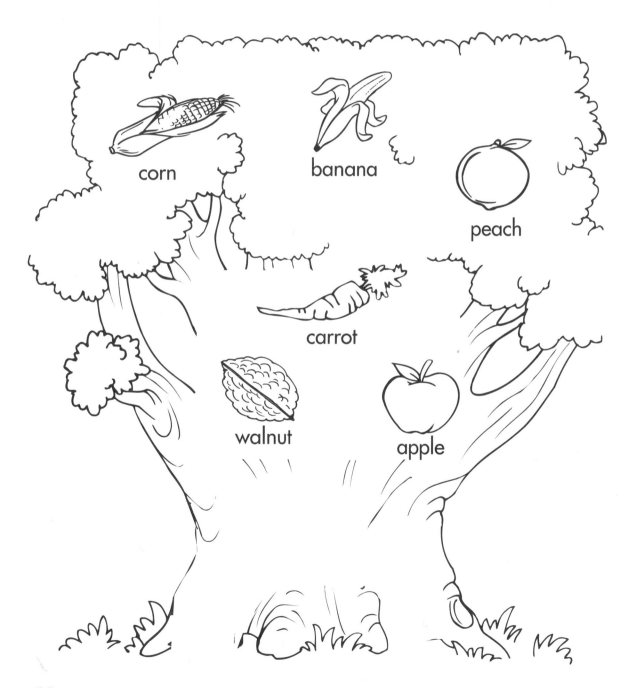

corn

banana

peach

carrot

walnut

apple

Name:_____

Words About Plants and Flowers

Directions: Use the Word Bank to find the words about plants and flowers. Circle the words in the puzzle. Look across and down.

t	s	c	e	s	u	b
e	b	w	a	t	e	r
a	r	d	k	l	b	c
r	o	o	t	s	p	m
t	s	s	b	t	l	s
c	e	i	l	e	a	f
e	j	f	o	m	n	s
m	g	r	o	w	t	o
t	s	b	m	n	i	a

Word Bank
roots

stem

rose

leaf

bloom

plant

grow

water

Name:_____

Words About Plants

We eat many plant parts. We may eat the leaves, the stem, the root, or the seeds.

Directions: Look at the pictures of the vegetables. Use the words in the Word Bank to write the name of the plant part that we eat. You may use the name of a plant part more than once.

Word Bank			
leaves	stem	root	seeds

1. _____

2. _____

3. _____

4. _____

5. _____

6. _____

Plants

153

Unit 6 Review

Directions: Write a sentence for each pair of synonyms.

1. funny/silly _____

_____

2. hurry/rush _____

_____

3. alike/same _____

_____

Directions: Circle the word that completes each sentence. Then, write the word on the line.

1. The math test was so _____ that I got an A.

   easy   hard

2. Jim was _____ to get a present from his grandparents.

   unhappy   glad

3. The colonists lived a _____ time ago.

   long   short

4. Pioneers traveled by _____ across the United States.

   car   wagon

5. My mother is the _____ waiting for me in the car.

   man   woman

6. The _____ writes the homework on the board.

   teacher   student

7. Some plants that we eat grow in the _____ .

   ground   air

Language Arts Words:
Antonyms.........................156–158, 164–166, 172–174

Social Studies Words:
Holidays...159, 167, 175

Science Words:
Food and Nutrition 160–162, 168–170, 176–178

Math Words:
Measurement 163, 171

Unit 7 Review 179

Words That Are Antonyms

Antonyms are words that have opposite meanings. **Dark** and **light** are opposites.

Directions: Write the antonym pairs from each sentence in the boxes.

Example: Many things are bought and sold at the market.

Name:_____

1. I thought I lost my dog, but someone found him.

2. The teacher will ask questions for the students to answer.

3. Airplanes arrive and depart from the airport.

4. The water in the pool was cold compared to the warm water in the whirlpool.

5. The tortoise was slow, but the hare was fast.

UNIT 7

Name:_____

Words That Are Antonyms

Antonyms are words that have opposite meanings. **Hot** and **cold** are antonyms. **Short** and **tall** are antonyms, too.

Directions: Draw a line from each word on the left to its antonym on the right.

sad	white
bottom	stop
black	fat
tall	top
thin	hard
little	found
cold	short
lost	hot
go	big
soft	happy

157

UNIT 7

Name:_____

Words That Are Antonyms

Directions: Tell a story about the picture by following the directions. Write one or two sentences for each answer.

Pet Store

1. Write about something that is happening quickly or slowly in the picture.

_____

_____

2. Use **top** or **bottom** in a sentence about the picture.

_____

_____

3. Tell about something hard and something soft in the picture. Use the word **but** in your sentence.

_____

_____

UNIT 7

Name:_____

Holiday Words

Fiction is something that is made up or not true. **Nonfiction** is about something that has really happened.

Directions: Read each story about the Fourth of July. Then, write whether it is fiction or nonfiction.

1. One sunny day in July, a dog named Stan ran away from home. He went up one street and down the other looking for fun, but all the yards were empty. Where was everybody? Stan kept walking until he heard

the sound of band music and happy people. Stan walked faster until he got to Central Street. There he saw men, women, children, and dogs getting ready to walk in a parade. It was the Fourth of July!

Fiction or nonfiction? _____

2. Americans celebrate the Fourth of July every year because it is the birthday of the United States of America. On July 4, 1776, the United States got its independence from Great Britain. Today, Americans celebrate this holiday with parades, picnics, and fireworks as they proudly wave the red, white, and blue American flag.

Fiction or nonfiction? _____.

UNIT 7

Name:_____

Food Words

Directions: This puzzle contains the names of foods listed on the menu. Circle the words. Look across and down. Then, color the pictures.

MENU
cheese   chicken
grapes   strawberries
bread   peaches
fish   pretzels

```
C  H  I  C  K  E  N  R  S
A  X  D  H  M  V  F  M  T
R  T  G  E  W  I  X  S  R
K  B  R  E  A  D  C  Q  A
N  I  A  S  T  P  O  F  W
O  B  P  E  R  J  S  I  B
P  R  E  T  Z  E  L  S  E
Y  I  S  Q  E  R  J  H  R
Q  P  E  A  C  H  E  S  R
E  Z  N  X  E  W  E  R  I
D  C  H  E  R  R  I  S  E
R  O  K  H  C  L  Z  Y  S
```

Name:_____

Food Words

Directions: Write the correct food word from the Word Bank under each picture.

Word Bank			
bread	cheese	eggs	fruit
meat	milk	supermarket	vegetables

1.

_____

2.

_____

3.

_____

4.

_____

5.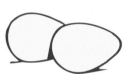

_____

6.

_____

Directions: Complete each sentence with a word from the Word Bank.

7. Mother buys food at the _____ .

8. I like pizza with _____ on it.

UNIT 7

Name:_____

Food Words

Directions: Circle the names of vegetables in green. Circle the names of drinks in red. Circle the names of desserts in blue.

water

corn

_____

peas

pie

cookie

carrot

_____

juice

milk

cake

Directions: Write each food word on the correct line.

Drinks	**Vegetables**	**Desserts**
_____	_____	_____
_____	_____	_____
_____	_____	_____

Name:_____

Measurement Words

An **inch** is a unit of length in the standard measurement system.

Directions: Use a ruler to measure each object to the nearest 1/4 inch. Write **in.** to stand for **inch**. The first two are done for you.

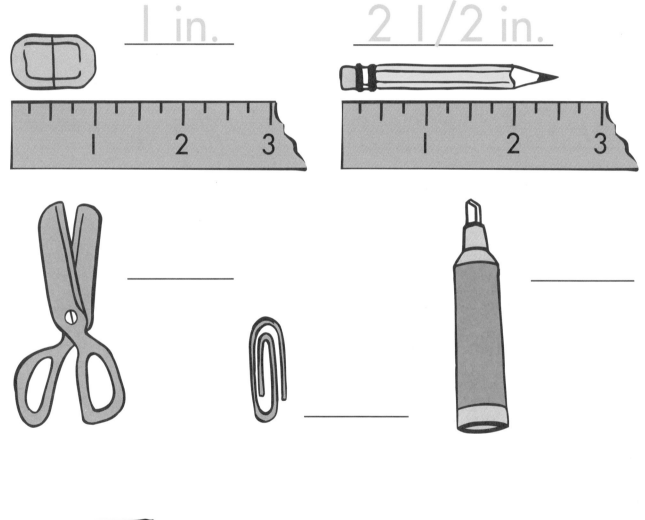

1 in.

2 1/2 in.

Name:_____

Words That Are Antonyms

Directions: In each sentence below, circle the incorrect word. Then, rewrite the sentence replacing the incorrect word with its antonym from the Word Bank. The first one is done for you.

Word Bank

happy	tall
full	tie
loud	lock
dangerous	

1. Swimming in the dark was (safe.)

   Swimming in the dark was dangerous.

2. The gorilla's scream sounded very quiet.

   _____

3. The packed room was empty.

   _____

4. My 6-foot brother is very short.

   _____

5. George, the funny clown, makes me very unhappy.

   _____

6. In an unsafe place, you should always unlock the door.

   _____

7. You need to untie your shoes before you run.

   _____

UNIT 7

Name:_____

Words That Are Antonyms

Directions: Read each word next to the picture. Draw a line from the word to its antonym.

dark   empty

hairy   dry

closed   happy

dirty   bald

sad   clean

full   light

wet   open

UNIT 7

Words That Are Antonyms

Directions: Read each sentence. Write the word from the Word Bank that is the antonym of the bold word.

Name:_____

Word Bank				
bottom	outside	black	summer	after
light	sister	clean	last	evening

1. Lisa has a new baby **brother**. _____

2. The class went **inside** for recess. _____

3. There is a **white** car in the driveway. _____

4. We went to the park **before** dinner. _____

5. Joe's puppy is **dirty**. _____

6. My name is at the **top** of the list. _____

7. I like to play outside in the **winter**. _____

8. I like to take walks in the **morning**. _____

9. The sky was **dark** after the storm. _____

10. Our team is in **first** place. _____

UNIT 7

Name:_____

Holiday Words

Valentine's Day	Fourth of July	Thanksgiving

Directions: Write the name of each holiday beside its picture. Remember that names of holidays begin with capital letters.

_____

_____

_____

UNIT 7

Name: _____

Food Words

A **calorie** is a unit for measuring the amount of energy a food can produce when taken into the body.

Directions: Read the menu. Then, answer the questions.

Menu

Chicken Nuggets.....300 calories		Apple.....................81 calories	
Pizza.....................445 calories		Carrots..................32 calories	
Taco.....................272 calories		Milk.....................120 calories	
Turkey Sandwich.....338 calories		Soda ....150 calories	
Cake.....................388 calories		Apple Juice...........87 calories	
Cookie ....68 calories			

1. Gavin chooses chicken nuggets, cake, and milk for lunch. How many calories does he eat? _____

2. Ramona has milk and an apple for breakfast. She has pizza and apple juice for lunch. Then, she has a taco and soda for dinner. How many calories does she eat in all? _____

3. Doug eats a turkey sandwich, carrots, cake, and milk for lunch. Ruben eats chicken nuggets, an apple, a cookie, and apple juice. Who eats more calories? _____
How many more? _____

4. Write the three items from the menu that you would choose to eat for lunch.

_____

5. How many total calories are there in your lunch?

_____

UNIT 7

Name:_____

Food Words

Directions: Read the story. Then, answer the questions. Try the recipe with the help of an adult.

Cows live on a farm. The farmer milks the cow to get milk. Many things are made from milk. We make ice cream, sour cream, cottage cheese, and butter from milk. Butter is fun to make! You can learn to make your own butter. First, you need cream. Put the cream in a jar and shake it. Then, you need to pour off the liquid. Next, you put the butter in a bowl. Add a little salt and stir! Finally, spread it on crackers and eat!

1. What animal gives us milk? _____

2. What four things are made from milk?

_____ _____ _____ _____

3. What did the story teach you to make? _____

4. Put the steps in order. Write the numbers 1, 2, 3, or 4 by the correct sentence.

_____ Spread the butter on crackers and eat!

_____ Shake the cream in a jar.

_____ Start with cream.

_____ Add salt to the butter.

 Food **169**

Name: _____

Food Words

The Pyramid Food Chart shows how much to eat from each food group. Tim has a turkey, cheese, and lettuce sandwich with mayonnaise. He also has an apple and some orange juice.

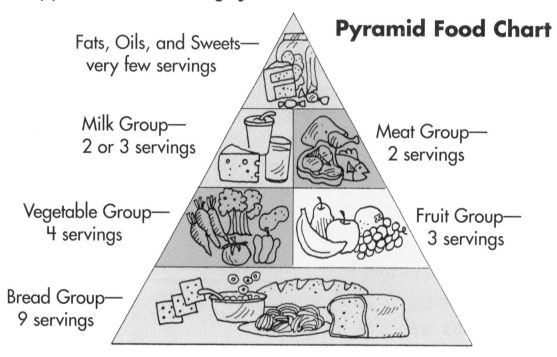

Pyramid Food Chart

Fats, Oils, and Sweets— very few servings

Milk Group— 2 or 3 servings

Meat Group— 2 servings

Vegetable Group— 4 servings

Fruit Group— 3 servings

Bread Group— 9 servings

Directions: Color in the graph to show how many servings of each food group Tim ate for lunch. (Hint: A serving of bread is one slice.)

Tim's Lunch

Number of Servings	Bread	Vegetable	Fruit	Milk	Meat	Fats
8						
7						
6						
5						
4						
3						
2						
1						

UNIT 7

Name:_____

Measurement Words

Directions: Write **feet**, **yards**, or **miles** on each line to tell how you would measure each thing.

1 foot = 12 inches
1 yard = 36 inches or 3 feet
1 mile = 1,760 yards

1. length of a river _miles_

2. height of a tree _____

3. width of a room _____

4. length of a football field _____

5. height of a door _____

6. length of a dress _____

7. length of a race _____

8. height of a basketball hoop _____

9. width of a window _____

10. distance a plane travels _____

Directions: Solve the problem.

Tara races Tom in the 100-yard dash. Tara finishes 10 yards in front of Tom. How many feet did Tara finish in front of Tom?

_____

Name:_____

Words That Are Antonyms

Directions: Complete each sentence with the correct antonym. Write it on the line. Use the clues in the picture and below each sentence. Then, color the picture.

UNIT 7

1. Spotty's suitcase is ___ .   _____
   (antonym for closed)

2. Spotty has a ___ on his face.   _____
   (antonym for frown)

3. His pillow is ___ .   _____
   (antonym for hard)

4. His coat is ___ .   _____
   (antonym for little)

5. Spotty packs his stuffed animal ___ . _____
   (antonym for first)

Name:_____

Words That Are Antonyms

Anna and Luke like to do opposite things. Help them design their new white t-shirts using antonyms.

Directions: Think of a pair of antonyms. Write one on each shirt. Draw pictures on the shirts to match the antonyms.

UNIT 7

Name:_____

Words That Are Antonyms

Directions: Read each sentence. Rewrite the sentence by changing the underlined word to its antonym.

The clown is <u>happy</u>.

1. _____

The boy swims <u>quickly</u>.

2. _____

The bell rings <u>loudly</u>.

3. _____

The popcorn is <u>hot</u>.

4. _____

Antonyms

174

Name:_____

Words About Holidays

In China, the most celebrated holiday is the **New Year**. The **Lantern Festival** is part of the celebration. That is when the Chinese people welcome the first full moon of the year. The Chinese New Year is fixed according to the lunar calendar. It occurs somewhere between January 30 and February 20. Each Chinese year is represented by one of 12 animals.

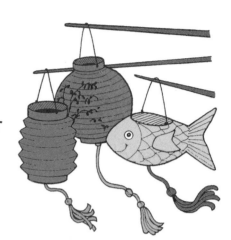

Look at the chart below to see what animal represents the year you were born.

RAT	OX	TIGER	HARE (RABBIT)	DRAGON	SNAKE	HORSE	RAM	MONKEY	ROOSTER	DOG	PIG
1900	1901	1902	1903	1904	1905	1906	1907	1908	1909	1910	1911
1912	1913	1914	1915	1916	1917	1918	1919	1920	1921	1922	1923
1924	1925	1926	1927	1928	1929	1930	1931	1932	1933	1934	1935
1936	1937	1938	1939	1940	1941	1942	1943	1944	1945	1946	1947
1948	1949	1950	1951	1952	1953	1954	1955	1956	1957	1958	1959
1960	1961	1962	1963	1964	1965	1966	1967	1968	1969	1970	1971
1972	1973	1974	1975	1976	1977	1978	1979	1980	1981	1982	1983
1984	1985	1986	1987	1988	1989	1990	1991	1992	1993	1994	1995
1996	1997	1998	1999	2000	2001	2002	2003	2004	2005	2006	2007
2008	2009	2010	2011	2012	2013	2014	2015	2016	2017	2018	2019

UNIT 7

Directions: The **Lantern Festival** is celebrated on the third day of the New Year. Make a colorful lantern to hang in your room.

1. Fold a brightly colored piece of construction paper vertically.

3. Open the paper. Bend the paper. Wrap it in a circle and staple it in place.

2. Cut strips from the folded side, stopping 2 inches from the open edge.

4. Cut out a long paper strip and staple it to the lantern to make a handle.

Name:_____

Food Words

Directions: Read each nutrition facts label. Use the labels to write the correct answers on the lines.

1. Serving size _____

2. Number of servings per container _____

3. Calories per serving _____

4. Number of calories per container _____

Nutrition Facts
Serving Size 1 cup (236g)
Servings Per Container About 3

Amount per serving	
Calories 180 Calories from Fat 70	
	% Daily Value*
Total Fat 8g	**12%**
Saturated Fat 3.5	**18%**
Cholesterol 30mg	**10%**
Sodium 920mg	**38%**
Total Carbohydrate 18g	**6%**
Dietary Fiber 2g	**8%**
Sugar 3g	
Protein 10g	

Nutrition Facts
Serving Size 1 cup (245g)
Servings Per Container About 2

Amount per serving	
Calories 380 Calories from Fat 200	
	% Daily Value*
Total Fat 22g	**33%**
Saturated Fat 13	**66%**
Cholesterol 60mg	**20%**
Sodium 1150mg	**48%**
Total Carbohydrate 28g	**9%**
Dietary Fiber 5g	**18%**
Sugar 1g	
Protein 17g	

Vitamin A 35%	•	Vitamin C 4%
Calcium 24%	•	Iron 20%

5. You eat 2 cups of this food. How many calories do you eat? _____

6. Shana wants to eat 500 calories for lunch. She has 1 serving of this food. How many more calories does she need to eat? _____

7. Roberto eats two servings. How much fat in grams does he consume? _____

   His daily intake of fat should be 30 g. Does he eat too little or too much? _____

   By how little/much? _____

Name:_____

Food Words

Directions: Look at the food items on the table. Then, answer the questions.

1. What food is sphere shaped? _____

2. What food has 4 sides and 4 corners that are all the same?

_____

3. What food has 6 sides that are all squares? _____

4. What food is an oval? _____

5. What food is a rectangular prism? _____

6. What food is a cylinder? _____

cake

plum   crackers   eggs

UNIT 7

Name:_____

Food Words

Directions: Color each piece of fruit that is cut into two equal parts. Write the name of each fruit you colored.

1. _____

2. _____

3. _____

4. _____

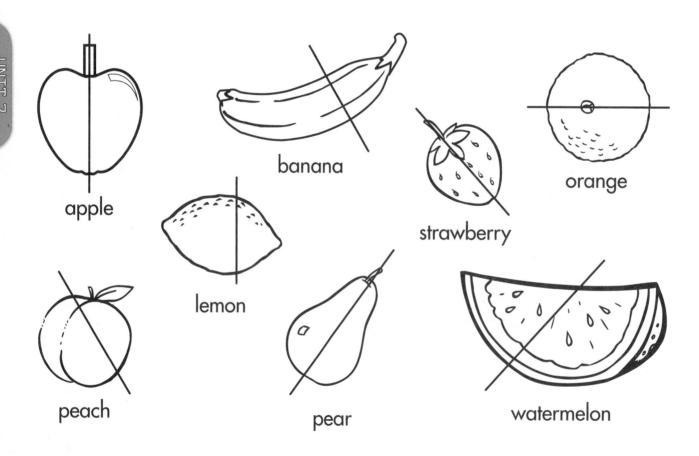

apple

banana

strawberry

orange

lemon

peach

pear

watermelon

Name:_____

Unit 7 Review

Directions: Think about a holiday that you like to celebrate. Write it on the line.

_____

Now, think about what you like to eat on this special day. Make up a menu that includes what you eat at breakfast, lunch, and dinner. Be sure to include items from each food group.

Breakfast	**Lunch**	**Dinner**
_____	_____	_____
_____	_____	_____
_____	_____	_____
_____	_____	_____
_____	_____	_____
_____	_____	_____
_____	_____	_____

UNIT 7

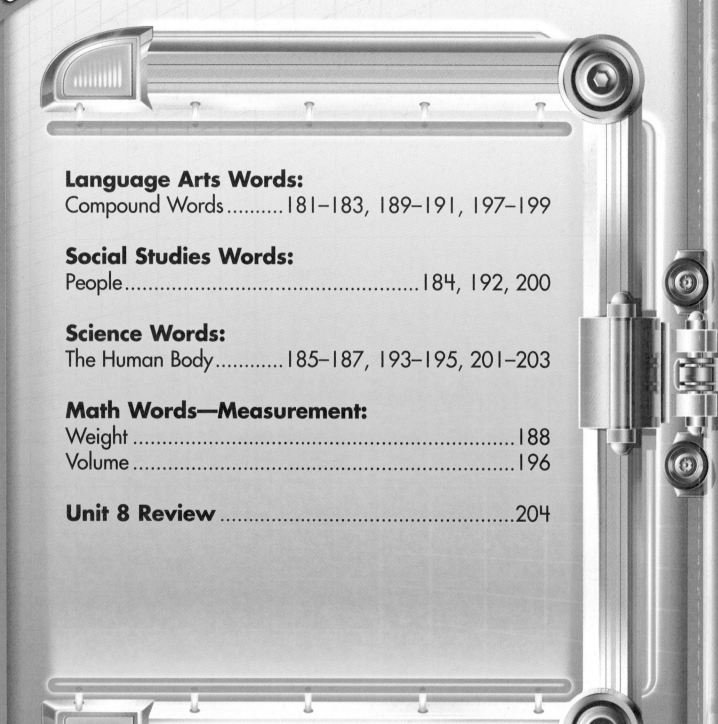

UNIT 8

Language Arts Words:
Compound Words 181–183, 189–191, 197–199

Social Studies Words:
People 184, 192, 200

Science Words:
The Human Body 185–187, 193–195, 201–203

Math Words—Measurement:
Weight 188
Volume 196

Unit 8 Review 204

Name:_____

Compound Words

Some short words can be put together to make one new word. The new word is called a **compound word**.

Example:

nut + shell = nutshell

Directions: Choose a word from the Word Bank to make a compound word that completes each sentence.

Word Bank					
board	bone	ground	prints	shake	house
brush	man	top	shell	ball	hive

Example:
>   The bird built its nest in the **treetop**.

1. We pitched our tent at the camp_____ .

2. You would not be able to stand up without your back_____ .

3. The police officer looked for finger_____ .

4. She placed the hair_____ in her purse.

5. It is important to have a firm hand_____ .

6. The teacher wrote on the chalk_____ .

7. The egg_____ is cracked.

8. Our whole family plays foot_____ together.

9. Be sure to put a top hat on the snow_____ .

10. Spot never sleeps in his dog_____ .

11. The beekeeper must check the bee_____ today.

Name:_____

Compound Words

Directions: Use the compound words in the Word Bank to answer the questions. The first one is done for you.

Word Bank				
sailboat	blueberry	bookcase	tablecloth	beehive
dishpan	pigpen	classroom	playground	bedtime
broomstick	treetop	fireplace	newspaper	sunburn

Which compound word means . . .

1. a case for books?

2. a berry that is blue?

3. a hive for bees?

4. a place for fires?

5. a pen for pigs?

6. a room for a class?

7. a pan for dishes?

8. a boat to sail?

9. a paper for news?

10. a burn from the sun?

11. the top of a tree?

12. a stick for a broom?

13. the time to go to bed?

14. a cloth for the table?

15. ground to play on?

bookcase

_____

_____

_____

_____

_____

_____

_____

_____

_____

_____

_____

_____

_____

_____

UNIT 8

Compound Words

Directions: Find one word in the Word Bank that goes with each of the words below to make a compound word. Write the compound words on the lines.

Word Bank

board	room	thing	side	bag
writing	book	hopper	toe	ball
class	where	work	out	basket

---

1. coat_____

2. snow_____

3. home _____

4. waste _____

5. tip _____

6. chalk _____

7. note_____

8. grass_____

9. school _____

10. with _____

Look at the words in the Word Bank that you did not use. Use those words to make your own compound words.

1. _____

2. _____

3. _____

4. _____

5. _____

UNIT 8

Name:_____

People Words

Directions: Find a word from the Word Bank to name each picture. Write it on the line below the picture.

Word Bank

baby   man   boy   woman   girl   men   family   children   people

1.

_____

4.

_____

7.

_____

2.

_____

5.

_____

8.

_____

3.

_____

6.

_____

9.

_____

Name:_____

Words About the Human Body

Directions: The letters in each word are mixed up. Unscramble the letters and write each word about the human body correctly. Use the Word Bank to help you.

Word Bank			
stomach	ears	skin	heart
fingers	skeleton	ankle	bones

1. ntloesek _____

2. sringef _____

3. sear _____

4. snobe _____

5. tareh _____

6. nisk _____

7. lenka _____

8. homcsat _____

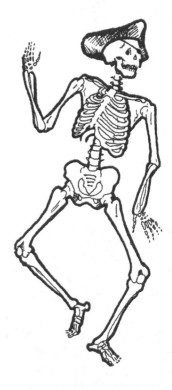

Name:_____

Words About the Human Body

Directions: Draw a line to match each word about the human body to its description on the right.

1. bones   This tells your body what to do.

2. lungs   You speak with this.

3. heart   This holds your head up.

4. mouth   It carries oxygen to your body.

5. neck   This helps you bend your arm.

6. brain   You use these to breathe.

7. elbow   These support and shape your body.

8. blood   It pumps blood.

UNIT 8

Name:_____

Words About the Human Body

Word Bank

| arms | chin | ears | eyes | feet |
| hand | legs | mouth | neck | nose |

Directions: Draw a picture of yourself. Use the words in the Word Bank to label the parts of your body.

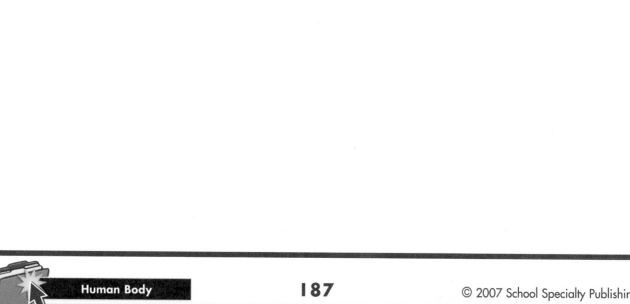

Name:_____

Words About Weight

Ounces and **pounds** are measurements of weight. An ounce is used to measure the weight of very light objects. A pound is used to measure the weight of heavier objects.

Example:

8 ounces   15 pounds

Directions: Decide if you would use ounces or pounds to measure the weight of each object. Circle your answer.

ounce   pound

ounce   pound

ounce   pound

ounce   pound

a chair: ounce   pound   **a table:** ounce   pound

a shoe: ounce   pound   **a shirt:** ounce   pound

UNIT 8

Name: _____

Compound Words

Directions: Look at the words below the pictures. Put the words together to make compound words. Write the new words on the lines. The first one is done for you.

1.

sail   +   boat   =   <u>sailboat</u>

2.

sun   +   glasses   =   _____

3.

bird   +   house   =   _____

4.

rain   +   coat   =   _____

UNIT 8

Name:_____

Compound Words

Directions: Use words from the Word Bank to write the compound word that matches each description.

Word Bank

gumdrop   peanut   cupcake

milkshake   popcorn   strawberry

1. This fruit is red. _____

2. This grows inside a shell. _____

3. This snack is made from corn. _____

4. This drink is sweet and cool. _____

5. This is a small candy. _____

6. This is baked in an oven. _____

Name:_____

Compound Words

Directions: Find the two words that make up each animal's name. Write them on the lines.

1.  seahorse

_____   _____

2.  goldfish

_____   _____

3.  bluebird

_____   _____

UNIT 8

Name:_____

People Words

Directions: Write a people word on the line to complete each sentence.

1. The _____ rang up the girl's groceries.

3. The _____ announced that dinner was ready.

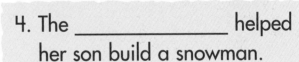

2. The _____ surprised his friend with a gift.

4. The _____ helped her son build a snowman.

UNIT 8

Name:_____

Words About the Human Body

Directions: Draw a line to match the sense to the body part that works with it.

taste	eyes
smell	ears
sight	nose
hearing	tongue
touch	skin

Directions: List three of your favorites for each sense. An example is given.

Taste _____pretzel_____

_____

Smell _____baking cookies_____

_____

Sight _____Mom_____

_____

Hearing _____barking dog_____

_____

Touch _____cold snow_____

_____

Human Body

193

UNIT 8

Name:_____

Words About the Human Body

Directions: Draw a line from each word to where it is on the body. Then, circle the words in the puzzle. Look across and down.

head   neck

chest   elbow

waist   knee

ankle   heel

T	T	E	H	E	A	D	K
N	A	L	N	E	C	K	H
F	N	B	N	R	H	R	E
K	K	O	K	N	E	E	E
Y	L	W	A	I	S	T	L
Z	E	L	D	Y	T	Q	F

UNIT 8

Name:_____

Words About the Human Body

Directions: Find and circle seven words about the human body. Look across and down. Then, write the words on the lines.

a	r	m	s	y	u	h	n
l	g	d	r	n	m	s	b
e	l	b	o	w	k	l	l
g	a	a	k	r	e	k	s
z	q	c	n	e	c	k	c
c	e	k	e	e	y	e	s
p	s	d	e	b	j	p	o

1. _____

2. _____

3. _____

4. _____

5. _____

6. _____

7. _____

Human Body

195

Name:_____

Words About Volume

Directions: Read about volume. Then, answer the questions.

Volume tells how much a container can hold. You can measure volume in many ways. One **cup** holds 8 ounces. One **pint** holds 2 cups. One **quart** holds 2 pints. One **gallon** holds 4 quarts.

8 ounces = 1 cup	2 pints = 1 quart
2 cups = 1 pint	4 quarts = 1 gallon

1. You should drink 8 cups of water a day. This keeps you healthy. How many quarts is this?

   a. 4 quarts

   b. 2 quarts

   c. 1 quart

2. Mary has had 2 pints of water today. How many more cups does she need to stay healthy? _____

3. The school orders 10 gallons of milk a day. This is the same as _____ pints.

4. A teacher buys 1 gallon of juice. The students drink 2 quarts. How many quarts are left? _____

Name:_____

Compound Words

Directions: Draw a line to separate the compound words into two words. Then, write a sentence using the compound word. The first one is done for you.

1. ant|hill

   The ants climbed the anthill.

2. pinwheel

   _____

3. doghouse

   _____

4. junkyard

   _____

5. notebook

   _____

6. birthday

   _____

7. mailbox

   _____

8. horseshoe

   _____

9. skateboard

   _____

10. cupcake

   _____

UNIT 8

Name:_____

Compound Words

Directions: Join words from the first column with words from the second column to make compound words. Then, write the new words on the lines.

grand	brows
snow	light
eye	stairs
down	string
rose	book
shoe	mother
note	ball
moon	bud

1. _____

2. _____

3. _____

4. _____

5. _____

6. _____

7. _____

8. _____

UNIT 8

Name:_____

Compound Words

Directions: Draw a line under the compound word in each sentence. Write the two words on the line that make up the compound word.

1. A firetruck came to help put out the fire.

_____

2. I will be nine years old on my next birthday.

_____

3. We built a treehouse at the back.

_____

4. Dad put a scarecrow in his garden.

_____

5. It is fun to make footprints in the snow.

_____

6. I like to read the comics in the newspaper.

_____

7. Cowboys ride horses and use lassos.

_____

UNIT 8

Name:_____

People Words

Directions: Write a sentence using each of the people words.

1. _____

   _____

   children

2.  _____

   _____

   girl

3. _____

   _____

   boy

4. _____

   _____

   baby

UNIT 8

Name:_____

Words About the Human Body

Directions: Use the Word Bank to write the name of each bone on the correct line.

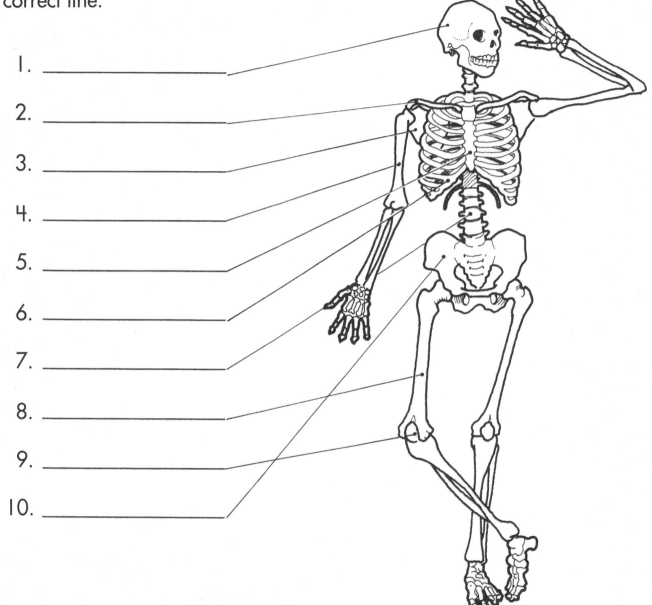

1. _____

2. _____

3. _____

4. _____

5. _____

6. _____

7. _____

8. _____

9. _____

10. _____

UNIT 8

Word Bank

hipbone	arm bone	backbone	rib
collarbone	breastbone	leg bone	skull
knee bone	shoulder blade		

Human Body   **201**   © 2007 School Specialty Publishing

Name:_____

Words About the Human Body

Directions: Find and circle the words in the puzzle about the human body. Look across and down.

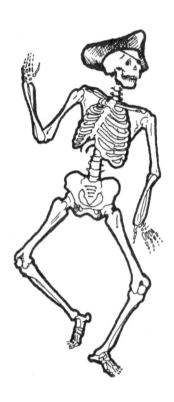

Word Bank

ribs

skull

skeleton

spine

pelvis

joints

muscle

b	s	a	t	s	i	p	o	j
o	s	m	r	r	i	b	s	o
m	u	s	c	l	e	b	s	i
e	s	k	e	l	e	t	o	n
s	b	u	s	p	i	n	e	t
p	e	l	v	i	s	r	s	s
t	i	l	e	s	z	y	j	k

UNIT 8

Name:_____

Words About the Human Body

Directions: Read about some of the major bones in your body. Then, draw a line from each bone to the part of the body where it is found.

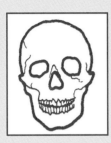

Skull
This protects your brain and gives shape to your face.

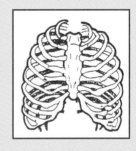

Ribs
These bones protect your heart, lungs, and liver.

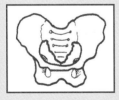

Pelvis
Your legs are attached to the pelvis.

Name:_____

Unit 8 Review

Directions: Circle the compound word in each row.

1. collarbone   ribs   skull

2. jacket   mittens   snowman

3. pelvis   backbone   knee

4. bedtime   pillow   blanket

5. recess   eraser   chalkboard

Directions: Write a sentence for each of the people word pairs.

1. boy/man

_____

2. girl/woman

_____

3. family/children

_____

UNIT 8

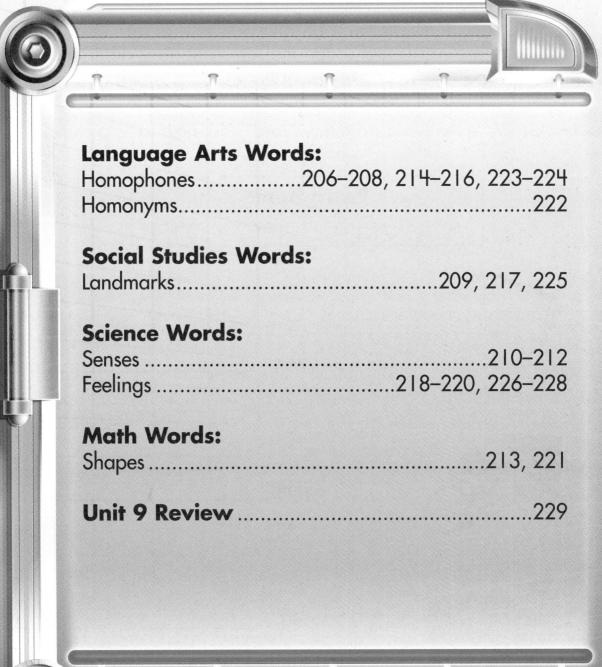

Language Arts Words:
Homophones...................206–208, 214–216, 223–224
Homonyms...222

Social Studies Words:
Landmarks.......................................209, 217, 225

Science Words:
Senses 210–212
Feelings 218–220, 226–228

Math Words:
Shapes 213, 221

Unit 9 Review 229

Name:_____

Words That Are Homophones

Homophones are words that sound the same but have different spellings and meanings. **Toe** and **tow** are homophones. So are **ate** and **eight**.

Directions: Write the word from the Word Bank next to its picture.

Word Bank			
so	see	blew	pear

1.

                sew _____

2.

                pair _____

3.

                sea _____

4.

                blue _____

UNIT 9

Name:_____

Words That Are Homophones

Directions: Read each word. Circle the picture that goes with the word.

1. sun

4. hi

2. ate

5. four

3. buy

6. hear

UNIT 9

Name:_____

Words That Are Homophones

Directions: Read the sentences. The bold words are homophones. Follow the directions to decorate a special birthday cake.

1. The baker **read** a recipe to bake a doggy cake. Color the plate he put it on **red**.

2. Draw a **hole** in the middle of the doggy cake. Then, color the **whole** cake yellow.

3. Look **for** the top of the doggy cake. Draw **four** candles there.

4. In the hole, draw what you think the doggy would really like.

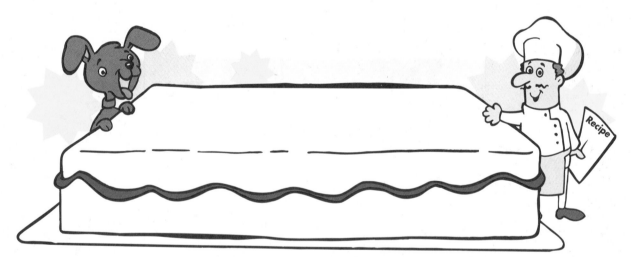

5. Write a sentence using the words **hole** and **whole**.

_____

6. Write a sentence using the words **read** and **red**.

_____

UNIT 9

Name:_____

Words About the Lincoln Memorial

Directions: Read about the Lincoln Memorial. Then, fill in the circle beside the answer that best completes each sentence.

The **Lincoln Memorial** honors Abraham Lincoln, our 16th president. Lincoln believed that all people were created equal. The memorial symbolizes this belief. Inside are two murals which represent freedom, brotherhood, unity, and charity. The building is surrounded by 36 columns. They represent the 36 states in the Union at the time of Lincoln's death. Many people visit this famous memorial in Washington, D.C.

1. The Lincoln Memorial honors

   Ⓐ   Lincoln, Nebraska.

   Ⓑ   Abraham Lincoln.

   Ⓒ   freedom.

3. The Memorial is in

   Ⓐ   Lincoln, Nebraska.

   Ⓑ   Springfield, Illinois.

   Ⓒ   Washington, D.C.

2. The columns represent

   Ⓐ   states of the Union.

   Ⓑ   justice.

   Ⓒ   strength.

4. Abraham Lincoln was our

   Ⓐ   king.

   Ⓑ   president.

   Ⓒ   brother.

UNIT 9

Name:_____

Words About Senses

hear   smell   taste   see   feel

Directions: Read each sentence. Then, write which sense would be used for each one.

1. Andrew reads his book. _____

2. Juicy red apples are delicious. _____

3. We knew a skunk was nearby. _____

4. I couldn't find my backpack. _____

5. The dog's bark kept us awake. _____

6. We ate brownies for dessert. _____

7. I like to listen to music. _____

8. Jon built a model airplane. _____

9. The odor from his sneakers was strong. _____

10. She tapped her friend on the shoulder. _____

Name:_____

Words About Senses

Directions: Color the pictures. Then, cut out the flowers at the bottom of the page. Pick one flower and look at the object word on it. Glue the flower on the vase that tells which sense you would mainly use with the object on that flower.

taste

hear

smell

see

feel

wind

cake

bell

ammonia

cloud

star

knock

perfume

raindrops

watermelon

UNIT 9

UNIT 9

Page left blank for cutting activity.

Name:_____

Shape Words

Directions: Use the words in the Word Bank to complete the puzzle about shapes.

Word Bank			
rectangle	circle	cube	diamond
sphere	triangle	cone	prism
cylinder	oval	square	

Across

1. A ball is this shape.
2. A three-dimensional shape with 6 sides that are all square.
4. A shape with no corners.
6. A party hat is this shape.
7. A shape with 3 sides and 3 corners.
8. A kite is this shape.
9. A rectangle box shape.

Down

1. A shape with 4 sides and 4 corners that are all the same.
3. A shape with 4 sides and 4 corners, 2 sides are long and 2 sides are short.
5. A round shape that is stretched out in the middle.
6. A soup can is this shape.

© 2007 School Specialty Publishing

UNIT 9

Name:_____

Words That Are Homophones

Homophones are words that sound the same but have different spellings and meanings.

Examples: Pear and **pair** are homophones.
To, **too**, and **two** are three homophones.

Directions: Draw a line from each word on the left to its homophone on the right.

blue	knight
night	too
beet	blew
write	see
hi	meet
two	son
meat	bee
sea	high
be	right
sun	beat

UNIT 9

Name:_____

Words That Are Homophones

Directions: Read each sentence. Then, write the correct word on the line. The first one is done for you.

1. **blue   blew**   She has ___blue___ eyes.

    The wind ___blew___ the barn down.

2. **eye   I**   He hurt his left _____ playing ball.

    _____ like to learn new things.

3. **see   sea**   Can you _____ the winner from here?

    He goes diving for pearls under the _____ .

4. **eight   ate**   The baby _____ the banana.

    Jane was _____ years old last year.

5. **one   won**   Jill _____ first prize at the science fair.

    I am the only _____ in my family with red hair.

6. **be   bee**   Jenny cried when a _____ stung her.

    I have to _____ in bed every night at eight o'clock.

7. **two to too**   My father likes _____ play tennis.

    I like to play, _____.

    It takes at least _____ people to play.

UNIT 9

Name: _____

Words That Are Homophones

Directions: Fill in the circle beside the word that names each picture.

1.
   ○ son
   ○ sun

2.
   ○ flower
   ○ flour

3.
   ○ too
   ○ two

4.
   ○ road
   ○ rode

5.
   ○ bare
   ○ bear

6.
   ○ wheel
   ○ we'll

7.
   ○ knows
   ○ nose

8.
   ○ pale
   ○ pail

9.
   ○ rose
   ○ rows

Homophones

216

Name:_____

Words About the Statue of Liberty

Directions: Read about the Statue of Liberty. Then, read each sentence below. If the sentence is true, put a **T** on the line. If it is false, put an **F** on the line.

> The **Statue of Liberty** is a symbol of the United States. It stands for freedom. The Statue of Liberty is located on an island in New York Harbor. It is the tallest statue in the United States.
>
> The statue is of a woman wearing a robe. She is holding a torch in her right hand. She is holding a book in her left hand. She is wearing a crown. The Statue of Liberty was a gift from the country of France.
>
> Each year, people come from all over the world to visit the statue. Not only do they look at it, they can also go inside the statue. At one time, visitors could go all the way up into the arm. In 1916, the arm was closed to visitors because it was too dangerous.

_____ 1. The Statue of Liberty is a symbol of the United States.

_____ 2. People cannot go inside the statue.

_____ 3. The statue was a gift from Mexico.

_____ 4. People used to be able to climb up into the statue's arm.

_____ 5. It is a very short statue.

_____ 6. The woman statue has a torch in her right hand.

_____ 7. People come from all over to see the statue.

 Landmarks

217

UNIT 9

Name:_____

Feeling Words

Directions: Use the Word Bank to find and circle the feeling words in the puzzle. Look across and down.

Word Bank

angry	happy	sick	friendly	mad	silly	tired
funny	sad	sleepy	worried	glad	safe	smart

```
W  H  A  P  P  Y  A  T  B  M
F  D  W  O  R  R  I  E  D  B
R  T  G  M  A  D  R  P  L  A
I  S  M  A  R  T  H  Q  R  N
E  H  S  L  E  E  P  Y  F  G
N  J  A  J  Q  K  F  T  U  R
D  T  I  R  E  D  S  S  N  Y
L  S  Q  B  N  I  I  I  N  O
Y  A  M  S  A  D  L  C  Y  D
E  F  I  C  B  G  L  K  E  U
Z  E  G  L  A  D  Y  S  L  M
```

UNIT 9

Name:_____

Feeling Words

Directions: Read the feeling words next to each picture. Choose the one that best describes how each person might be feeling. Write a sentence for each picture.

Example:

| sick
tired
happy |  | The girl

___is happy._____ |

| content
angry
sleepy |  | 1. The lady

_____ |

| funny
tired
glad |  | 2. The man

_____ |

| hungry
sleepy
sad |  | 3. The boy

_____ |

UNIT 9

Name:_____

Feeling Words

Directions: Write a sentence for each feeling word in the Word Bank.

Word Bank			
surprised	happy	sad	angry
excited	shy	scared	sorry

_____

_____

_____

_____

_____

_____

_____

UNIT 9

Name:_____

Shape Words

Directions: Find the shapes that are in the picture. Use the clues to find the shapes that are described.

1. Color the shapes blue that have 4 sides and 4 corners that are all the same.

2. Color the shapes red that have no corners and are ball-shaped.

3. Color the shapes yellow that have 4 sides and 4 corners, but the angles are not the same.

4. Color the shapes green that have 4 sides. Two of the sides are long and 2 are short.

5. Color the three-dimensional shapes orange that have 6 sides and each side is a square.

6. Color the shapes purple that are round and the middles are stretched out.

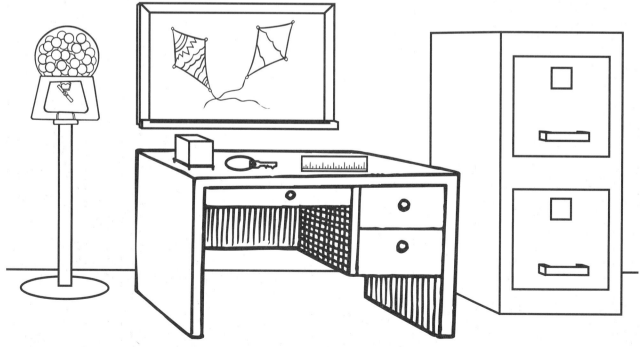

Shapes

221

UNIT 9

Name:_____

Words That Are Homonyms

Homonyms are words that are spelled and pronounced the same but have different meanings.

Directions: Read each word. Find the two pictures that show what the word means. Then, draw lines from both pictures to the word.

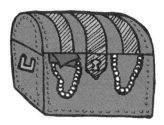

dress

pen

chest

UNIT 9

Name:_____

Words That Are Homophones

Directions: Use the words in the Word Bank to complete the puzzle about homophones.

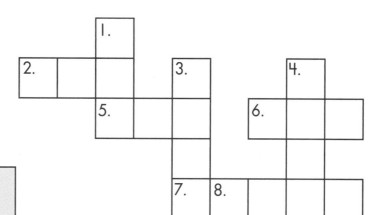

Word Bank

see	knew
sea	right
one	write
won	meet
new	meat

Across

2. _____, two, three

5. We _____ the game!

6. You do this with your eyes.

7. You do this with your pencil.

10. People eat this.

Down

1. Not old

3. I _____ you would like this.

4. We will _____ at 8:00.

8. Not left

9. Smaller than an ocean

UNIT 9

Name:_____

Words That Are Homophones

Directions: Use the words in the Word Bank to complete the puzzle about homophones.

Word Bank
blew
blue
too
two
to
sun
son
right
write
be
bee

Across

1. Julia _____ out the candles.
4. Three days ago, she was stung by a _____ .
5. After _____ days she felt better.

Down

1. She has on _____ shoes for her party.
2. She will _____ a letter to her grandma.
3. Julia is a girl, so she is not her mother's _____ .

Homophones   224   © 2007 School Specialty Publishing

Name:_____

Words About Landmarks

The United States has many historical landmarks. One of these landmarks is the **Golden Gate Bridge**, built in 1937. Stretching 1.7 miles, it is a symbol of San Francisco. Beneath the bridge, the San Francisco Bay and Pacific Ocean connect. People can cross the bridge by car, bicycle, or foot. It is painted bright orange so it can be seen in the fog.

Directions: Pretend you just visited the Golden Gate Bridge. Write a note telling your friend about it. Write your message on the left side. Write your friend's name and address on the right side.

VISIT

San Francisco

United States 25¢

Golden Gate Bridge • San Francisco, California

Landmarks

Name:_____

Feeling Words

Directions: Read the story. Then, fill in the circle beside the phrase that completes each sentence.

It is a rainy day. Mom tells Tosh to stay inside until the weather clears up. Tosh lies on his bed and pouts. Now and then, he checks to see if the rain has stopped.

1. Tosh probably wants to   ◯ go outside and play.

                              ◯ lie in bed all day.

2. Tosh probably feels   ◯ happy.

                              ◯ bored and grumpy.

3. When it stops raining,   ◯ angry.
   Tosh will probably feel
                              ◯ glad.

UNIT 9

Name:_____

Feeling Words

Word Bank		
annoyed	angry	proud
sleepy	bored	confused

Directions: Complete each sentence with a word from the Word Bank.

1. The alarm went off too early. I am still _____ .

2. I am so _____ of winning the spelling bee.

3. I am _____ . What did you say your name was?

4. I am _____ that you tore up the newspaper, Rex!

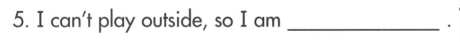

5. I can't play outside, so I am _____ .

6. I am _____ that a gopher ate all my plants!

UNIT 9

Name:_____

Feeling Words

Directions: Use feeling words to complete each sentence.

1. When I spend time with my friends, I feel _____ .

2. When I don't do something well, I feel _____ .

3. When I get a good grade, I feel _____ .

4. When my friend and I fight, I feel _____ .

UNIT 9

Name:_____

Unit 9 Review

Directions: Draw a picture of a robot using the shapes in the Word Bank. Label the parts of your robot.

Word Bank					
rectangle	triangle	square	oval	circle	diamond

Directions: Circle the correct word that completes each sentence. Then, write it on the line.

1. I _____ spaghetti for dinner.
   eight   ate

2. I _____ my mom calling me.
   here   hear

3. The monkey climbs _____ up in the tree.
   high   hi

4. She likes to _____ her own clothes.
   so   sew

UNIT 9

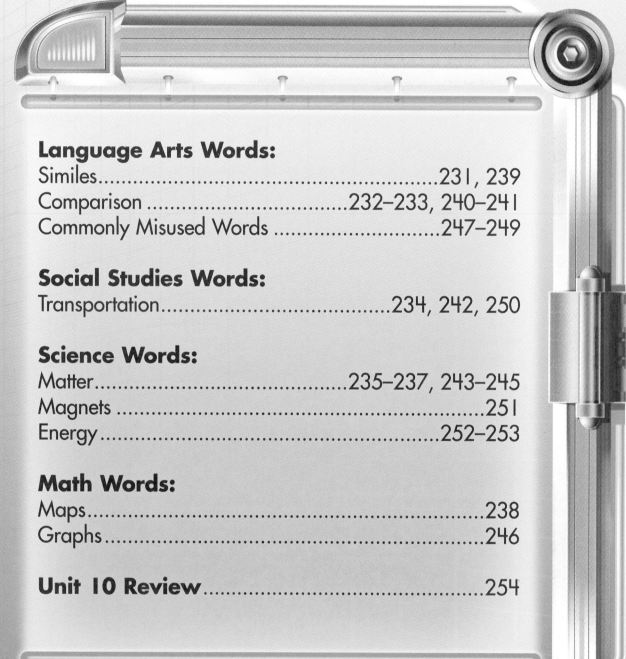

UNIT 10

Language Arts Words:
Similes..231, 239
Comparison 232–233, 240–241
Commonly Misused Words 247–249

Social Studies Words:
Transportation................................234, 242, 250

Science Words:
Matter.................................235–237, 243–245
Magnets 251
Energy 252–253

Math Words:
Maps...238
Graphs...246

Unit 10 Review..254

Name:_____

Words Used in Similes

A **simile** is a figure of speech that compares two different things. You can use the words **like** or **as** in similes.

Directions: Draw a line to the picture that goes with each set of words.

1. as hard as a

2. as hungry as a

3. as quiet as a

4. as soft as a

5. as easy as

6. as light as a

7. as tiny as an

UNIT 10

Name:_____

Words That Compare

Words that end in **-er** compare two things. Words that end in **-est** compare more than two things.

Directions: Read each sentence. Circle the correct word that describes how each plant has grown.

1. A sunflower grew 3 inches. A daisy grew 2 inches.
   The sunflower is _____ than the daisy.
   a. shorter   b. taller

2. Tomato plant A grew up 2 inches. Tomato plant B grew up 1 inch.
   Tomato plant A is _____ than tomato plant B.
   a. smaller   b. taller

3. The students cut the grass around the garden. They let the grass behind the school and in the playground grow.
   The grass around the garden is the _____ .
   a. shortest   b. tallest

4. A student weighed a carrot from the garden. It weighs 3 pounds. A cucumber from the same garden weighs 2 pounds.
   The carrot is _____ than the cucumber.
   a. lighter   b. heavier

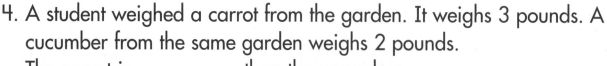
UNIT 10

Name:_____

Words That Compare

Directions: Write the correct words on the lines to complete the chart.

Word	-er compares two	-est compares more than two
1. tall	_____	_____
2. _____	faster	_____
3. _____	_____	lightest
4. strong	_____	_____
5. _____	bigger	_____

Directions: Using the chart, write the correct comparison word on the line to complete each sentence.

6. That tree is _____ than the bush.

   The tree is the _____ one in the forest.

7. His car is the _____ in the race.

   Dad's car is _____ than my bike.

8. The feather is the _____ item in the box.

   A feather is _____ than a pencil.

UNIT 10

Name:_____

Transportation Words

Directions: Look at the numbered pictures. Write the numbers of the pictures beside each question. There may be more than one correct answer for each question.

What can carry more than one person?   _____

What moves on wheels?   _____

What moves on just two wheels?   _____

What makes a very loud noise?   _____

What moves through water?   _____

What has a motor to make it run?   _____

What can hold large, heavy objects?   _____

What can travel very fast?   _____

What has to be pushed or pulled?

1	2	3
4	5	6
7	8	9
10	11	12

UNIT 10

Transportation

Name:_____

Words About Matter

All things are made of matter. Matter takes up space. It can take three forms: solid, liquid, or gas.

Solids have shape and volume. They do not change shape easily.

Liquids have volume, but they have no shape of their own. They take the shape of the container they are in.

Gases have no shape or volume. Most gases are invisible.

Directions: Find and circle the words in each word search that are examples of each kind of matter. Look across, down, and diagonally. Then, write the words on the lines.

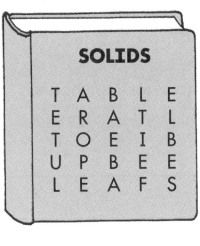

SOLIDS

```
T A B L E
E R A T L
T O E I B
U P B E E
L E A F S
```

LIQUIDS

```
A P O P K
B C O L A
J U I C E
A M L I T
W A T E R
```

GASES

```
A B T O E P
C I G L T O
E B R A H D
O X Y G E N
W O T E R T
H E L I U M
```

_____   _____   _____

_____   _____   _____

_____   _____   _____

_____   _____   _____

_____   _____   _____

_____   _____   _____

UNIT 10

Words About Matter

Directions: Water is a type of matter. Water turns into a solid at a temperature of 32°F. This is called the freezing point. Does all water freeze at 32°F? Do the experiment to find out.

You will need:

2 small paper cups
4 teaspoons salt
water
marking pen
freezer

1. Fill both cups with water.

2. Mix 4 teaspoons of salt in one of the cups. Write **salt** on that cup.

3. Put both cups in the freezer. Check on them every hour for four hours.

I found out . . .
the cup of plain water _____

_____

the cup of salt water _____

_____

What happened?

When the temperature of water gets very cold, the particles of water hook together to make ice crystals. Salt gets in the way of this process, and an even lower temperature is needed before ice crystals will form.

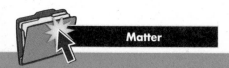
UNIT 10

Name:_____

Words About Matter

Directions: Follow the instructions to mix a solid and a liquid to make clay.

Ingredients:
        1 cup salt
        2 cups flour
        3/4 cup water

Mix the salt and flour. Then, add the water. DO NOT eat the clay. Use your hands to mix the clay. Now, roll it out. What can you make with your clay?

1. Circle the main idea:
        Do not eat the clay.
        Mix a solid and a liquid to make clay.

2. What is the liquid ingredient in the clay? _____

3. Is the clay a solid or a liquid? _____

Name:_____

Map Words

Directions: Look at the map. Pretend you are standing in the town square. Circle the correct letter to answer each question.

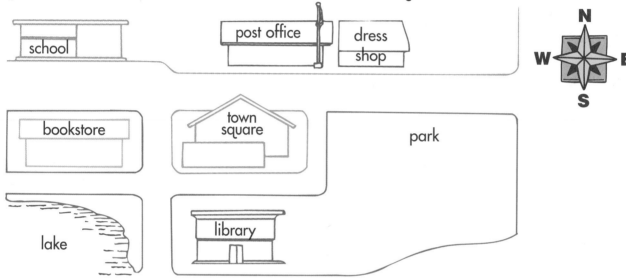

1. What direction is the library from you?
   a. North
   b. West
   c. South

2. What direction must you go to reach the post office?
   a. East
   b. North
   c. West

3. Which direction must you go to get to the park?
   a. North
   b. West
   c. East

4. You are standing at the school facing the post office. Which direction must you turn to get to the lake?
   a. right
   b. left

5. Draw a bus in the street south of the school.

6. Draw a tree in the middle of the park.

Name:_____

Words Used in Similes

Directions: Look at each picture. Write a sentence that uses a simile. Use the word under the picture.

Example:

cold

My hands are as

cold as ice.

1.

hard

_____

_____

2.

slow

_____

_____

3.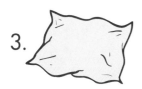

soft

_____

_____

4.

happy

_____

UNIT 10

Name:_____

Words That Compare

The suffixes **-er** and **-est** can be used to compare. Use **-er** when you compare two things. Use **-est** when you compare more than two things.

Examples: The puppy is **smaller** than its mom.
This puppy is the **smallest** puppy in the litter.

Directions: Complete each sentence using a word that compares. Add **-er** or **-est** to the base word under each line.

Base Word

1. The dog is _____ than the puppy.
   loud

2. The tan puppy is the _____ in the litter.
   old

3. I think cats are _____ than dogs.
   neat

4. You can run _____ than my dog.
   fast

5. Those are the _____ words I have ever heard.
   kind

6. You are _____ than your brother.
   tall

UNIT 10

Name:_____

Words That Compare

Directions: Read each sentence. Choose the correct word. Then, write it on the line.

big
bigger
biggest

1. The town made the _____ snowman on record.
2. Emmett made a _____ snowman.
3. Sara helped him make it even _____ .

fast
faster
fastest

1. The snowman's head fell off and started to roll very _____ .
2. It was the _____ rolling snowball anyone had ever seen.
3. It rolled _____ than they could run.

white
whiter
whitest

1. As the snowball rolled closer, Mr. Wetzel's face became even _____ .
2. After it snowed all night, the town was the _____ it had ever been.
3. Mr. Wetzel's face turned _____ when he saw the snowball rolling toward his candy store.

UNIT 10

Name:_____

Transportation Words

Directions: Read the descriptions in Column A. Choose a transportation word from Column B that matches each description. Then, write the number of the answer in the correct square. The first one is done for you.

Column A

A. Filled with helium
B. Runs on gasoline
C. Powered by wind
D. Burns coal or wood
E. Runs on nuclear energy
F. Moves on snow or ice
G. Moves by pedals
H. Powered by oars
I. Pulled by horses or oxen

Column B

1. rowboat
2. sailboat
3. steam locomotive
4. blimp
5. submarine
6. wagon
7. sled
8. bicycle
9. car

A 5	B ___	C ___
D ___	E ___	F ___
G ___	H ___	I ___

Add the numbers across, down, and diagonally.
What answer do you get? _____

UNIT 10

Name:_____

Words About Matter

Directions: Read about rain. Then, follow the instructions.

Clouds are made up of little drops of ice and water. They push and bang into each other. Then, they join together to make bigger drops. More raindrops cling to them. They become heavy and fall quickly to the ground.

Write **first**, **second**, **third**, **fourth**, and **fifth** on the lines to put the events in order.

_____ More raindrops cling to them.

_____ Clouds are made up of little drops of ice and water.

_____ They join together and make bigger drops that begin to fall.

_____ The drops of ice and water bang into each other.

_____ The drops become heavy and fall quickly to the ground.

UNIT 10

Name:_____

Words About Matter

Directions: Water exists in three different forms: solid, liquid, and gas. Read the story. Then, find and circle the bold words in the puzzle. Look across, down, and diagonally.

Have you ever felt **grass** early in the **morning**? It feels very **wet**. The water is not rain. It is **dew**! When the sun rises in the morning, it warms the **air**. Some of the **water** in the **warm** air **evaporates**. It changes into a gas. These "floating" water **molecules** fall to the **cool** grass. The warm molecules land on the grass and become a **liquid** again. This is called **condensation**.

```
R S A C O N W M O L G T M
C O N D E N S A T I O N O
A W L E S B O G R T G S L
L A D W G A I R R M R W E
I T R T C X W E T B A A C
Q E V A P O R A T E S L U
U R M O R S O D X R S B L
I U L J G C H L D C F N E
D S M O R N I N G E S R S
```

© 2007 School Specialty Publishing

UNIT 10

Name:_____

Words About Matter

Directions: Answer the questions about these three modes of transportation.

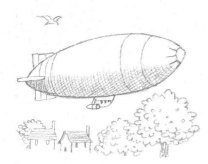

blimp

boat

bulldozer

1. Which is filled with gas? _____

2. Which floats on water? _____

3. Which moves solid matter from one place to another? _____

4. Which floats in the air? _____

5. Which moves on land? _____

UNIT 10

Name:_____

Words About Graphs

A **graph** has rows. A **row** goes across.

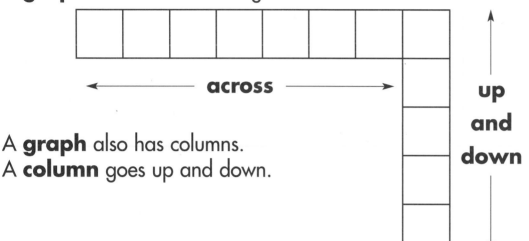

← **across** →

up and down

A **graph** also has columns.
A **column** goes up and down.

This graph shows how many fish are at the pet store each week.

First Saturday	🐟	🐟	🐟			
Second Saturday	🐟	🐟	🐟	🐟	🐟	🐟
Third Saturday	🐟	🐟	🐟	🐟		
Fourth Saturday	🐟	🐟				

Directions: Color the fish at the store on the third Saturday **red**. Color the fish at the store on the first Saturday **blue**, the second Saturday **yellow**, and the fourth Saturday **green**. How many fish did the store have on the first Saturday? _____ second Saturday? _____ third Saturday? _____ fourth Saturday? _____

Name:_____

Commonly Misused Words

The word **their** is the possessive form of **they**. In other words, it refers to something that belongs to **them**.

The word **there** means "at or in that place."

The word **they're** means "they are."

Examples: The kids hold **their** basketballs.
Tim is looking over **there**.
They're about to start playing.

Directions: Write **their**, **there**, or **they're** on each line to finish the sentence correctly.

1. Look over _____ !

2. The Smiths are having _____ yard sale.

3. _____ selling a good bike.

4. I will ask my mom to go _____ .

UNIT 10

Name:_____

Commonly Misused Words

Its is a pronoun. It means "belonging to it." It does not have
an apostrophe.

Example: The elephant lifted **its** trunk.

It's is a contraction. It means "it is." It does have an apostrophe.

Example: **It's** fun to see the animals.

Directions: Write **its** or **it's** on each line to finish the sentence correctly.

1. The elephant did _____ best trick.

2. _____ difficult to stand on that small box.

3. The lion swished _____ tail.

4. Don't worry. _____ not a dangerous lion.

UNIT 10

Name:_____

Commonly Misused Words

Your means "belonging to you." It does not have an apostrophe.

Example: I am **your** friend.

You're is a contraction.
It means "you are."
It does have an apostrophe.

Example: **You're** my best friend.

Directions: Write **your** or **you're** on each line to finish the sentence correctly.

1. We can sell lemonade at _____ house.

2. We'll use lemons from _____ tree.

3. It looks like _____ having fun.

4. If _____ thirsty, have some lemonade!

5. Let me fill _____ glass for you.

Name:_____

Transportation Words

Directions: Circle the correct answer that completes each sentence.

1. A large truck used for moving furniture is called a
   a. dump truck.
   b. van.
   c. pickup truck.

2. A large vehicle for transporting children to school is called a
   a. bus.
   b. yacht.
   c. jet.

3. A long line of boxcars that runs on a track is called a
   a. submarine.
   b. train.
   c. bicycle.

4. A vehicle that moves through water is called a
   a. ship.
   b. tank.
   c. sled.

5. A vehicle pulled by horses or oxen is called a
   a. hot air balloon.
   b. tricycle.
   c. wagon.

UNIT 10

Name:_____

Words About Magnets

Every magnet has a north and a south **pole**. The north pole of one magnet attracts and pulls the south pole of another magnet. Two poles that are the same (two north poles or two south poles) do not attract each other. Instead, they push away from each other.

Directions: Using the information above, continue labeling the horseshoe and bar magnets below with **N** (for north) and **S** (for south). Then, color the magnets that are attracted to each other.

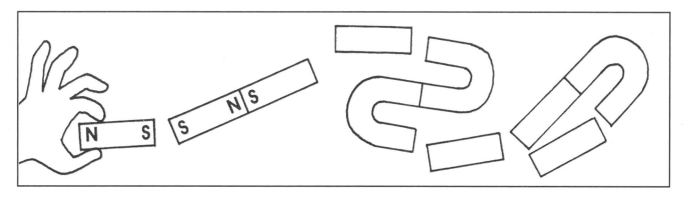

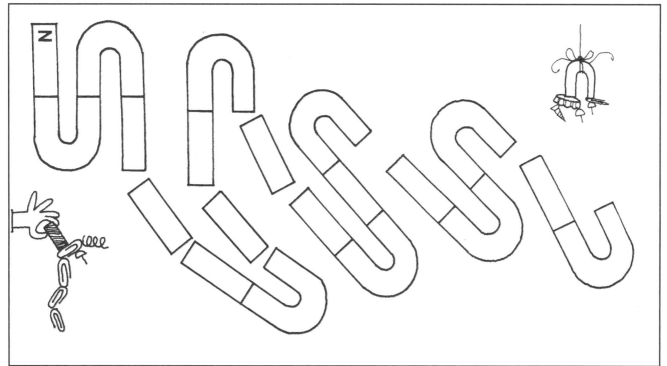

UNIT 10

Name:_____

Words About Energy

Directions: Use the words in the Word Bank to write the sources of energy above the correct cauldron. Then, color the pictures.

Word Bank

lamp	alarm	camp stove
candle	furnace	curling iron
trumpet	buzzer	flashlight

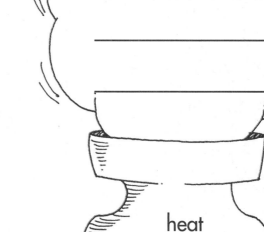

heat

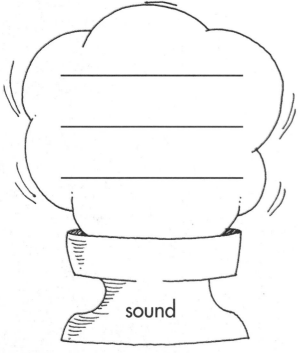

sound

light

Name:_____

Words About Energy

Directions: Read about energy. Then, find and circle the bold words in the puzzle. Look across, down, and diagonally.

When **rays** of **sun** hit the earth, the earth absorbs or reflects the heat. Darker surfaces absorb the **radiation**. Lighter surfaces **reflect** the radiation. That is why you feel cooler when you wear light-colored clothing in the **summer**.

r	r	u	a	p	t	n	d	s	s
s	h	i	j	w	s	d	s	u	c
r	a	d	i	a	t	i	o	n	d
e	a	e	r	b	k	d	h	o	l
f	s	y	e	s	u	m	m	e	r
l	c	n	s	o	l	g	j	e	e
e	y	b	s	r	e	k	e	r	a
c	u	t	m	b	a	w	n	s	d
t	i	a	p	b	q	l	o	h	s

Name:_____

Unit 10 Review

Directions: Fill in the graph to show how many times during the week you used each mode of transportation.

	Sunday	Monday	Tuesday	Wednesday	Thursday	Friday	Saturday
bicycle							
car							
bus							
scooter							
other? _____							

Directions: Write sentences using the words from the Word Bank.

Word Bank				
gas	its	lightest	magnets	north

_____

_____

_____

_____

_____

UNIT 10

Language Arts Words:
Plurals..............................256–258, 264–266, 272–274

Social Studies Words:
Jobs 259, 267, 275

Science Words:
Simple Machines 260–262, 268–270, 276–278

Math Words:
Tangrams...263
Shapes 271

Unit 11 Review..279

Name:_____

Words That Are Plural

Some words name only one person or thing, such as the word **ball**. Other words name more than one thing, such as the word **balls**.

Words that name more than one thing are called **plurals**. Plurals often are made by adding **–s** to the end of a word.

Directions: Write the plurals of each word. Then, draw a second item to make each picture plural.

1.

jet _____

2.

doll _____

3.

car _____

4.

game _____

5.

duck _____

6.

drum _____

7.

top _____

8.

horn _____

UNIT 11

Name:_____

Words That Are Plural

Directions: Write the words on the fish in the correct tank. Then, color the fish.

| kites | mitten | star | cats | bird | rocks | girls | lunch |

One

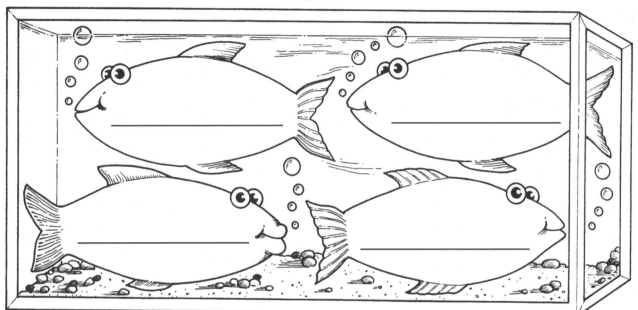

More Than One (Plural)

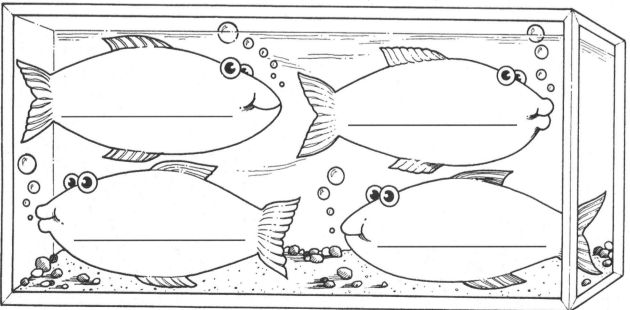

Name:_____

Words That Are Plural

Directions: Read the words in the Word Bank. If the word means **one**, write it on the paint jar. If the word means **more than one**, write it on the paintbrushes.

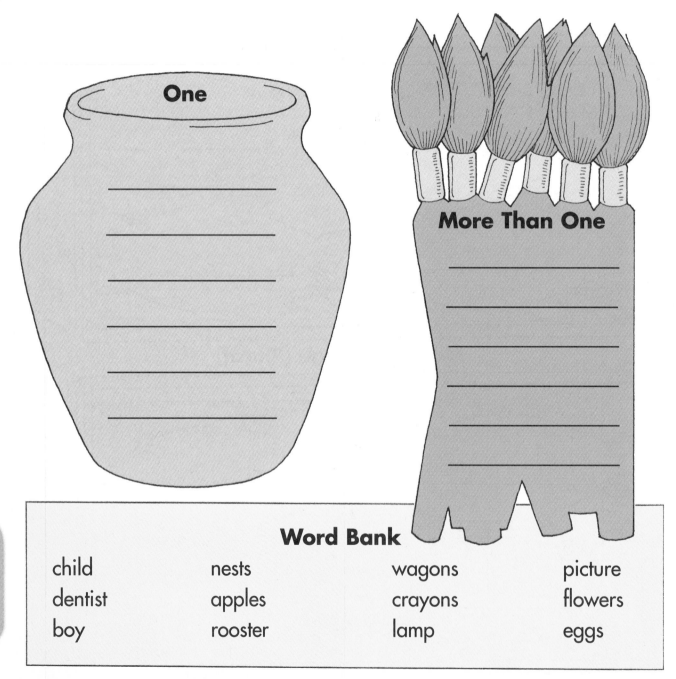

One

More Than One

Word Bank

child	nests	wagons	picture
dentist	apples	crayons	flowers
boy	rooster	lamp	eggs

UNIT 11

Name:_____

Job Words

Word Bank			
baker	catcher	mover	painter
photographer	pitcher	reporter	writer

Directions: Use the words in the Word Bank to complete each sentence.

1. A person who bakes is called a _____ .

2. The _____ writes stories for children.

3. The baseball _____ pitches balls to the batter.

4. A television _____ reports the news.

5. My family hired a _____ to move our furniture.

6. The _____ painted a picture of the trees in the park.

7. These photographs were taken by a _____ .

8. A _____ catches the ball in his glove.

UNIT 11

Name:_____

Words About Simple Machines

Simple machines are tools that make work easier. Simple machines help us lift, pull, split, fasten, and cut things. These machines use energy to work and have few or no moving parts. We use simple machines every day, such as when we open a door, turn on the water faucet, or open a can of soup.

Directions: Read the descriptions of the simple machines. Then, draw a line to match each description to the correct picture.

nail

Lever – has two parts; the arm moves and the fulcrum supports the arm but does not move

wagon

Inclined plane – a flat surface with one end higher than the other

ladder

Wedge – two inclined planes placed back-to-back; used to split or cut

screw

Wheel and Axle – helps turn something more easily

pulley

Pulley – able to change the direction of force used to do work

shovel

Screw – used to hold things together

UNIT 11

Name:_____

Words About Simple Machines

Directions: Use the words in the Word Bank to complete each sentence.

Word Bank		
inclined plane	wedge	lever
screw	wheel and axle	pulley

1. A ramp is an _____ .

2. A seesaw is an example of a _____ .

3. A knife is a _____ .

4. The bottom of a light bulb is a _____ .

5. A skateboard is an example of a _____ .

6. A _____ is used to raise and lower a flag.

UNIT 11

Name:_____

Words About Simple Machines

A **wedge** is a type of inclined plane. It is made up of two inclined planes joined together to make a sharp edge. A wedge can be used to cut things. Some wedges are pointed.

Directions: Color only the pictures of wedges.

UNIT 11

Name:_____

Words About Tangrams

Directions: Read about tangrams. Then, answer the questions.

A **tangram** is a set of seven shapes. The shapes can be put together to make a square. A tangram set has five triangles, one square, and one parallelogram. Each piece is called a **tan**.

This game is from China. People use the shapes to make pictures of animals. They make the animals while they tell stories. You can make a rabbit, a goose, a wolf, and even an alligator.

1. How many shapes are in a tangram set? _____

2. How many of the shapes are triangles? _____

3. What other two shapes are in a tangram set?

_____

4. What is each piece of a tangram set called? _____

5. What country do tangrams come from? _____

6. What are tangrams used to tell? _____

Name:_____

Words That Are Plural

A **plural** is a word that means more than one person or thing. Add **-s** or **-es** to the end of a word to make it plural.

Add **s** to these words. cup — cups sink — sinks stove — stoves table — tables

Add **es** to words that end in **s**, **x**, **sh** or **ch**. glass — glasses box — boxes dish — dishes bench — benches

Directions: Write a sentence using the plural of each word.

1. house _____

2. bush _____

3. dress _____

4. lamp _____

UNIT 11

Name:_____

Words That Are Plural

Directions: Read the story. Then, circle the correct word that completes each sentence.

Angela learned a lot about sharks when her class visited the city aquarium. She learned that sharks are fish. Some sharks are as big as an elephant, and some can fit into a small paper bag. Sharks have no bones. They have hundreds of teeth, and when they lose them, they grow new ones. They eat animals of any kind. Whale sharks are the largest of all fish.

1. **Shark / Sharks** are fish.

2. Sharks have no **bones / bone**.

3. They have hundreds of **tooth / teeth**.

4. They eat **animal / animals** of any kind.

5. Sharks can be as big as an **elephants / elephant**.

6. Others can fit into a paper **bags / bag**.

© 2007 School Specialty Publishing

Name:_____

Words That Are Plural

Some words have special plural forms.

Example: leaf — leaves

Directions: Read the words in the Word Bank. The words on the right are special plurals. Complete each sentence with one of these plurals.

> **Word Bank**
> tooth — teeth
> child — children
> foot — feet
> mouse — mice
> woman — women
> man — men

1. I lost my two front ___ ___ ___ ___ ___ !

2. My sister has two pet ___ ___ ___ ___ .

3. My mother and her sister are nice ___ ___ ___ ___ ___ .

4. The circus clown had big ___ ___ ___ ___ .

5. The teacher played a game with the

___ ___ ___ ___ ___ ___ ___ .

6. Little boys grow up to be ___ ___ ___ .

UNIT 11

Name:_____

Job Words

Directions: Draw a line from each job in the circle to the person it names.

nurse

police officer

clerk

doctor

teacher

barber

Words About Simple Machines

A **lever** is a simple machine used to lift or move things. It has two parts. The **arm** is the part that moves. The **fulcrum** supports the arm but does not move.

Directions: Label the parts of this lever.

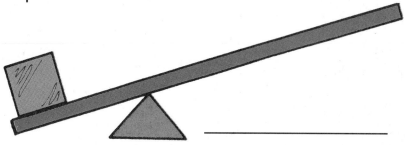

Directions: The letters in each word are mixed up. Unscramble the letters to write the names of these kinds of levers.

rbowcra

serlip

_____

_____

emrahm

sorciss

_____

_____

UNIT 11

Name:_____

Words About Simple Machines

Directions: Levers help make our work easier. Color all the levers. Then, find and circle their names in the puzzle. Look across and down.

```
c a n o p e n e r a
r s d d l j k l m n
o h s c i s s o r s
w v h b e z x c a w
b t o b r o o m k l
a d v n s u k f s w
r u e h a m m e r g
w f l h g f a d s v
```

UNIT 11

Name:_____

Words About Simple Machines

An **inclined plane** has a slanted surface. It is used to move things from a low place to a high place. Some inclined planes are smooth. Others have steps.

Directions: Color the inclined planes in the picture.

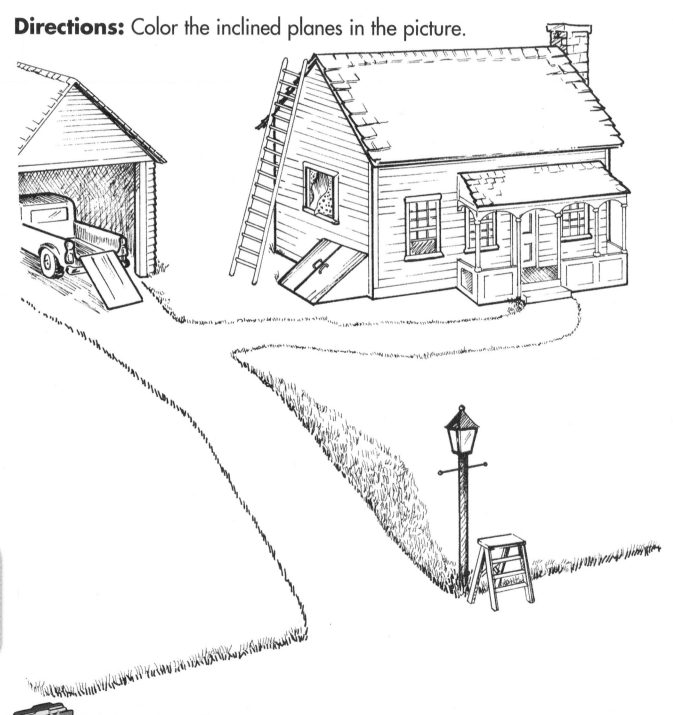

Name:_____

Shape Words

Directions: The objects on the left are CDs. Color the CDs. Then, draw a line from each CD to the case on the right that matches it. The shapes may be **tilted**, **flipped**, or **turned**.

1.

2.

3.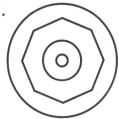

4.

5.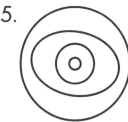

A.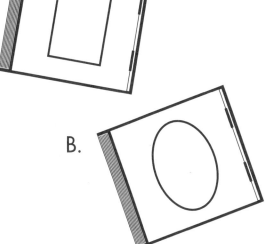

B.

C.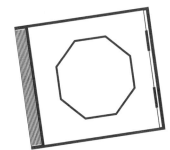

D.

E.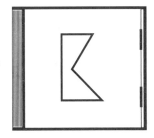

UNIT 11

Name:_____

Words That Are Plural

Directions: Read the sentences. Write the noun you find in each sentence. If it is a plural noun, circle it.

Example: (socks) My socks do not match.

1. _____ The birds could not fly.

2. _____ Some apples are tart.

3. _____ My mother likes to cook.

4. _____ Swimming in the lake is fun.

5. _____ The flowers grow quickly.

6. _____ The eggs are colorfully decorated.

7. _____ It is easy to ride a bicycle.

8. _____ My cousin is very tall.

9. _____ The boy went fishing.

10. _____ My parents went out to eat.

11. _____ Her ankle is swollen.

12. _____ My brother was born today.

13. _____ The slide is steep.

14. _____ The doctor was late.

Name:_____

Words That Are Plural

To show more than one of something, add **-s** to most words.
Examples: one dog   **two dogs**   one book   **two books**

Some words are different. For words that end in **x**, use **-es** to show more than one.
Examples: one fox   **two foxes**   one box   **two boxes**

Some words become different words when they show more than one.
Example: one mouse   **two mice**

Some words stay the same when they show more than one.
Examples: one deer   **two deer**   one fish   **two fish**

Directions: Write the word that names each picture to complete the sentences.

1. The  run fast.   _____

2. The  are eating.   _____

3. Have you seen any  today?   _____

4. Where do the  live?   _____

5. Did you ever have  for pets?   _____

UNIT 11

Name:_____

Words That Are Plural

Directions: Complete each line of the poem with plural words. Make sure each line of the poem rhymes!

Two little _____
Ran around twice.

Then, two red _____
Jumped out of some boxes.

Last came two _____ ,
What were they doing here?

The animals come until the day ends.
I welcome them, for they are my friends.

Name:_____

Job Words

Directions: What do you want to do when you grow up? Write about the job. Then, draw a picture of yourself doing the job.

_____

_____

_____

_____

_____

_____

_____

UNIT 11

Name:_____

Words About Simple Machines

Directions: Use the words in the Word Bank to write the name of the simple machine under each picture.

1.

_____

3.

_____

2.

_____

4.

_____

Word Bank

inclined plane   wedge   lever   wheel and axle

UNIT 11

Name:_____

Words About Simple Machines

Directions: Read the sentences. Fill in the circle below the name of the simple machine that matches each description.

1. Two inclined planes are joined together. The planes make a sharp edge that can cut.

      wedge   lever   wheel and axle
       ○   ○   ○

2. It is used to lift or move things. It has an arm that moves and a fulcrum that doesn't move.

     wheel and axle   lever   inclined plane
        ○   ○   ○

3. It has a slanted surface. It is used to move things from a low place to a high place.

      lever   inclined plane   wedge
       ○   ○   ○

4. It has a rod that goes through a wheel. It helps move things from place to place.

      pulley   lever   wheel and axle
       ○   ○   ○

5. This is made of a wheel and rope. It lets you move loads up or down.

      lever   pulley   wedge
       ○   ○   ○

UNIT 11

Name:_____

Words About Simple Machines

Directions: This crossword puzzle has words for simple machines. Use the picture clues to help you fill in the squares.

Unit 11 Review

Directions: Write the plural of each word. Then, write a sentence using each plural.

1. drum _____

_____

2. box _____

_____

3. machine _____

_____

4. house _____

_____

5. teacher _____

_____

6. tooth _____

_____

7. lever _____

_____

8. square _____

_____

UNIT 11

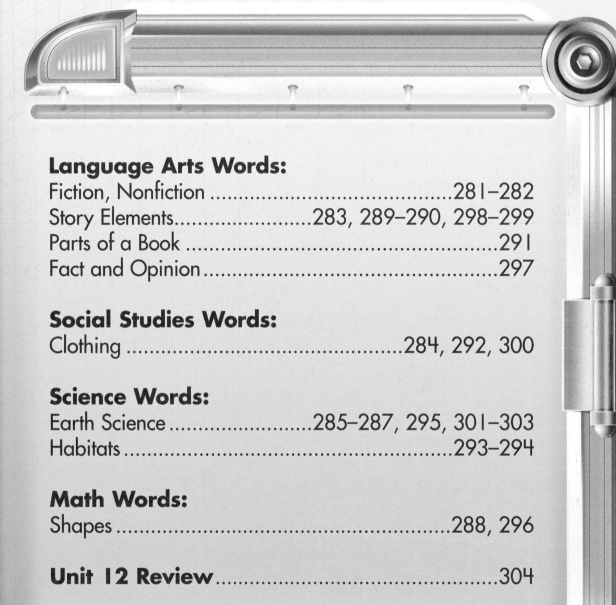

UNIT 12

Language Arts Words:
Fiction, Nonfiction 281–282
Story Elements......................283, 289–290, 298–299
Parts of a Book 291
Fact and Opinion..297

Social Studies Words:
Clothing 284, 292, 300

Science Words:
Earth Science 285–287, 295, 301–303
Habitats 293–294

Math Words:
Shapes 288, 296

Unit 12 Review...304

Name:_____

Story Words

Fiction is a made-up story. **Nonfiction** is a true story.

Directions: Read the stories about two famous baseball players. Write **fiction** or **nonfiction** in the baseball bats.

1. In 1998, Mark McGwire played for the St. Louis Cardinals. He liked to hit homeruns. On September 27, 1998, he hit home run number 70, to set a new record for the most home runs hit in one season. The old record was set in 1961 by Roger Maris, who later played for the St. Louis Cardinals (1967 to 1968), when he hit 61 home runs.

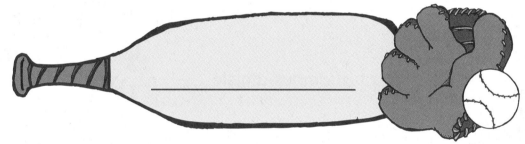

2. The Mighty Casey played baseball for the Mudville Nine and was the greatest of all baseball players. He could hit the cover off the ball with the power of a hurricane. But, when the Mudville Nine was behind 4 to 2 in the championship game, Mighty Casey struck out with the bases loaded. There was no joy in Mudville that day because the Mudville Nine had lost the game.

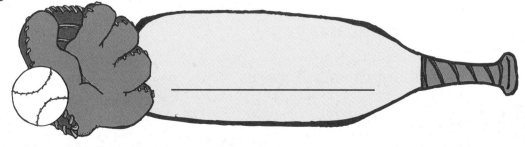

Genres

281

Name:_____

Story Words

Directions: Read about fiction and nonfiction books. Then, look at each different type of book listed. Write **F** if the book is fiction. Write **NF** if the book is nonfiction.

There are many kinds of books. Some books have make-believe stories about princesses and dragons. Some books contain nursery rhymes, like Mother Goose. These are fiction.

Some books contain facts about space and plants. And still other books have stories about famous people in history like Abraham Lincoln. These are nonfiction.

_____ 1. nursery rhyme

_____ 2. fairy tale

_____ 3. true life story of a famous athlete

_____ 4. Aesop's fables

_____ 5. dictionary entry about foxes

_____ 6. book about national monuments

_____ 7. story about a talking tree

_____ 8. story about how a
tadpole becomes a frog

_____ 9. story about animal habitats

_____ 10. riddles and jokes

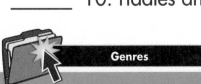

Name:_____

Story Words

The **main idea** tells about the whole picture.

Directions: Fill in the circle beside the sentence that tells the main idea of each picture.

1. ○ She saw a shooting star.

   ○ She likes to climb hills.

   ○ She likes to stay up late.

2. ○ Skateboarding can be done anywhere.

   ○ Skateboarding is easy.

   ○ Skateboarders should wear helmets.

3. ○ Grandpa is a great storyteller.

   ○ Grandpa is boring.

   ○ Grandpa is funny.

4. ○ Mom made me a birthday cake.

   ○ We ate ice cream.

   ○ I opened presents.

UNIT 12

Clothing Words

Word Bank			
glasses	jacket	mittens	pants
skirt	slippers	sneakers	socks

Directions: Use the words in the Word Bank to complete the sentences.

1. Be sure to tie the laces of your _____ so you won't trip and fall.

2. I put on my _____ before I put on my shoes.

3. On a cool day, my _____ keeps me warm.

4. In the winter, I wear long _____ to keep my legs warm.

5. A bathrobe and _____ are comfortable to wear at night.

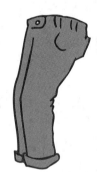

6. Mr. Jesse wears _____ to read the newspaper.

7. My sister wore a pleated _____ and a sweater.

8. In the winter, _____ keep my hands warm.

Name:_____

Words About Landforms

Directions: Use the words in the Word Bank to solve the riddles. Then, color the pictures.

Word Bank

| lake | island | plain | river | mountain | peninsula |

1.

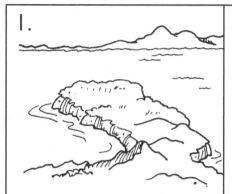

I have water on three sides. I am a

_____ .

3.

I have water all around me. I am an

_____ .

5.

I am wet and have land all around me. I am a

_____ .

2.

I am long and narrow and flow through the land. I am a

_____ .

4.

I am raised land, larger than a hill. I am a

_____ .

6.

I am low and flat. I am a

_____ .

UNIT 1.2

Name:_____

Words About the Ocean Floor

Directions: Have you ever wondered what is under the sand on a beach? Some beaches are really layers of rocks, pebbles, shells, and sand. Follow the instructions to create your own ocean floor.

You will need:
sand
rocks
shells
pebbles
a glass jar
water

1. Put the sand, rocks, shells, and pebbles in the glass jar. Add the same amount of each material.

2. Fill the jar to the top with water.

3. Close the lid tightly!

4. Shake the jar 10 times.

5. Set the jar aside for one day.

6. Draw a picture of the jar and its contents.

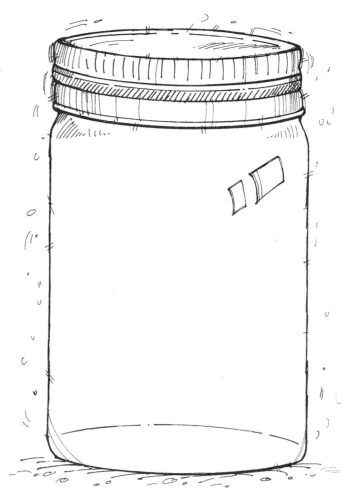

Earth Science

UNIT 12

Name:_____

Words About Rocks

Directions: Go outside and gather a pile of rocks. Follow the instructions below.

Size
Arrange your rocks in three piles by size. Count the rocks in each pile.
Number of large rocks _____
Number of medium rocks _____
Number of small rocks _____

Color
Arrange your rocks in three piles by color. Count the rocks in each pile.
Number of dark-colored rocks _____
Number of medium-colored rocks _____
Number of light-colored rocks _____
List every color you see on these rocks. _____

_____

Feel
Arrange your rocks in three piles by feel. Count the rocks in each pile.
Number of smooth rocks _____
Number of rough rocks _____
Number of rough and smooth rocks _____

Name:_____

Shape Words

Directions: A class goes to the sandbox on the playground. They take a cylinder, a cone, a cube, and a prism.

   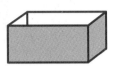

cylinder   **cone**   **cube**   **prism**

They pack sand in the shapes and then build structures. Look at the picture below. Use the picture to write the name of the shape the children used to make each part.

Part 1 was made with the _____ .

Part 2 was made with the _____ .

Part 3 was made with the _____ .

Part 4 was made with the _____ .

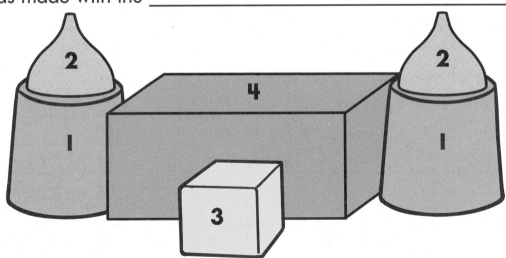

Create a structure of your own using the shapes at the top of the page.

Name:_____

Story Words

A story has a **setting** that tells where and when the story takes place.

Directions: Read the story. Then, answer the questions about the setting.

The Amazon jungle is a huge rain forest in South America. It is full of gigantic green trees, thick jungle vines, and many species of dangerous animals. It is very humid in the jungle.

1. What is the weather like in the Amazon jungle?

   _____

2. Where is the Amazon jungle located?

   _____

3. Would it be easy to travel in the Amazon jungle? Why or why not?

   _____

   _____

   _____

4. Does it rain a lot in the Amazon jungle?

   _____

Story Elements

289

Name:_____

Story Words

A **main idea** tells what the story is about. The **supporting details** tell more about the main idea.

A **character** is the person, animal, or object that a story is about. You cannot have a story without a character.

Directions: Read the story below. Then, answer the questions.

The cake is done. Dad takes it from the oven. Dylan and Dana want to frost the cake. "I want to use white frosting," says Dylan. "I want to use red frosting," says Dana. "We will use both your ideas," says Dad. "We will have pink frosting!"

1. Which sentence tells the main idea?

   The cake will have red frosting.

   Pink frosting is made of red and white frosting.

2. What is one supporting detail? _____

3. Who are two characters in the story? _____

Name:_____

Words About Books

A **book** has many parts. The **title** is the name of the book. The **author** is the person who wrote the book. The **illustrator** is the person who drew the pictures. The **table of contents** is located at the beginning of the book. It lists what is in the book. The **glossary** is a little dictionary in the back to help you with unfamiliar words. Books are often divided into smaller sections of information called **chapters**.

Directions: Look at one of your books. Write the parts you see below.

1. The title of my book is _____ .

2. The author is _____ .

3. The illustrator is _____ .

4. My book has a table of contents.   Yes or No

5. My book has a glossary.   Yes or No

6. My book is divided into chapters.   Yes or No

Parts of a Book   **291**   © 2007 School Specialty Publishing

UNIT 12

Name:_____

Clothing Words

Directions: Circle the pictures that are articles of clothing.

hat

coat

mittens

bike

duck

bird

lion

cat

ball

gloves

cap

shirt

tree

grass

bush

leaf

dress

skirt

UNIT 2

Clothing

Name:_____

Words About Animal Habitats

Directions: Read the story. Then, write each animal's name under **water** or **land** to tell where it lives.

Animals live in different **habitats**. A habitat is the place of an animal's natural home. Many animals live on land and others live in water. Most animals that live in water breathe with gills.
Animals that live on land breathe with lungs.

fish	shrimp	giraffe	dog
cat	eel	whale	horse
bear	deer	shark	jellyfish

WATER

1. _____   4. _____

2. _____   5. _____

3. _____   6. _____

LAND

1. _____   4. _____

2. _____   5. _____

3. _____   6. _____

UNIT 12

Name:_____

Words About Animal Habitats

Directions: Read the story. Then, read the bird names in the Word Bank. Write each bird name under **land** or **water** to tell where it lives.

land? water?

Carlos and Joshua learned that some birds like living near land and others like living near the water. They decided to write a book about land birds and water birds, but they needed some help. They looked in the library to find out which birds live near water and which birds live near land.

Word Bank			
blue jay	cardinal	duck	goose
hummingbird	parrot	pelican	puffin
roadrunner	swan	eagle	penguin

LAND	**WATER**
1. _____	1. _____
2. _____	2. _____
3. _____	3. _____
4. _____	4. _____
5. _____	5. _____
6. _____	6. _____

Name:_____

Words About Sand

Directions: Read about sand. Use the bold words to find and circle the words about sand in the puzzle. Look across and down. Then, color the picture.

Have you ever felt warm **sand** on a **beach**? Sand is made of weathered **rocks**. The **weathering** is caused by **rain** and wind. The rocks are broken into **fragments** and carried to the sea. **Waves** deposit the particles on the beach. Heavier rocks sink to the bottom **layer**. Lighter particles stay on top. This is what you feel under your feet!

s	c	r	a	y	u	e	i	o	f
s	t	b	o	a	e	m	s	s	r
d	b	l	e	h	y	e	s	a	a
w	e	a	t	h	e	r	i	n	g
a	a	y	d	t	g	a	n	d	m
v	c	e	t	e	w	i	e	f	e
e	h	r	f	s	b	n	r	s	n
s	j	k	l	k	s	c	r	b	t
t	e	s	b	e	r	o	c	k	s

Name:_____

Shape Words

Directions: Draw a line from each word to the correct shapes.

Use a red line for circles.
Use a blue line for squares.

Use a yellow line for rectangles
Use a green line for triangles.

Circle   **Square**   **Triangle**   **Rectangle**

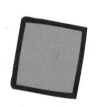

Name:_____

Story Words

A **fact** is something that can be proven. An **opinion** is a belief about something that cannot be proven.

Directions: Read about recycling. Then, follow the instructions.

What do you throw away every day? What could you do with these things? You could change an old greeting card into a new card. You could make a puppet with an old paper bag. Old buttons make great refrigerator magnets. You can plant seeds in plastic cups. Cardboard tubes make perfect rockets. So, use your imagination!

1. Write **F** next to each fact and **O** next to each opinion.

_____ Cardboard tubes are ugly.

_____ Buttons can be made into refrigerator magnets.

_____ An old greeting card can be changed into a new card.

_____ Paper-bag puppets are cute.

_____ Seeds can be planted in plastic cups.

_____ Rockets can be made from cardboard tubes.

2. What could you do with a cardboard tube? _____

_____

Name:_____

Story Words

In some paragraphs, the order of the sentences is very important. **Transition words**, such as **first**, **then**, **now**, and **finally**, offer clues to help show the sequence of the sentences.

Directions: Read about how to make a snowman. Circle the transition words. Then, write the numbers 1, 2, 3, or 4 in each box to show the correct sequence.

It is fun to make a snowman. First, find things for the snowman's eyes and nose. Dress warmly. Then, go outdoors. Roll a big snowball. Now, roll another to put on top of it. Roll a small snowball for the head. Finally, put on the snowman's face.

Name:_____

Story Words

Something that is **real** could actually happen. Something that is **fantasy** is not real. It could not happen.

Examples:
  Real: Dogs can bark.
  Fantasy: Dogs can fly.

Directions: Look at the sentences. Write **real** or **fantasy** next to each one.

1. My cat can talk to me. _____

2. Witches ride brooms and cast spells. _____

3. Dad can mow the lawn. _____

4. I ride a magic carpet to school. _____

5. I have a man-eating tree. _____

6. My sandbox has toys in it. _____

7. Mom can bake chocolate chip cookies. _____

8. Mark has tomatoes and corn in his garden. _____

9. Jack grows candy and ice cream in his garden. _____

10. I make my bed every day. _____

11. Write your own real sentence. _____

_____

12. Write your own fantasy sentence. _____

_____

Name:_____

Clothing Words

Directions: Read the story. Use context clues to figure out the missing words. Write a word from the Word Bank to complete each sentence. Then, answer the questions.

Word Bank			
socks	scarf	sweaters	mittens

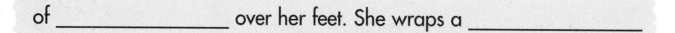

Maria bundles up. She sticks her arms through

two _____ . She tugs three pairs

of _____ over her feet. She wraps a _____

around her neck. At last, she pulls her _____ onto

her hands. Maria goes outside to play. Nobody is warmer than Maria.

1. What clue words helped you figure out sweaters?

_____

2. What clue words helped you figure out mittens?

_____

Name:_____

Words About Soil

Most soil is made of particles of sand, clay, rocks, or organic matter. **Organic matter** is made of dead plants and leaves.

Directions: This truck is moving loads of soil. Follow the trail. Circle the words that name things that help make soil.

leaves

plastic

sand

metal

clay

wheels

rocks

Name:_____

Words About Soil

Directions: Read about soil and earthworms. Use the bold words to find and circle the words in the puzzle. Look across and down.

Soil that has earthworms will be rich and healthy with lots of **organic** matter. The **earthworm** is not a picky eater. It will eat anything organic, from dead leaves to banana peels. Its waste is called **compost**. Earthworms **dig**, **mix**, and **fertilize** the soil. **Plants** love this kind of soil.

```
d  i  m  j  f  d  u  d  d  g
s  d  i  g  e  c  d  c  d  h
g  h  x  d  r  b  f  c  o  j
e  e  a  r  t  h  w  o  r  m
c  r  y  d  i  u  n  m  g  d
y  s  d  v  l  d  d  p  a  j
s  f  f  u  i  l  a  o  n  k
u  n  k  m  z  b  h  s  i  f
i  m  l  q  e  h  l  t  c  n
p  l  a  n  t  s  y  j  c  s
```

Name:_____

Words About Gardening

Directions: Read about garden soil. Then, read each sentence. If it is a fact, write **F**. If it is an opinion, write **O**.

Before you start a garden, make sure you have good soil. It should be easy to turn. To do this, break it up with a shovel. This will allow the water to move through it. You can add old grass clippings and dead leaves to the soil to give it nutrients. If you take the time to create good soil, you will have a beautiful garden!

1. Soil smells wonderful. _____

2. Grass clippings and dead leaves are good for soil. _____

3. Good soil makes a beautiful garden. _____

4. A shovel is hard to use. _____

5. Breaking up the soil allows the water to move through it. _____

UNIT 12

Name:

Unit 12 Review

Directions: Write a story about an animal. Answer the questions to help you get started.

Is your story fiction or nonfiction? _____

What is the main idea of your story? _____

Where does your story take place? _____

What is the animal's habitat? _____

Does the character in your story have a name? _____

_____
Title

_____
Author

_____

_____

_____

_____

_____

_____

UNIT 12

Words That Are Nouns

A **noun** names a person, place, or thing.

Directions: The boy found many things in the old trunk. Circle the nouns in each row.

1. look — sit — (kite) — (photo)
2. (block) — (hammer) — (letter) — kneel
3. cry — (hat) — (dress) — smile
4. (basket) — (doll) — eat — run
5. (fiddle) — (book) — sing — (blanket)

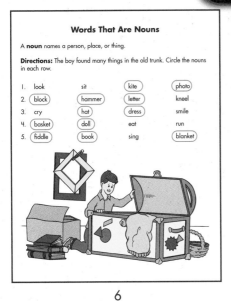

6

Words That Are Nouns

Directions: Read the sentences. Circle the nouns. Then, write the nouns next to the pictures.

1. Our (family) likes to go to the (park). — family / park
2. We play on the (swings). — swings
3. We eat (cake). — cake
4. We drink (lemonade). — lemonade
5. We throw the (ball) to our (dog). — ball / dog
6. Then we go (home). — home

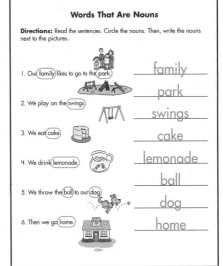

7

Words That Are Nouns

Directions: Read the sentences. Fill in the circle below each noun.

1. First, the boy had to feed his puppy.
2. He got fresh water for his pet.
3. Next, the boy poured some dry food into a bowl.
4. He set the dish on the floor in the kitchen.
5. Then, he called his dog to come to dinner.
6. The boy and his dad worked in the garden.
7. The father turned the dirt with a shovel.
8. The boy carefully dropped seeds into little holes.
9. Soon, tiny plants would sprout from the soil.
10. Sunshine and showers would help the radishes grow.

8

Words About Family

Directions: Use the Word Bank to find the words that name family members. Circle the words in the puzzle. Look across and down.

Word Bank			
mother	father	grandpa	grandma
sister	brother	baby	puppy

```
G L S I S T E R
R Y T B P N X F
A G R A N D P A
N Q L B H B G T
D N T Y Z M Y H
M P U P P Y G E
A N M O T H E R
B R O T H E R X
```

9

Words About Birds

Directions: Use the words in the Word Bank to complete the puzzle about birds.

Across

2. Birds are ___warm___ -blooded animals.
3. Birds lay ___eggs___ from which baby birds are hatched.
5. Like human beings, birds use ___lungs___ to breathe.

Down

1. Birds are covered with ___feathers___ to keep them warm and dry.
4. A bird's mouth is called a ___bill___ .

Word Bank				
feathers	bill	lungs	eggs	warm

10

Words About Birds

Directions: The eggs in the nest contain the names of different birds. Fill in the names in the puzzle. The last letter of one name becomes the first letter of the next name. For example, the last letter of **parrot** is **t**, so that is the first letter of the next word, **turkey**.

Start at the outside edge and spiral in toward the center. The first three are done for you.

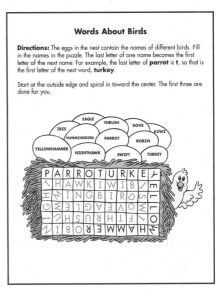

11

Words About Birds

A **fact** is a statement that is true. It can be proven. Here is a fact: Birds have wings. An **opinion** is a statement based on feeling or belief. It cannot be proven. Here is an opinion: My canary is pretty.

Directions: Read the statements about birds. Write **F** next to each fact. Write **O** next to each opinion.

- F 1. Birds have two feet.
- F 2. All birds lay eggs.
- O 3. Parrots are too noisy.
- F 4. All birds have feathers and wings.
- O 5. It would be great to be a bird and fly south for the winter.
- F 6. Birds have hard beaks or bills instead of teeth.
- O 7. Pigeons are fun to watch.
- F 8. Some birds cannot fly.
- O 9. Parakeets make good pets.
- F 10. A penguin is a bird.

12

Words About Counting

Directions: Each basket a player makes is worth two points. Help your home team win by counting by twos to beat the other team's score.

Home   **two**   Visitor

four
six
eight
ten
twelve
fourteen
sixteen
eighteen
twenty
twenty-two
twenty-four
twenty-six
twenty-eight
thirty
thirty-two

Winner!

Final Score	
Home	thirty-two
Visitor	**thirty**

13

Words That Are Pronouns

Pronouns are words that can be used instead of nouns. **She**, **he**, **it**, and **they** are pronouns.

Directions: Read each sentence. Then, write **she**, **he**, **it**, or **they** on the line to replace the underlined word or words.

1. <u>Dan</u> likes funny jokes. _He_ likes funny jokes.
2. <u>Peg and Sam</u> went to the zoo. _They_ went to the zoo.
3. <u>My dog</u> likes to dig in the yard. _It_ likes to dig in the yard.
4. <u>Sara</u> is a very good dancer. _She_ is a very good dancer.
5. <u>Fred and Ted</u> are twins. _They_ are twins.

14

Words That Are Pronouns

Directions: Read each sentence. Then, write each sentence again using the correct pronoun to replace the underlined word or words.

1. <u>Tommy</u> packed sandwiches and apples.
   He packed sandwiches and apples.
2. Tommy hiked along <u>the trail</u>.
   Tommy hiked along it.
3. <u>Ed and Larry</u> caught up with Tommy.
   They caught up with Tommy.
4. <u>Rita</u> met the boys at the trail's end.
   She met the boys at the trail's end.
5. <u>Tommy</u> sent Bill one of his photos later.
   He sent Bill one of his photos later.
6. <u>The boys</u> ate their lunches under a tree.
   They ate their lunches under a tree.
7. After lunch, <u>Rita</u> gave the boys a cookie.
   After lunch, she gave the boys a cookie.

15

Words That Are Pronouns

Use the pronouns **I** and **we** when talking about the person or people doing an action.

Example: I can roller skate. **We** can roller skate.

Use **me** and **us** when talking about something that is happening to a person or people.

Example: They gave **me** the roller skates. They gave **us** the roller skates.

Directions: Circle the correct pronoun that completes each sentence. Then, write it on the line.

Example: _We_ are going to the picnic together.   **(We)** Us
1. _I_ am finished with my science project.   **(I,)** Me
2. Eric passed the football to _me_.   **(me,)** I
3. They ate dinner with _us_ last night.   we, **(us)**
4. _I_ like spinach better than ice cream.   **(I,)** Me
5. Mom came in the room to tell _me_ good night.   **(me,)** I
6. _We_ had a pizza party in our backyard.   Us, **(We)**
7. They told _us_ the good news.   **(us,)** we
8. Tom and _I_ went to the store.   me, **(I)**
9. She is taking _me_ with her to the movies.   I, **(me)**
10. Katie and _I_ are good friends.   **(I,)** me

16

Words About Friends

Directions: Friends are great! Use the Word Bank to find the words that describe a good friend. Circle them in the puzzle. Look across, down, diagonally, and backward.

Word Bank			
smart	funny	gentle	nice
helpful	honest	polite	kind

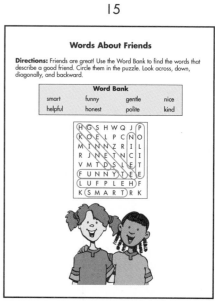

17

ANSWER key

Words About Fish

Fish live almost anywhere there is water. Although fish come in many different shapes, colors, and sizes, they are alike in many ways.

- All fish have backbones.
- Fish breathe with gills.
- Most fish are cold-blooded.
- Most fish have fins.
- Many fish have scales.
- Some fish have funny names.

Directions: The letters in each fish name are mixed up. Unscramble the letters and write each name correctly on the line. Use the clues to help you. Then, use your imagination to draw each fish.

Pictures will vary.

__parrot fish__ rparto fish (a talking bird)	__lionfish__ oinlfish (king of the beasts)	__kingfish__ gknifish (opposite of queen)
__butterfly fish__ tbturelfy fish (an insect with colorful wings)	__goatfish__ ogatfish (a nanny- or a billy-)	__porcupinefish__ opprucneifish (animal with quills)

18

Words About Fish

Most fish have ways to protect themselves from danger. Two of these fish are the **trigger fish** and the **porcupinefish**. The trigger fish lives on the ocean reef. When it sees danger, it swims into its private hole, puts its top fin up and squeezes itself in tight. Then, a predator cannot take it from its hiding place. The porcupinefish also lives on the ocean reef. When it senses danger, it puffs up like a balloon by swallowing air or water. When it puffs up, poisonous spikes stand out on its body. After the danger is gone, it deflates its body.

Directions: Complete the sentences about trigger fish and porcupinefish.

1. Trigger fish and porcupinefish live on the __ocean reef__.

2. The trigger fish swims into its private __hole__.

3. The porcupinefish puffs up like a __balloon__.

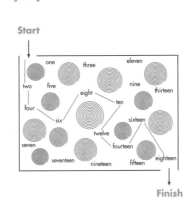

19

Words About Fish

Directions: Read about sea horses. Then, answer the questions.

Sea horses are fish, not horses. A sea horse's head looks like a horse's head. It has a tail like a monkey's tail. A sea horse looks very strange.

1. (Circle the correct answer.)
   A sea horse is a kind of

   horse.

   monkey.

   (fish.)

2. What does a sea horse's head look like?

   __A sea horse's head looks__
   __like a horse's head.__

3. What makes a sea horse look strange?

   a. __It has a head like a horse's head.__

   b. __It has a tail like a monkey's tail.__

20

Words About Counting

Directions: Trace a path following the even numbers (two, four, six, etc.) to get through the maze.

Start

one three eleven
two five eight ten nine thirteen
four six sixteen
seven twelve fourteen eighteen
seventeen nineteen fifteen

Finish

21

Words That Are Nouns

	Word Bank			
books	bus	chalkboard	classroom	crayons
desk	pencil	playground	school	teacher

Directions: Use the words in the Word Bank to complete each sentence. Write the correct noun on the line.

1. There are many kinds of __books__ to read in school.
2. Miss Lopez is my second-grade __teacher__.
3. You can color pictures with __crayons__.
4. Children sit in a __classroom__ to learn.
5. I ride to school on the __bus__.
6. There are swings and slides on our school __playground__.
7. There is a __school__ building next to the park.
8. The teacher writes sentences on the __chalkboard__.
9. I write a story with a __pencil__.
10. My __desk__ is in the front of the classroom.

22

Words That Are Nouns

A **noun** names a person, place, or thing.

Directions: Circle the two nouns in each sentence.

Example: (Mom) reads a (book).

1. The (bird) flew to its (nest).

2. The (kite) was high in the (air).

3. The (children) played a (game).

4. The (books) fell on the (ground).

5. The (monkey) climbed a (tree).

23

307

Words That Are Nouns

Directions: The cookie jars hold different kinds of nouns. Read the nouns on the cookies. Decide if they are people, places, or things. Then, write each noun on the correct jar.

People
teacher
friend
mom
sister

Places
beach
school
park
library

Things
jar
toad
bird
box

beach
teacher
school
jar
friend
park
toad
library
bird
mom
box
sister

24

Words About Home

Word Bank				
bedroom	blanket	bathroom	dishes	house
kitchen	sink	stove	table	yard

Directions: Write the correct word from the Word Bank beside each picture.

1. kitchen
4. house
2. bathroom
5. bedroom
3. table
6. dishes

Directions: Use the words in the Word Bank to complete each sentence.

7. Mark has a swing set in his back ___yard___.
8. I use a ___blanket___ to keep warm when it is cold.
9. Mother cooks dinner on the ___stove___.
10. You can wash your hands in the ___sink___.

25

Words About Insects

Sometimes, two small words can be put together to make one new word. The new word is called a **compound word**.

Some insect names are compound words:

fire + fly = firefly
water + bug = waterbug

Directions: Find the two words that make up each insect's name. Write the two words on the lines. Then, color the insects.

1. butterfly
   ___butter___ ___fly___

Color the pictures.

2. grasshopper
   ___grass___ ___hopper___

3. ladybug
   ___lady___ ___bug___

26

Words About Insects

All insects have these body parts:

Head at the front
Thorax in the middle
Abdomen at the back
Six **legs**—three on each side of the thorax
Two **eyes** on the head
Two **antennae** attached to the head
Some insects also have **wings**.

Directions: Draw your favorite insect. Include all the body parts listed above.

Pictures will vary.

27

Words About Insects

Directions: Read about ladybugs. Then, answer the questions.

A ladybug is a kind of beetle. Ladybugs can be found all over the world. There are more than 4,500 kinds of ladybugs! Ladybugs are small insects. They are usually yellow, orange, or red and have small black spots on their backs. Their bright colors help protect them from predators.

Ladybugs are very good for gardens. They are considered good luck because they eat other insects that damage plants.

1. Where can ladybugs be found? found all over the world.
2. What color are ladybugs? Ladybugs are yellow, orange, or red.
3. Why are ladybugs brightly colored? Ladybugs are brightly colored to protect them from predators.
4. What do ladybugs eat? Ladybugs eat insects.
5. Why are ladybugs good for gardens? Ladybugs eat insects that damage plants.

28

Unit 1 Review

Directions: Read each sentence. Write **F** next to each fact. Write **O** next to each opinion. Then, underline the nouns.

F 1. Lemonade is a drink made from lemons.
O 2. My grandma is a very nice woman.
F 3. A porcupinefish can puff up like a balloon.
O 4. The children like to play on the playground.
O 5. An ibis is a pretty bird.
F 6. My house has two bathrooms.
F 7. Some insects have wings.
F 8. A bird uses its bill to pick up food.
O 9. Planting seeds with my dad is fun.
O 10. A sea horse is a kind of strange fish.

29

Words That Are Verbs

A **verb** is the action word in a sentence. A verb tells what someone or something does. **Run, sleep,** and **jump** are verbs.

Directions: Circle the verb in each sentence.

1. We (play) baseball every day.
2. Susan (pitches) the ball very well.
3. Mike (swings) the bat harder than anyone.
4. Chris (slides) into home base.
5. Laura (hits) a home run.

31

Words That Are Verbs

A **verb** can tell when something happens. Sometimes, **-ed** is added at the end of a verb to tell that something has already happened.

Example: Let's **play** at my house today. We **played** at your house yesterday.

Directions: Circle the correct verb that completes each sentence. Then, write it on the line.

1. Today, I will ___wash___ my dog, Fritz.
   (wash)   washed
2. Last week, Fritz ___cried___ when we said, "Bath time, Fritz."
   cry   (cried)
3. My sister likes to ___help___ wash Fritz.
   (help)   helped
4. One time she ___cleaned___ Fritz by herself.
   clean   (cleaned)
5. Fritz will ___look___ a lot better after his bath.
   (look)   looked

32

Words That Are Verbs

Some verbs do not show action. Instead, they link the subject with the second part of the sentence. These types of verbs are **linking verbs**. **Am, is, are, was,** and **were** are linking verbs.

Examples: Many people **are** collectors.
His collection **is** large.

Directions: Underline the linking verb in each sentence.

1. I <u>am</u> happy.
2. Toy collecting <u>is</u> a nice hobby.
3. Mom and dad <u>are</u> helpful.
4. The rabbit <u>is</u> beautiful.
5. Itsy and Bitsy <u>are</u> stuffed mice.
6. Monday <u>was</u> special.
7. I <u>was</u> excited.
8. The class <u>was</u> impressed.
9. The elephants <u>were</u> gray.
10. My friends <u>were</u> a good audience.

33

Words About Community Places

Word Bank					
bakery	bank	library	post office	school	hospital

Directions: Read each clue. Write the word from the Word Bank that names the place being described. Write the word on the line.

1. Save your cash. Bring it here.
   It will grow year to year. ___bank___
2. French bread, muffins, chocolate cake.
   Here's the place where people bake. ___bakery___
3. Here's the place to learn to read.
   Our teacher will help us succeed. ___school___
4. Come inside and take a look.
   When you leave, check out a book. ___library___
5. Buy some stamps. Mail a letter.
   To do these things, there's no place better. ___post office___
6. Come here if you need health care.
   A doctor will be waiting there. ___hospital___

34

Words About Reptiles

A **reptile** is a cold-blooded animal with scaly skin and a backbone. A **snake** is a reptile.

Directions: Read about snakes. Then, write the correct answers to complete each sentence.

There are many facts about snakes that might surprise someone. A snake's skin is dry. Most snakes are shy. They will hide from people. Snakes eat mice and rats. They do not chew them up. Snakes' jaws drop open to swallow their food whole.

1. A snake's skin feels ___dry___.

2. Most snakes are ___shy___.

3. Snakes eat
   a. ___mice___
   b. ___rats___

35

Words About Reptiles

There are about 6,000 kinds of reptiles. They range in length from 2 inches to almost 30 feet. Even though reptiles seem quite different, they all breathe with lungs, are cold-blooded, have scaly skin, and have a backbone.

Directions: In the Reptile House at the zoo, each animal needs to be placed in the correct area. Read the information about each reptile. Then, read the clues to write the name of each reptile in its area.

Giant Tortoise	Reticulated Python	Saltwater Crocodile	Komodo Dragon
can live over 100 years. It can hide under its shell for protection.	is the longest snake. One was almost 33 feet long.	is one of the largest reptiles. It can weigh 1,000 pounds.	is a dragon-like reptile. It is the largest living lizard.

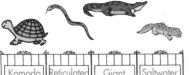

| Komodo Dragon | Reticulated Python | Giant Tortoise | Saltwater Crocodile |

Clues: • The snake is between the largest lizard and the largest member of the turtle family.
• A relative of the alligator is on the far right side.

36

Words About Reptiles

Directions: Circle each word along the trail that names a reptile.

START HERE!

lizard | cat | snake
whale
ant | alligator | snail
dog
duck | turtle | eagle
horse
tortoise | fox | crocodile

37

Words About Counting

Directions: Follow the directions in each column to write the missing number words.

Write the number word that is one less.

1. _fifteen_ , sixteen
2. _three_ , four
3. _one_ , two
4. _two_ , three
5. _nine_ , ten
6. _ten_ , eleven
7. _four_ , five
8. _thirteen_ , fourteen
9. _five_ , six
10. _twelve_ , thirteen
11. _six_ , seven

Write the number word that is one greater.

12. six, _seven_
13. five, _six_
14. nine, _ten_
15. eleven, _twelve_
16. two, _three_
17. four, _five_
18. one, _two_
19. twelve, _thirteen_
20. nineteen, _twenty_
21. ten, _eleven_
22. three, _four_

38

Words That Are Verbs

A **verb** is a word that can show action.

Examples: I **jump**. He **kicks**. He **walks**.

Directions: Underline the verb in each sentence. Then, write it on the line.

1. Our school plays games on Field Day. _plays_
2. Juan runs 50 yards. _runs_
3. Carmen hops in a sack race. _hops_
4. Paula tosses a ball through a hoop. _tosses_
5. One girl carries a jellybean on a spoon. _carries_
6. Lola bounces the ball. _bounces_
7. Some boys chase after balloons. _chase_
8. The children cheer for the winners. _cheer_

39

Words That Are Verbs

Directions: Circle the verb in each sentence.

1. The woman (paints) a picture.

2. The puppy (chases) its ball.

3. The students (go) to school.

4. Butterflies (fly) in the air.

5. The baby (drinks) from a cup.

40

Words That Are Verbs

Directions: Fill in the bubble beside the verb that best matches each picture.

Example:

(A) drop
(B) help
(C) climb
(D) slide

1.
● mix
(B) fix
(C) eat
(D) chew

2.
(A) lake
(B) boil
(C) bake
(D) lick

3.
(A) drink
(B) glass
(C) milk
● spill

4.
● hug
(B) laugh
(C) tug
(D) cook

41

Words About Libraries

Directions: Read the paragraph below. Then, find and circle the bold words in the puzzle. Look across, down, and diagonally.

A **library** is a great place to visit in the **summer**. It provides **books** and other items for **education** and **fun**. The **librarian** is helpful and friendly. Most libraries have summer programs, such as **reading** contests, summer **movies**, and **story** times. It is hard to believe this great place is **free**!

42

Words About Mammals

Directions: A **mammal** is a warm-blooded animal with hair or fur. Write the mammal name from the Word Bank beside the correct picture. The first one is done for you.

Word Bank

fox   rabbit   bear   squirrel   mouse   deer

1. squirrel
2. rabbit
3. bear
4. mouse
5. fox
6. deer

43

Words About Mammals

Directions: Use the words in the Word Bank to find and circle orange the names of three animals that would make good pets. Circle blue the names of three wild animals. Circle green the two animals that live on a farm. Also, find and circle the animal sounds.

Word Bank

BEAR   CAT   LION   SHEEP   BIRD   DOG   COW   TIGER

```
A  M  E  O  W  N  L  I  O  N
B  M  D  O  G  X  I  I  S  O
A  R  B  E  A  R  V  L  M  H
R  M  R  M  O  O  U  S  E  K
K  C  A  B  B  I  R  D  S  E
I  O  T  T  I  G  E  R  M  P  Q
B  W  N  O  W  W  R  Q  N  E  N
D  N  C  P  H  H  I  D  U  D  N
F  K  C  A  T  T  R  O  A  R  M
```

44

Words About Zoo Animals

Directions: Write the name of the animal that answers each riddle on the line. Use the pictures and animal names to help you.

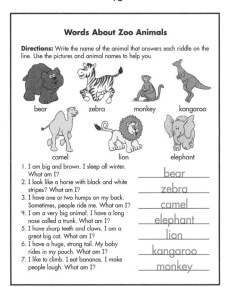

bear   zebra   monkey   kangaroo

camel   lion   elephant

1. I am big and brown. I sleep all winter. What am I? — bear
2. I look like a horse with black and white stripes? What am I? — zebra
3. I have one or two humps on my back. Sometimes, people ride me. What am I? — camel
4. I am a very big animal. I have a long nose called a trunk. What am I? — elephant
5. I have sharp teeth and claws. I am a great big cat. What am I? — lion
6. I have a huge, strong tail. My baby rides in my pouch. What am I? — kangaroo
7. I like to climb. I eat bananas. I make people laugh. What am I? — monkey

45

Words About Counting

Directions: Write the missing number words on the lines.

1. Count by twos:

two   four   six   eight   ten

2. Count by fives:

five   ten   fifteen   twenty   twenty-five   thirty

3. Count by tens:

ten   twenty   thirty   fourty   fifty

46

Words That Are Verbs

Directions: Write a sentence that tells what happens in each picture. Use the **verb** under the picture. The first one is done for you.

1. falls   breaks   cleans

A glass falls off the table.
Suggested sentences:
The glass breaks.
The girl cleans up.

2.

fixes   cuts   lifts

Suggested sentences:
Dad fixes the lawnmower.
She cuts the grass.
The boy lifts the bag.

47

Words That Are Verbs

Directions: Underline the verb in each sentence.

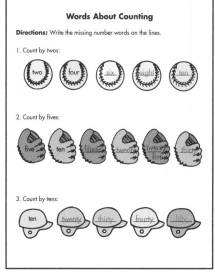

1. The tigers slept in the hot sun.

2. The lion cubs played by the fence.

3. The elephant ate the salty peanuts.

4. The ducks swam in the deep lake.

48

Words That Are Verbs

Directions: Read the two sentences in each story. Then, use the verb under the last picture to write one more sentence to tell what happens next.

1. Today is Mike's birthday.

   Mike asked four friends to come.

   cut   Suggested sentence:
   Mike's mom cut the birthday cake.

2. Edith's dog walked in the mud.

   He got mud in the house.

   cleaned   Suggested sentence:
   Edith cleaned the mess.

49

Words About Community Places

Directions: Look at the pictures. Circle the word that names each community place.

1.

   (pet store)
   bakery
   florist

2.

   (bakery)
   library
   post office

3.

   florist
   post office
   (school)

50

Words For Animal Young

Directions: Use the story about baby animals to complete the chart below. Write the kind of animal that belongs with each special baby name.

> Many animals are called special names when they are young. A baby deer is called a **fawn**. A baby cat is called a **kitten**.
> Some young animals have the same name as other kinds of baby animals. A baby elephant is a **calf**. A baby whale is a **calf**. A baby giraffe is a **calf**.
> A baby cow is a **calf**.
> Some baby animals are called **cubs**. A baby lion, a baby bear, a baby tiger, and a baby fox are all called **cubs**.
> Some baby animals are called **colts**. A young horse is a **colt**. A baby zebra is a **colt**. A baby donkey is a **colt**.

calf	cub	colt
elephant	lion	horse
whale	bear	zebra
giraffe	tiger	donkey
cow	fox	

51

Words For Animal Young

Directions: Look at the pictures of the mother animals and their babies. Write **calf**, **cub**, or **colt** on the line to name each baby.

1. colt

4. calf

2. cub

5. calf

3. colt

6. cub

52

Name:_____

Words For Animal Young

Directions: Read the story about baby animals. Then, write the word from the story that completes each sentence.

Baby cats are called **kittens**. They love to play. A baby dog is a **puppy**. Puppies chew on old shoes. They run and bark. A baby sheep is a **lamb**. Lambs eat grass. A baby duck is a **duckling**. Ducklings swim with their wide, webbed feet. Baby horses are **foals**. A foal can walk the day it is born! A baby goat is a **kid**. Some people call children **kids**, too!

1. A baby cat is called a ___kitten___.

2. A baby dog is called a ___puppy___.

3. A baby sheep is a ___lamb___.

4. ___Ducklings___ swim with webbed feet.

5. A ___foal___ can walk the day it is born.

6. A baby goat is a ___kid___.

53

Unit 2 Review

Directions: Circle the verb in each sentence. Underline the community place.

1. There (are) hundreds of books at the library.

2. We (eat) delicious desserts from the bakery.

3. We (buy) our fish at the pet store.

4. He (visits) the reptile house at the zoo.

5. Children (learn) lots of new things at school.

Directions: Write a sentence to tell what you know about each topic below.

1. reptiles ___Sentences will vary.___

2. mammals _____

3. animal young _____

54

312

Words That Are Adjectives

An **adjective** is a word that describes a noun. It can tell how a person, place, or thing looks, tastes, sounds, or feels.

Directions: Choose two words from the Word Bank that describe each person. Then, complete each sentence.

Word Bank					
surprised	upset	happy	caring	kind	confused

1. The girl is <u>kind</u> and <u>caring</u> because she <u>Sentences will vary.</u>

2. Mother is <u>surprised</u> and <u>happy</u> because she <u>Sentences will vary.</u>

3. Father is <u>upset</u> and <u>confused</u> because he <u>Sentences will vary.</u>

56

Words That Are Adjectives

Use an **adjective** that best describes a noun or pronoun. Be specific.

Example: David had a nice birthday.
David had a **fun** birthday.

Directions: Read each sentence. Write the sentence again, replacing **nice** or **good** with a better adjective from the Word Bank.

Word Bank					
sturdy	new	great	chocolate	delicious	special

1. David bought a nice pair of in-line skates.
<u>David bought a great pair of in-line skates.</u>

2. He received a nice helmet.
<u>He received a sturdy helmet.</u>

3. He got nice kneepads.
<u>He got new kneepads.</u>

4. Dad baked a good cake.
<u>Dad baked a delicious cake.</u>

5. David made a good wish.
<u>David made a special wish.</u>

6. Mom served good ice cream.
<u>Mom served chocolate ice cream.</u>

57

Words That Are Adjectives

An **adjective** is a word that describes a noun.

Example: Yolanda has a **tasty** lunch.

Directions: Color each space that has an adjective. Do not color the other spaces.

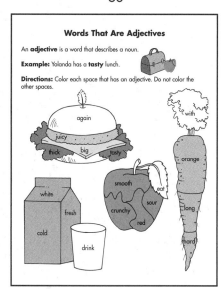

58

Words About Community Helpers

Directions: Use the words in the Word Bank to answer each clue. Write the answer on the line.

Word Bank			
captain	dentist	fireman	doctor
plumber	police	teacher	baker

1. I think I have a cavity in my tooth. Who can help me?
<u>dentist</u>

2. My mom needs to order a wedding cake for my uncle. Who can help her?
<u>baker</u>

3. I hurt my ankle during gym class. Who can help me?
<u>doctor</u>

4. My pipes are leaking. Who can help me?
<u>plumber</u>

59

Weather Words

Directions: Use the words in the Word Bank to complete the puzzle about weather.

Word Bank
clouds
lightning
outside
rainy
snow
storm
sunny
thunder
weather

Crossword answers:
7 across: sunny
2 across: weather
4 across: lightning
8 across: outside
6 across: rainy
5 across: storm
9 down: snow
1 down: thunder
3 down: clouds
8 down: outside

Across

2. The conditions outside, like sunshine or rain

4. Flash of light seen during a storm

5. Wind and rain make a _____.

6. An umbrella is needed when the weather is _____.

7. There are no clouds on a bright, _____ day.

8. The opposite of inside

Down

1. A loud noise heard during a rainstorm

3. White, puffy objects that float in the sky

9. Frozen rain that falls in the winter

60

Weather Words

Directions: Write a sentence about each picture. Use weather words from the Word Bank.

Word Bank					
windy	cool	cold	rainy	wet	cloudy

1. <u>Sentences will vary.</u>

2. _____

3. _____

4. _____

61

Weather Words

Directions: Use the Word Bank to write the weather word that completes each sentence. Put a period at the end of the telling sentences and a question mark at the end of the asking sentences.

Word Bank		
rainbow	wind	blizzard
rain	hot	sun

Example:

Do flowers grow in the ___sun___ [?]

1. The ___wind___ almost blew me away [.]

2. This huge umbrella protects me from the ___rain___ [.]

3. During the ___blizzard___ , the snow was blowing hard [.]

4. Did you see the beautiful ___rainbow___ after it rained [?]

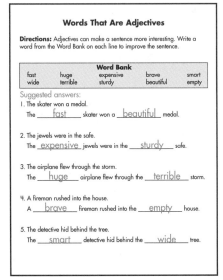

62

Ordinal Number Words

Ordinal numbers tell the order in a series. **First**, **second**, and **third** are ordinal numbers.

Directions: Follow the instructions to color the train cars. The first car is the engine.

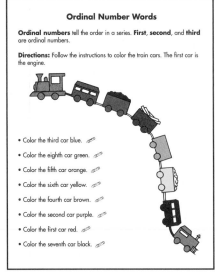

- Color the third car blue.
- Color the eighth car green.
- Color the fifth car orange.
- Color the sixth car yellow.
- Color the fourth car brown.
- Color the second car purple.
- Color the first car red.
- Color the seventh car black.

63

Words That Are Adjectives

Directions: Adjectives can make a sentence more interesting. Write a word from the Word Bank on each line to improve the sentence.

Word Bank				
fast	huge	expensive	brave	smart
wide	terrible	sturdy	beautiful	empty

Suggested answers:

1. The skater won a medal.
   The ___fast___ skater won a ___beautiful___ medal.

2. The jewels were in the safe.
   The ___expensive___ jewels were in the ___sturdy___ safe.

3. The airplane flew through the storm.
   The ___huge___ airplane flew through the ___terrible___ storm.

4. A fireman rushed into the house.
   A ___brave___ fireman rushed into the ___empty___ house.

5. The detective hid behind the tree.
   The ___smart___ detective hid behind the ___wide___ tree.

64

Words That Are Adjectives

Directions: Write an adjective on each line. Draw a picture to match each sentence.

1. The _____ flag waved over the _____ building.

   Adjectives and pictures will vary.

4. A _____ lion searched for food in the _____ jungle.

2. We saw _____ fish in the _____ aquarium.

5. Her _____ car was parked by the _____ van.

3. The _____ dog barked and chased the _____ truck.

6. The _____ building was filled with _____ packages.

65

Words That Are Adverbs

Describing words can also tell about an action. These words are called **adverbs**.

Examples: The turtle moved **slowly**.
The rabbit moved **quickly**.

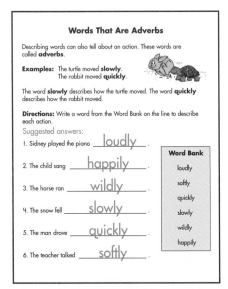

The word **slowly** describes how the turtle moved. The word **quickly** describes how the rabbit moved.

Directions: Write a word from the Word Bank on the line to describe each action.

Suggested answers:

1. Sidney played the piano ___loudly___.

2. The child sang ___happily___.

3. The horse ran ___wildly___.

4. The snow fell ___slowly___.

5. The man drove ___quickly___.

6. The teacher talked ___softly___.

Word Bank
loudly
softly
quickly
slowly
wildly
happily

66

Words About Community Helpers

The people who work in your community do important jobs.

Directions: Write a sentence to show what you know about each community helper.

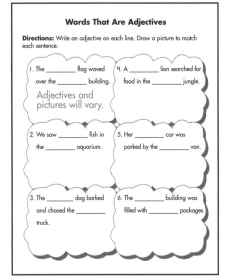

1. police officer ___Sentences will vary.___

2. doctor _____

3. mayor _____

4. dentist _____

5. firefighter _____

6. teacher _____

67

Winter Words

Directions: Fill in the circle beside the word that best completes each sentence.

It was a _____ winter day. Alicia
    1
and her brother Randy hurried out

in their warm _____ . They played
          2

in the _____ . They made a
    3

big _____ .
   4

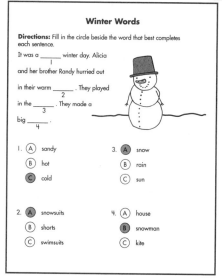

1. (A) sandy   3. (A) snow
   (B) hot   (B) rain
   (C) cold   (C) sun

2. **(A) snowsuits**   4. (A) house
   (B) shorts   **(B) snowman**
   (C) swimsuits   (C) kite

68

Spring Words

Directions: Fill in the circle beside the word that best completes each sentence. Then, write the word on the line.

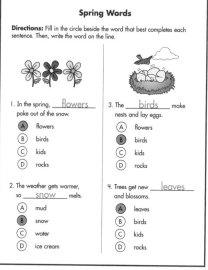

1. In the spring, _flowers_ poke out of the snow.
   (A) flowers
   (B) birds
   (C) kids
   (D) rocks

2. The weather gets warmer, so _snow_ melts.
   (A) mud
   (B) snow
   (C) water
   (D) ice cream

3. The _birds_ make nests and lay eggs.
   (A) flowers
   (B) birds
   (C) kids
   (D) rocks

4. Trees get new _leaves_ and blossoms.
   (A) leaves
   (B) birds
   (C) kids
   (D) rocks

69

Summer Words

Directions: Fill in the circle beside the word that best completes each sentence.

It is a _____ summer day. The
   1
children are out of _____ . It is
          2
time to have _____ . The _____
       3   4
is the best place to be!

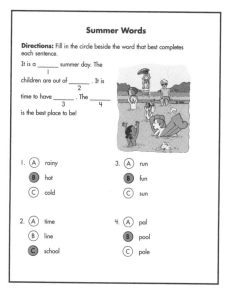

1. (A) rainy   3. (A) run
   (B) hot   **(B) fun**
   (C) cold   (C) sun

2. (A) time   4. (A) pal
   (B) line   **(B) pool**
   (C) school   (C) pole

70

Ordinal Number Words

Directions: Look at the treats in the box. Circle the ordinal number for each treat.

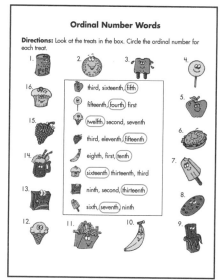

third, sixteenth, (fifth)
fifteenth, (fourth) first
(twelfth) second, seventh
third, eleventh, (fifteenth)
eighth, first, (tenth)
(sixteenth) thirteenth, third
ninth, second, (thirteenth)
sixth, (seventh) ninth

71

Words That Are Adverbs

Directions: Read the sentences about the picture. Circle the words that are adverbs. Then, color the picture.

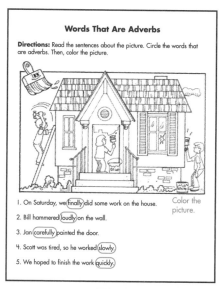

Color the picture.

1. On Saturday, we (finally) did some work on the house.
2. Bill hammered (loudly) on the wall.
3. Jan (carefully) painted the door.
4. Scott was tired, so he worked (slowly).
5. We hoped to finish the work (quickly).

72

Words That Are Adverbs

An **adverb** describes a verb. It tells how, when, or where an action takes place.

Examples: The space shuttle blasted off **yesterday**. (when)
It rose **quickly** into the sky. (how)
We watched **outdoors**. (where)

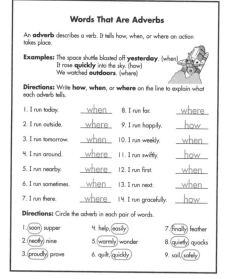

Directions: Write **how**, **when**, or **where** on the line to explain what each adverb tells.

1. I run today. _when_   8. I run far. _where_
2. I run outside. _where_   9. I run happily. _how_
3. I run tomorrow. _when_   10. I run weekly. _when_
4. I run around. _where_   11. I run swiftly. _how_
5. I run nearby. _where_   12. I run first. _when_
6. I run sometimes. _when_   13. I run next. _when_
7. I run there. _where_   14. I run gracefully. _how_

Directions: Circle the adverb in each pair of words.

1. (soon) supper   4. help, (easily)   7. (finally) feather
2. (neatly) nine   5. (warmly) wonder   8. (quietly) quacks
3. (proudly) prove   6. quilt, (quickly)   9. sail, (safely)

73

Words That Are Adverbs

Directions: Complete each sentence with an adverb from the Word Bank.

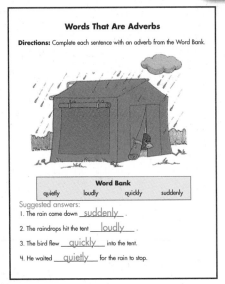

Word Bank

quietly   loudly   quickly   suddenly

Suggested answers:
1. The rain came down __suddenly__.
2. The raindrops hit the tent __loudly__.
3. The bird flew __quickly__ into the tent.
4. He waited __quietly__ for the rain to stop.

74

Words for Community Helpers

Directions: Use the words in the Word Bank to write the names of two community helpers that fit each description.

Word Bank

mathematician	veterinarian	teacher	chef
police officer	nurse	doctor	accountant
mail carrier	seamstress	librarian	tailor
delivery person	farmer	umpire	zookeeper

1. Place importance on books — teacher / librarian
2. Work with needle and thread — seamstress / tailor
3. Work with food — farmer / chef
4. Make sure people follow rules — police officer / umpire
5. Deliver mail and packages — mail carrier / delivery person
6. Take care of medical needs — nurse / doctor
7. Work with animals — veterinarian / zookeeper
8. Use numbers often — mathematician / accountant

75

Autumn Words

Directions: Fill in the circle beside the word that best completes each sentence. Then, write the word on the line.

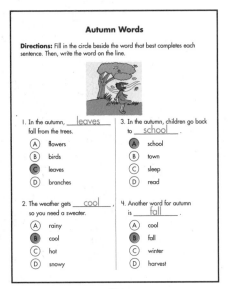

1. In the autumn, __leaves__ fall from the trees.
   (A) flowers
   (B) birds
   (C) leaves
   (D) branches

2. The weather gets __cool__ so you need a sweater.
   (A) rainy
   (B) cool
   (C) hot
   (D) snowy

3. In the autumn, children go back to __school__.
   (A) school
   (B) town
   (C) sleep
   (D) read

4. Another word for autumn is __fall__.
   (A) cool
   (B) fall
   (C) winter
   (D) harvest

76

Words About Seasons

Directions: Write three words on the lines to tell about each season.

Spring — Answers will vary.

Summer

Fall

Winter

77

Words About Seasons

Directions: Use the words in the Word Bank to complete the puzzle about the seasons.

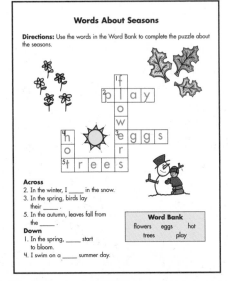

Puzzle answers: play, flowers, eggs, hot, trees

Across
2. In the winter, I _____ in the snow.
3. In the spring, birds lay their _____.
5. In the autumn, leaves fall from the _____.

Down
1. In the spring, _____ start to bloom.
4. I swim on a _____ summer day.

Word Bank

flowers   eggs   hot   trees   play

78

Unit 3 Review

Directions: Use the Word Bank to write the job word that completes each sentence. Then, circle the two adjectives in each sentence.

Word Bank

zookeeper   plumber   mathematician   nurse   seamstress

1. The (smart) __mathematician__ solves the (difficult) problems.
2. The (talented) __seamstress__ sews a (beautiful) dress.
3. The (caring) __nurse__ takes care of her (sick) patient.
4. The (busy) __zookeeper__ feeds the (hungry) animals.
5. The (handy) __plumber__ fixes the (leaky) sink.

Directions: Use the Word Bank to write the weather word that completes each sentence.

Word Bank

clouds   weather   lightning   sunny

1. I saw __lightning__ flash outside my window.
2. A __sunny__ day is perfect for a picnic.
3. The rain __clouds__ were thick and dark.
4. When the __weather__ is cold, you should dress warmly.

79

Words That Are Articles

Articles are words that come before nouns. **A** and **an** are articles. Use **a** before a word that begins with a consonant. Use **an** before a word that begins with a vowel.

Example: A man ran fast. He was **an** energetic man.

Directions: Circle the correct article that completes each sentence.

1. Our class had **(a)** / **an** picnic in the park.
2. Miss Lee passed **an** / **(a)** ball to me.
3. We saw **a** / **(an)** anthill by the trees.
4. **(A)** / **An** woman fished by the pond.
5. Today was **(a)** / **an** fun day.

81

Words That Are Articles

Directions: Read each sentence. Write **a** or **an** on the line to complete the sentence.

1. My family went to ___a___ zoo to see some wild animals.
2. We saw ___an___ elephant that was really big.
3. ___A___ lion waved its tail at us as we walked by.
4. There was ___an___ alligator that showed us its large teeth.
5. There were monkeys swinging playfully from the branches of ___a___ tree.
6. My family had ___a___ great day!

82

Words That Are Articles

Directions: Write **a** or **an** beside each word.

Examples: a turtle
an owl

1. ___a___ kangaroo   9. ___a___ tiger
2. ___an___ ostrich   10. ___a___ cat
3. ___a___ frog   11. ___an___ ant
4. ___a___ goat   12. ___a___ zebra
5. ___a___ lion   13. ___a___ pig
6. ___an___ elephant   14. ___a___ dog
7. ___a___ snail   15. ___a___ whale
8. ___a___ bat   16. ___a___ skunk

83

Words About the United States

Directions: Study the map of the United States. Follow the instructions.

1. Draw a star on the state where you live.
2. Draw a line from your state to the Atlantic Ocean.
3. Draw a triangle in the Gulf of Mexico.
4. Draw a circle in the Pacific Ocean.
5. Color each state that borders your state a different color.

Answers and colors will vary.

84

Words About Day and Night

Directions: Read the words in the Word Bank. If they relate to day, write them under the sun. If they relate to night, write them under the moon.

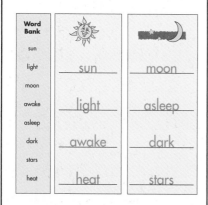

Word Bank	☀	🌙
sun	sun	moon
light	light	asleep
moon	awake	dark
awake	heat	stars
asleep		
dark		
stars		
heat		

85

Time of Day Words

Directions: Fill in the circle beside the word that answers each question.

1. Which word means "not light"?
   - (A) **dark**
   - (B) hot
   - (C) cool

2. Which word means "full of sun"?
   - (A) **sunshine**
   - (B) dark
   - (C) sunny

3. Which word means "the early hours of night"?
   - (A) morning
   - (B) dawn
   - (C) **evening**

4. Which word is "the time when the sun comes up"?
   - (A) **sunrise**
   - (B) sunset
   - (C) sunshine

5. Which word means "middle of the day"?
   - (A) dawn
   - (B) dusk
   - (C) **noon**

6. Which word means "middle of the night"?
   - (A) **midnight**
   - (B) midday
   - (C) night

86

Space Words

Directions: Read each clue. Find the matching word in the puzzle and write it on the line. Connect the puzzle dots in the same order as your answers. Then, color the picture.

Clues

1. The planet we live on ___Earth___
2. The closest star ___sun___
3. They shine in the sky at night. ___stars___
4. Earth is a ___planet___.
5. Planets, stars, and moons are in ___space___
6. Time when the sun shines ___day___
7. A group of stars ___constellation___
8. A person who travels in space ___astronaut___
9. The path a planet follows to travel around the sun ___orbit___
10. It gives us light at night. ___moon___
11. People who study the stars ___astronomers___
12. You use this to see the stars. ___telescope___
13. Time when the sun does not shine ___night___
14. We feel this from the sun. ___heat___

Color the picture.

Earth, sun, night, heat, stars, planet, space, day, constellation, moon, orbit, astronomers, telescope, astronaut

87

Time Words

Directions: Circle each mouse if it has a time word.

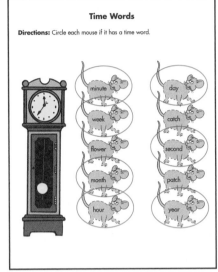

minute, week, flower, month, hour, day, catch, second, patch, year

88

Words With Prefixes

A **prefix** is a word part that goes at the beginning of a base word to change the word's meaning. The prefix **re-** means "again."

Example: **Refill** means "to fill again."

Directions: Look at the pictures. Read the base words. Add the prefix **re** to the base word to show that the action is being repeated. Write the new word on the line.

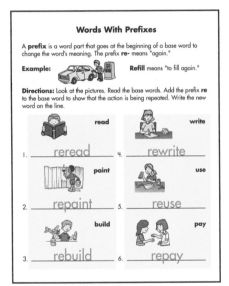

1. read — reread
2. paint — repaint
3. build — rebuild
4. write — rewrite
5. use — reuse
6. pay — repay

89

Words With Prefixes

The prefixes **un-** and **dis-** mean "not" or "the opposite of."

Unlocked means "not locked."

Dismount is the opposite of "mount."

Directions: Look at the pictures. Circle the word that tells about each picture. Then, write the word on the line.

1. tied / (untied) — untied
2. happy / (unhappy) — happy
3. safe / (unsafe) — unsafe
4. like / (dislike) — dislike
5. (obey) / disobey — obey
6. honest / (dishonest) — dishonest

90

Words With Prefixes

The prefix **un-** means "not." The prefix **mis-** means "bad or wrong."

Directions: Change the meaning of the sentences by adding the prefixes to the bold words. Write the new word on the line to complete each sentence.

1. The boy was **lucky** because he **read** the directions.
   The boy was (un) ___unlucky___ because he (mis) ___misread___ the directions.

2. When Mary **behaved**, she felt **happy**.
   When Mary (mis) ___misbehaved___, she felt (un) ___unhappy___.

3. Mike **understood** because he was **familiar** with the book.
   Mike (mis) ___misunderstood___ because he was (un) ___unfamiliar___ with the book.

91

Words About Your State

Directions: The United States of America has 50 states. Think about your own state. Answer the questions.

1. What is the name of your state?
   ___Answers will vary.___

2. What is your state capital?
   _____

3. What is the name of your city or town?
   _____

4. What is special about your state?
   _____
   _____
   _____

THANK YOU FOR VISITING OUR GREAT STATE

92

Space Words

Directions: Read the paragraph. Then, use the bold words to answer the questions.

There are eight planets that move around the sun. Our planet is **Earth**. Earth is closest to **Mars** and **Venus**. **Jupiter** is the largest planet. It is many times larger than Earth. **Saturn** is the planet with seven rings around it. The smallest planet is called **Mercury**!

1. How many planets are there?   three   (eight)   seven

2. I am your planet. _____Earth_____

3. We are closest to Earth. __Mars__   __Venus__

4. I am the largest planet. _____Jupiter_____

5. I am the planet with seven rings. _____Saturn_____

6. I am the smallest planet. _____Mercury_____

7. Draw three red rings around Saturn.

93

Words About Planets

In our solar system, eight planets circle the sun. **Mercury** is the planet closest to the sun, followed by the planets **Venus**, **Earth**, and **Mars**. These four planets are called the **inner solar system**. The **outer solar system** is made up of **Jupiter**, **Saturn**, **Uranus**, and **Neptune**.

Directions: Write the names of the planets on the lines according to their distances from the sun. Then, color the picture.

Neptune	Jupiter	Earth	Mercury
Venus	Uranus	Saturn	Mars

Color the picture.

Mercury, Venus, Earth, Mars, Jupiter, Saturn, Uranus, Neptune

94

Space Words

Directions: Read each sentence. Write the correct word on the line from the Word Bank.

Word Bank
Mercury
Earth
Jupiter
planets
sun
star

1. Our solar system has eight of these. _____planets_____

2. This is a planet with land and water. _____Earth_____

3. This is a huge star you see during the day. _____sun_____

4. This is the beginning of a popular lullaby, "Twinkle, twinkle, little _____star_____."

5. This is the smallest planet. _____Mercury_____

6. This is the largest planet. _____Jupiter_____

95

Time Words

A clock has two hands to tell us the time.
The big hand is called the **minute hand**.
The little hand is called the **hour hand**.

Directions: Color the minute hand purple. Color the hour hand yellow. Then, **write minute hand** or **hour hand** on the line to complete each sentence correctly.

On this clock, the _hour hand_ is pointing to the number 9.

The _minute hand_ is pointing to the number 12.

That is how a clock tells us it is 9 o'clock.

 On this clock, the _minute hand_ is pointing to the number 12.
The _hour hand_ is pointing to the number 3.
That is how a clock tells us it is 3 o'clock.

96

Words With Suffixes

A **suffix** is a word part that is added to the end of a word to change its meaning.
The suffix **-ful** means "full of." **Wonderful** means "full of wonder."
The suffix **-less** means "without." **Comfortless** means "without comfort."
The suffix **-ness** means "a state of being." **Sadness** means "being sad."
The suffix **-ly** means "in this way." **Carefully** means "in a careful way."

Directions: Add the suffixes to the base words to make new words. Write the new words on the lines.

1. color + ful = _colorful_

2. help + less = _helpless_

3. quiet + ly = _quietly_

4. nice + ly = _nicely_

5. fit + ness = _fitness_

97

Words With Suffixes

A **suffix** is a word part that goes at the end of a word to change its meaning.

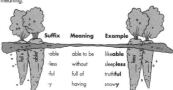

Suffix	Meaning	Example
-able	able to be	like**able**
-less	without	sleep**less**
-ful	full of	truth**ful**
-y	having	snow**y**

Directions: Circle the suffix in each word.

Example: fluff(y)

1. rain(y)
2. blame(less)
3. peace(ful)
4. thought(ful)
5. enjoy(able)
6. care(less)
7. like(able)
8. help(ful)
9. sill(y)

Directions: Write a word on the line for each meaning.

1. full of hope _hopeful_
2. without hope _hopeless_
3. without power _powerless_
4. having rain _rainy_
5. able to break _breakable_
6. full of cheer _cheerful_

98

Words With Suffixes

Directions: Add the suffixes to the base words to make new words. Write the words on the lines.

1. help + ful = helpful
2. care + less = careless
3. clean + ness = cleanness
4. wind + y = windy
5. love + ly = lovely
6. break + able = breakable

Directions: Use the new words from above to complete the sentences.

1. Flying a kite works best on a __windy__ day.
2. My mother never lets my brother near __breakable__ things in the store.
3. Sally is always __helpful__ to her mother.
4. I earned an allowance for the __cleanness__ of my room.
5. The flowers are __lovely__ .
6. It is __careless__ to cross the street without looking both ways.

99

Words About the United States

Directions: Read the state facts. Use the map to locate each state. Then, follow the directions to color the map.

1. The Liberty Bell rang at the first reading of the Declaration of Independence. It is in Philadelphia, Pennsylvania. Color Pennsylvania red.
2. The Statue of Liberty is in New York Harbor. Color New York blue.
3. Rhode Island is the smallest state. Color Rhode Island yellow.
4. Florida is called "The Sunshine State." Color Florida orange.
5. Idaho is famous for its potatoes. Color Idaho brown.
6. Hawaii was the 50th state to join the United States. This state is made of eight main islands. Color Hawaii green.
7. Montana means "mountain" in Spanish. Color Montana purple.

100

Space Words

Word Bank			
	astronomer	Earth	moon
sun	planets	stars	space

Directions: Use the words in the Word Bank to complete the sentences.

1. A constellation is a group of __stars__ .
2. You can see the __moon__ in the night sky.
3. Mars is one of the eight __planets__ .
4. An __astronomer__ studies the stars.
5. We live on the planet __Earth__ .
6. You cannot see the __sun__ shine at night.
7. Rockets can fly into __space__ .

101

Space Words

If you look in the sky on a clear night, you may see groups of stars. People draw imaginary lines between those stars to form pictures of animals, people, or things. Each picture is called a **constellation**. One constellation is called **The Big Dipper**. It looks like a cup with a long handle.

Directions: Connect the stars from 1 to 7 to make The Big Dipper.

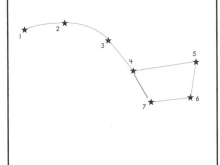

102

Space Words

Directions: Read about Kim the astronomer. Then, fill in the circle beside the word that correctly completes each sentence.

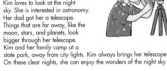

Kim loves to look at the night sky. She is interested in astronomy. Her dad got her a telescope. Things that are far away, like the moon, stars, and planets, look bigger through her telescope. Kim and her family camp at a state park, away from city lights. Kim always brings her telescope. On these clear nights, she can enjoy the wonders of the night sky.

1. The study of stars and planets is called _____ .
   - (A) astronomy
   - (B) geology
   - (C) math

2. Things in the sky look bigger with a _____ .
   - (A) microscope
   - (B) telescope
   - (C) magnifying glass

3. Kim enjoys clear nights in a _____ .
   - (A) city
   - (B) state park
   - (C) small town

103

Unit 4 Review

Directions: Write the letter of each description on the right that matches the words on the left.

1. __e__ a
2. __i__ minute hand
3. __l__ sunrise
4. __f__ Hawaii
5. __j__ Gulf of Mexico
6. __k__ ness
7. __c__ second, minute, hour
8. __h__ The Big Dipper
9. __b__ stars
10. __g__ astronomer
11. __d__ unsafe, disobey, reread
12. __a__ Jupiter

a. The largest planet
b. Things you see in the night sky
c. Time words
d. Words with prefixes
e. Use this article before a word that begins with a consonant.
f. State made up of eight main islands
g. A person who studies the stars
h. A constellation
i. The big hand on a clock
j. The body of water near Texas
k. A suffix that means "a state of being"
l. The time when the sun comes up

104

Words That Are Prepositions

Prepositions are words that show a connection between a noun or pronoun and another word. **Across** and **between** are prepositions.

Directions: Follow the directions to complete the picture.

- Draw a matching black circle across from the black circle.
- Draw a triangle between the circles.
- Draw a big circle around all the shapes.
- Color funny hair on the outside of the big circle.
- Write your clown's name beside him.
- Color your clown.

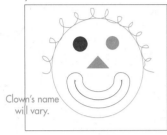

Clown's name will vary.

106

Words That Are Prepositions

Directions: Use a preposition from the first box and words from the second box to complete each sentence. The first one is done for you.

between	around	inside	outside	behind	across

the yard	the house	the table	the school	the box
the hill	the picture	the field	the puddle	the park

Suggested answers:
1. Our garden grows __behind the house__ .
2. We like to play __outside the school__ .
3. The street is __beside the field__ .
4. Can you run __across the yard__ ?
5. Let's ride bikes __around the park__

107

Words That Are Prepositions

Directions: Draw a line from each sentence to its picture. Then, complete each sentence with the word under the picture. Write the word on the line.

Example:

He is walking __behind__ the tree.

1. We stay __inside__ when it rains.

2. She drew a dog __beside__ his house.

3. She stands __between__ her friends.

4. They walked __across__ the bridge.

5. Let the cat go __outside__ .

6. Draw a circle __around__ the fish.

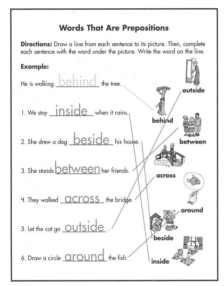

outside

behind

between

across

around

beside

inside

108

Words About Continents

Continents are huge landmasses on the earth. The map shows the seven continents.

Directions: Complete each sentence by writing the correct continent on the line. Use the map to help you. Then, color the map.

1. The continent east of Antarctica is __Australia__ .
2. The continent east of South America is __Africa__ .
3. The continent farthest south is __Antarctica__ .
4. We live on the continent of __Answers will__ vary.
5. There are __seven__ continents.

Color the map.

109

Words About Living and Nonliving Things

Living things need air, food, and water to live. **Nonliving** things are not alive.

Directions: Write each word from the Word Bank in the correct category.

	Living		Nonliving
1.	hen	1.	car
2.	bird	2.	truck
3.	kitten	3.	nest
4.	cow	4.	boat
5.	dog	5.	rock
6.	tree	6.	plane

Word Bank		
car	kitten	cow
truck	nest	plane
hen	boat	dog
bird	rock	tree

110

Words About Living and Nonliving Things

Directions: Write each word from the Word Bank in the correct category.

	Living		Nonliving
1.	flower	1.	book
2.	tree	2.	camera
3.	boy	3.	car
4.	dog	4.	chair
5.	horse	5.	bread
6.	ant	6.	shoe

Word Bank					
flower	book	boy	dog	chair	bread
tree	camera	car	horse	ant	shoe

111

Words About Living and Nonliving Things

Directions: Use yellow to color the spaces that have words about living things. Use blue to color the spaces that have words about nonliving things.

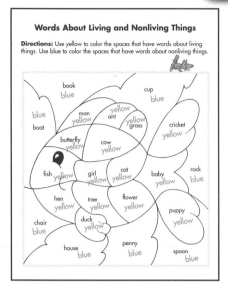

book blue
cup blue
blue boat
man yellow
yellow ant
yellow grass
cricket yellow
butterfly yellow
cow yellow
fish yellow
girl yellow
cat yellow
baby yellow
rock blue
hen yellow
tree yellow
flower yellow
puppy yellow
chair blue
duck yellow
house blue
penny blue
spoon blue

112

Money Words

"One dollar" can be written as $1.00.

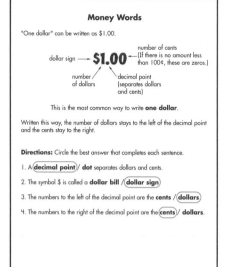

dollar sign → **$1.00** ← number of cents (If there is no amount less than 100¢, these are zeros.)

number of dollars

decimal point (separates dollars and cents)

This is the most common way to write **one dollar**.

Written this way, the number of dollars stays to the left of the decimal point and the cents stay to the right.

Directions: Circle the best answer that completes each sentence.

1. A **decimal point** / **dot** separates dollars and cents.

2. The symbol $ is called a **dollar bill** / **dollar sign**

3. The numbers to the left of the decimal point are the **cents** / **dollars**

4. The numbers to the right of the decimal point are the **cents** / **dollars**.

113

Words That Are Prepositions

Directions: Use the words in the Word Bank to answer each question.
Suggested answers:

1. Where is the slice of pizza? The slice of pizza is in front of the girl.

2. Where is the boy sitting? The boy is sitting by the girl.

3. Where is the trash can? The trash can is next to the table.

4. Where is the silverware? The silverware is near the napkins.

Word Bank
next to
near
by
beside
in front of
behind

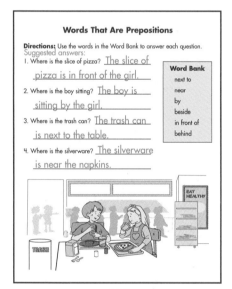

114

Words That Are Prepositions

Directions: Draw a ball where it belongs in each picture.

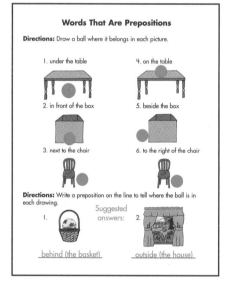

1. under the table
2. in front of the box
3. next to the chair
4. on the table
5. beside the box
6. to the right of the chair

Directions: Write a preposition on the line to tell where the ball is in each drawing.

1. Suggested answers: 2.

behind (the basket)   outside (the house)

115

Words That Are Prepositions

Directions: Follow the instructions to complete the picture. The prepositions will tell you where to draw things in the room.

Draw a ▢ between the two 👡👡 . Color it red.

Draw a 🪑 under the window. Color it green.

Draw three big 🌼 on the wall. Color them orange.

116

Words About Continents

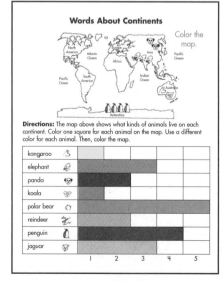

Color the map.

North America, Atlantic Ocean, Asia, Pacific Ocean, Africa, Pacific Ocean, South America, Indian Ocean, Australia, Antarctica

Directions: The map above shows what kinds of animals live on each continent. Color one square for each animal on the map. Use a different color for each animal. Then, color the map.

		1	2	3	4	5
kangaroo						
elephant						
panda						
koala						
polar bear						
reindeer						
penguin						
jaguar						

117

Words About Living and Nonliving Things

Directions: Look at each picture. Fill in the correct circle beside the word to show whether each thing is living or nonliving.

1. ○ Living ● Nonliving	5. ● Living ○ Nonliving	9. ○ Living ● Nonliving
2. ● Living ○ Nonliving	6. ● Living ○ Nonliving	10. ○ Living ● Nonliving
3. ● Living ○ Nonliving	7. ● Living ○ Nonliving	11. ○ Living ● Nonliving
4. ● Living ○ Nonliving	8. ● Living ○ Nonliving	12. ● Living ○ Nonliving

118

Words About Plants

Directions: Read the instructions and use the words in the Word Bank to complete the chart. Start at the arrow.

Word Bank
flower
root
leaf
stem
seed

→					flower
	stem				
			leaf		
	seed				
					root

1. Go right 5 spaces. Then go down 3 spaces and left 5 spaces. Write the word that names what grows into a new plant here.
2. Now go up 2 spaces. Then go right 6 spaces and down 3 spaces. Write the word that names the part of the plant that is underground here.
3. Now go up 3 spaces. Then go left 3 spaces and down 1 space. Write the word that names the part of the plant that makes the food here.
4. Now go right 2 spaces. Then go up 1 space and left 4 spaces. Write the word that names the part of the plant that carries food and water to the rest of the plant here.
5. Now go down 2 spaces. Then go right 5 spaces and up 3 spaces. Write the word that names the part of the plant that makes the seeds here.

119

Words About Plants

Directions: Read the story. Then, complete the sentences.

Weed is the word used for any plant that grows where it is not wanted. Grasses that grow in your flower or vegetable garden are weeds. An unwanted flower growing in your lawn is also a weed. Dandelions are this kind of weed.

People do not plant weeds. They grow very fast. If you do not pull them out or kill them, weeds will crowd out the plants that you want to grow. The seeds of many kinds of weeds are spread by the wind. Birds and other animals also carry weed seeds.

1. A weed is any plant that grows where it is not wanted

2. One kind of flowering weed is the dandelion

3. Two things that spread the seeds of weeds are
Suggested answer:
the wind and birds or other animals

120

Money Words

Directions: Read the words on the coins. To fill the piggy bank, find the words and circle them. Look across, down, and diagonally.

Coins: money bank, earn count, quarter, dime, dollar savings, nickel penny, coins cents

```
Q U A M S B R I D P L
T U D S O A M B S E C
A S A V I N G S P N O
B A S R O K E C E A I
A C E N T S I Y N T N
L O T L R E H S N O S
N I C K E L R D Y R Q
P F K E N Q U I L D U
D O L L A R Q V E I E
O M G A M R S G J M D
P E R C O U N T O E R
```

121

Words That Are Prepositions

Directions: Use a preposition to tell where the cat is in each sentence. The first one is done for you.

1. The cat is behind the box.

Suggested answers:

2. The cat is inside the cage.

3. The cat is between the dogs.

4. The cat is beside the mouse.

5. The cat is in front of the door.

122

Words That Are Prepositions

Prepositions show a connection between a noun and another word. Some prepositions are **on**, **in**, **to**, **toward**, **over**, and **behind**.

Directions: Read the story. Then, circle the prepositions.

Molly had the bat (in) her hands. The catcher had his mask (on) his face. He crouched (behind) home plate. Everyone had their eyes (on) the pitcher. Roy yelled, "Hit it (toward) second base!" Molly listened. She hit the ball so hard that it went (over) the fence. Molly raced (to) first base.

123

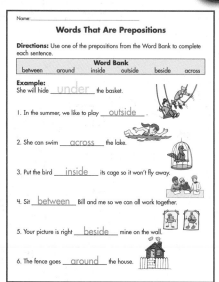

Words That Are Prepositions

Directions: Use one of the prepositions from the Word Bank to complete each sentence.

Word Bank

between   around   inside   outside   beside   across

Example:
She will hide __under__ the basket.

1. In the summer, we like to play __outside__ .

2. She can swim __across__ the lake.

3. Put the bird __inside__ its cage so it won't fly away.

4. Sit __between__ Bill and me so we can all work together.

5. Your picture is right __beside__ mine on the wall.

6. The fence goes __around__ the house.

124

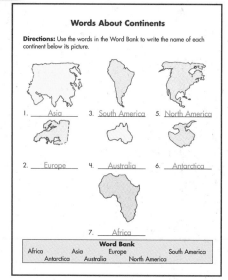

Words About Continents

Directions: Use the words in the Word Bank to write the name of each continent below its picture.

1. __Asia__   3. __South America__   5. __North America__

2. __Europe__   4. __Australia__   6. __Antarctica__

7. __Africa__

Word Bank

Africa   Asia   Europe   South America
Antarctica   Australia   North America

125

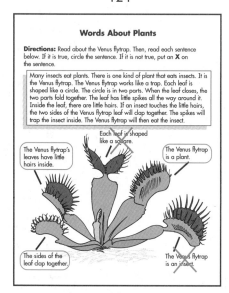

Words About Plants

Directions: Read about the Venus flytrap. Then, read each sentence below. If it is true, circle the sentence. If it is not true, put an **X** on the sentence.

Many insects eat plants. There is one kind of plant that eats insects. It is the Venus flytrap. The Venus flytrap works like a trap. Each leaf is shaped like a circle. The circle is in two parts. When the leaf closes, the two parts fold together. The leaf has little spikes all the way around it. Inside the leaf, there are little hairs. If an insect touches the little hairs, the two sides of the Venus flytrap leaf will clap together. The spikes will trap the insect inside. The Venus flytrap will then eat the insect.

Each leaf is shaped like a square.

The Venus flytrap's leaves have little hairs inside.

The Venus flytrap is a plant.

The sides of the leaf clap together.

The Venus flytrap is an insect.

126

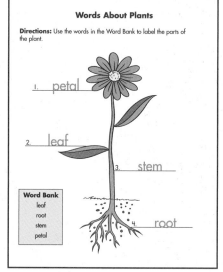

Words About Plants

Directions: Use the words in the Word Bank to label the parts of the plant.

1. __petal__

2. __leaf__

3. __stem__

4. __root__

Word Bank

leaf
root
stem
petal

127

Words About Plants

Directions: Use a word from the Word Bank to complete each sentence. Then, color the picture.

Max and Gina spent the morning at the park. They planted a __tree__ . First, they dug a hole. They took the tree out of the container. They loosened the __roots__ gently so that they had room to grow in the ground. Max and Gina put the tree in the hole. The __trunk__ of the tree was slim and weak, so they staked it. Soon, the top __branches__ would be strong and full of leaves.

Color the picture.

Word Bank

trunk
branches
tree
roots

128

Unit 5 Review

Directions: Circle the correct word that completes each sentence. Then, write the word on the line.

1. A plant grows from a __seed__ .
   petal   (seed)

2. Elephants and __pandas__ live in Asia.
   (pandas)   koalas

3. Trees, people, and animals are __living__ things.
   (living)   nonliving

4. We stay __inside__ to keep dry when it rains.
   outside   (inside)

5. Four __quarters__ equal $1.00.
   dimes   (quarters)

6. A car, a book, and a __chair__ are examples of nonliving things.
   cat   (chair)

7. The children ran __toward__ the school to return to class.
   (toward)   behind

8. There are __seven__ continents.
   eleven   (seven)

9. My baby sister sits __under__ an umbrella to protect herself from the sun.
   (under)   next to

10. The __root__ of a plant lives underground.
    (root)   leaf

129

Words That Are Synonyms

Synonyms are words with nearly the same meaning.

Directions: Draw a line to match each word on the left with its synonym on the right.

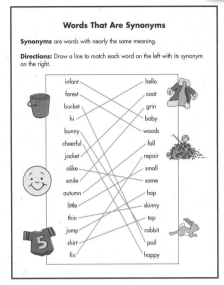

infant — baby
forest — woods
bucket — pail
hi — hello
bunny — rabbit
cheerful — happy
jacket — coat
alike — same
smile — grin
autumn — fall
little — small
thin — skinny
jump — hop
shirt — top
fix — repair

131

Words That Are Synonyms

Directions: Read the story. Then, write a synonym from the Word Bank to complete each sentence.

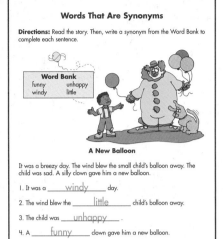

Word Bank
funny   unhappy
windy   little

A New Balloon

It was a breezy day. The wind blew the small child's balloon away. The child was sad. A silly clown gave him a new balloon.

1. It was a ___windy___ day.

2. The wind blew the ___little___ child's balloon away.

3. The child was ___unhappy___ .

4. A ___funny___ clown gave him a new balloon.

132

Words That Are Synonyms

Directions: Read the sentences that tell about each picture. Draw a circle around the word that means the same as the bold word.

1. The child is **unhappy**.
hungry   (sad)

4. The flowers are **lovely**.
(pretty)   green

2. The baby was very **tired**.
(sleepy)   hurt

5. The **funny** clown made us laugh.
glad   (silly)

3. The ladybug is so **tiny**.
(small)   red

6. We saw a **scary** tiger.
(frightening)   ugly

133

Words About Early America

Although the lives of the colonists were different than ours today, many of their needs were the same.

Directions: Unscramble the names of objects we use today. The first letter of each word is underlined. Then, draw a line to match similar objects of the past and present. Color the pictures.

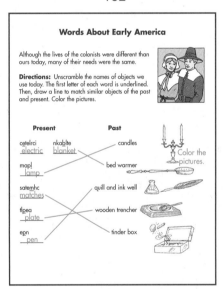

Present

cetelrci
electric

nkablte
blanket

mapl
lamp

satemhc
matches

tlpea
plate

epn
pen

Past

candles
bed warmer
quill and ink well
wooden trencher
tinder box

Color the pictures.

134

Words About Trees

Directions: Read the words in the Word Bank. These things all come from trees! Circle the words in the puzzle. Look across and down. Then, color the picture.

Word Bank
syrup   lumber   medicine
fruit   furniture   shelter
nuts   paper   rubber

Color the picture.

```
P S H E L T E R F
A R U B B E R L R
P K N U T S L U U
E S Y R U P W M I
R N N M M V J B T
  M E D I C I N E
  F U R N I T U R E
```

135

325

Words About Leaves

This tricky tree has four different kinds of leaves: ash, poison ivy, silver maple, and white oak.

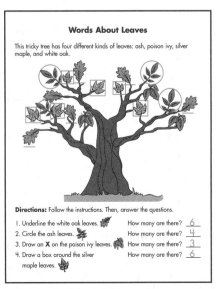

Directions: Follow the instructions. Then, answer the questions.

1. Underline the white oak leaves.   How many are there? __6__
2. Circle the ash leaves.   How many are there? __4__
3. Draw an **X** on the poison ivy leaves.   How many are there? __3__
4. Draw a box around the silver maple leaves.   How many are there? __6__

136

Words About Leaves

Directions: Gather some leaves. Put your leaves into groups by type. Then, answer the questions.

white oak   red oak   pine   ash

elm   silver maple   red maple

1. How many white oak leaves did you find? _Answers will vary._
2. How many red oak leaves did you find? _____
3. How many pine needles did you find? _____
4. How many ash leaves did you find? _____
5. How many elm leaves did you find? _____
6. How many silver maple leaves did you find? _____
7. How many red maple leaves did you find? _____
8. What other kinds of leaves did you find? Use a book to help you name them. Write their names here. _____

137

Fraction Words

Directions: Read each fraction. Draw a line from the fraction to the shape with that amount shaded.

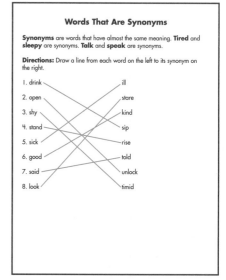

1. one-fourth
2. two-fourths
3. one-half
4. one-third
5. two-thirds

138

Words That Are Synonyms

Directions: Circle the two words in each line that have almost the same meaning.

1. (gooey) (sticky) hard
2. slow (hurry) (rush)
3. (slope) (hill) sled
4. (stop) green (end)
5. treat (pledge) (promise)
6. (piece) (bit) pie
7. excuse (easy) (simple)
8. (complete) (whole) pile

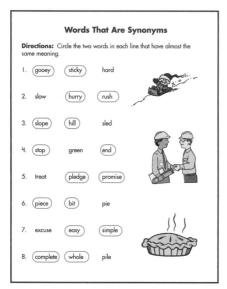

139

Words That Are Synonyms

Synonyms are words that have almost the same meaning. **Tired** and **sleepy** are synonyms. **Talk** and **speak** are synonyms.

Directions: Draw a line from each word on the left to its synonym on the right.

1. drink   ill
2. open   stare
3. shy   kind
4. stand   sip
5. sick   rise
6. good   told
7. said   unlock
8. look   timid

140

Words That Are Synonyms

Directions: Circle the synonym of the bold word in each sentence.

1. I am **happy** to write you a letter.
   (glad) sad

2. I hope my grandma will like this **gift**.
   (present) toaster

3. I always **laugh** when I watch my silly kitten.
   (chuckle) worry

4. My friend loves to **talk** on the telephone.
   draw (chat)

5. The little boy was **charming** to his grandmother.
   (delightful) naughty

6. Can you please **sew** this fabric together?
   hitch (stitch)

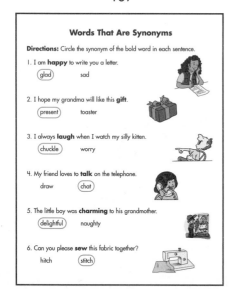

141

Words About Early America

Directions: Read the story. Circle the correct word that completes each sentence. Then, color the map.

From about 1760 to 1850, pioneers moved westward across the United States. They traveled in big covered wagons along several trails. Some started in a swampy area in Nauvoo, Illinois. Others started in Independence, Missouri. Some trails are marked on the map below.

1. In the 1800s, pioneers moved toward the **eastern** / (**western**) part of the United States.
2. They traveled by **train** / (**wagon.**)
3. The city of Independence is in **Illinois** / (**Missouri.**)

Color the map.

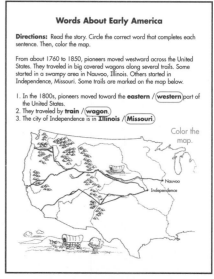

Nauvoo
Independence

142

326

143

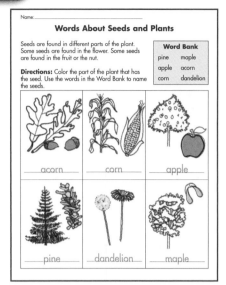

144

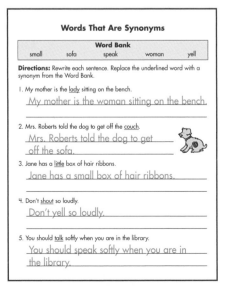

147

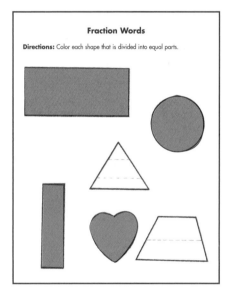

146

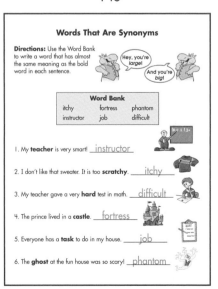

148

Words That Are Synonyms

Directions: Read the sentences. Use the Word Bank to write the synonym of each underlined word.

Word Bank

friend   tired   story
presents   little

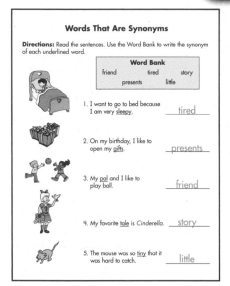

1. I want to go to bed because I am very <u>sleepy</u>.   _tired_

2. On my birthday, I like to open my <u>gifts</u>.   _presents_

3. My <u>pal</u> and I like to play ball.   _friend_

4. My favorite <u>tale</u> is Cinderella.   _story_

5. The mouse was so <u>tiny</u> that it was hard to catch.   _little_

149

Words About Native Americans

Directions: Use the pictures of the Native American houses to answer each riddle. Then, color the pictures.

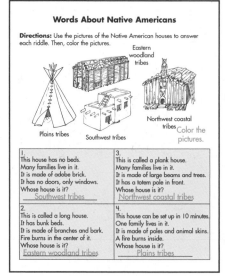

Eastern woodland tribes

Plains tribes   Southwest tribes   Northwest coastal tribes

Color the pictures.

1.
This house has no beds.
Many families live in it.
It is made of adobe brick.
It has no doors, only windows.
Whose house is it?
Southwest tribes

3.
This is called a plank house.
Many families live in it.
It is made of large beams and trees.
It has a totem pole in front.
Whose house is it?
Northwest coastal tribes

2.
This is called a long house.
It has bunk beds.
It is made of branches and bark.
Fire burns in the center of it.
Whose house is it?
Eastern woodland tribes

4.
This house can be set up in 10 minutes.
One family lives in it.
It is made of poles and animal skins.
A fire burns inside.
Whose house is it?
Plains tribes

150

Words About Trees

Many different foods come from trees. People and animals eat this food.

Directions: Color the pictures of foods that come from trees.

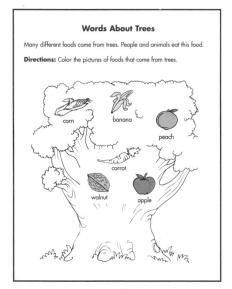

corn   banana   peach   carrot   walnut   apple

151

Words About Plants and Flowers

Directions: Use the Word Bank to find the words about plants and flowers. Circle the words in the puzzle. Look across and down.

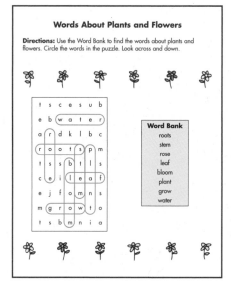

t	s	c	e	s	u	b
e	b	w	a	t	e	r
a	r	d	k	l	b	c
r	o	o	t	s	p	m
t	s	s	b	t	l	s
c	e	i	l	e	a	f
e	j	f	o	m	n	s
m	g	r	o	w	t	o
t	s	b	m	n	i	a

Word Bank

roots
stem
rose
leaf
bloom
plant
grow
water

152

Words About Plants

We eat many plant parts. We may eat the leaves, the stem, the root, or the seeds.

Directions: Look at the pictures of the vegetables. Use the words in the Word Bank to write the name of the plant part that we eat. You may use the name of a plant part more than once.

Word Bank

leaves   stem   root   seeds

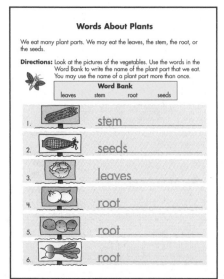

1. _stem_
2. _seeds_
3. _leaves_
4. _root_
5. _root_
6. _root_

153

Unit 6 Review

Directions: Write a sentence for each pair of synonyms.

1. funny/silly _Sentences will vary._

2. hurry/rush _____

3. alike/same _____

Directions: Circle the word that completes each sentence. Then, write the word on the line.

1. The math test was so _easy_ that I got an A.
   (easy)   hard

2. Jim was _glad_ to get a present from his grandparents.
   unhappy   (glad)

3. The colonists lived a _long_ time ago.
   (long)   short

4. Pioneers traveled by _wagon_ across the United States.
   car   (wagon)

5. My mother is the _woman_ waiting for me in the car.
   man   (woman)

6. The _teacher_ writes the homework on the board.
   (teacher)   student

7. Some plants that we eat grow in the _ground_.
   (ground)   air

154

Words That Are Antonyms

Antonyms are words that have opposite meanings. **Dark** and **light** are opposites.

Directions: Write the antonym pairs from each sentence in the boxes.

Example: Many things are bought and sold at the market.

bought	sold

1. I thought I lost my dog, but someone found him.

lost	found

2. The teacher will ask questions for the students to answer.

ask	answer

3. Airplanes arrive and depart from the airport.

arrive	depart

4. The water in the pool was cold compared to the warm water in the whirlpool.

cold	warm

5. The tortoise was slow, but the hare was fast.

slow	fast

156

Words That Are Antonyms

Antonyms are words that have opposite meanings. **Hot** and **cold** are antonyms. **Short** and **tall** are antonyms, too.

Directions: Draw a line from each word on the left to its antonym on the right.

sad — white
bottom — stop
black — fat
tall — top
thin — hard
little — found
cold — short
lost — hot
go — big
soft — happy

157

Words That Are Antonyms

Directions: Tell a story about the picture by following the directions. Write one or two sentences for each answer.

1. Write about something that is happening quickly or slowly in the picture.

   Sentences will vary.

2. Use **top** or **bottom** in a sentence about the picture.

3. Tell about something hard and something soft in the picture. Use the word **but** in your sentence.

158

Holiday Words

Fiction is something that is made up or not true. **Nonfiction** is about something that has really happened.

Directions: Read each story about the Fourth of July. Then, write whether it is fiction or nonfiction.

1. One sunny day in July, a dog named Stan ran away from home. He went up one street and down the other looking for fun, but all the yards were empty. Where was everybody? Stan kept walking until he heard the sound of band music and happy people. Stan walked faster until he got to Central Street. There he saw men, women, children, and dogs getting ready to walk in a parade. It was the Fourth of July!

   Fiction or nonfiction? _fiction_

2. Americans celebrate the Fourth of July every year because it is the birthday of the United States of America. On July 4, 1776, the United States got its independence from Great Britain. Today, Americans celebrate this holiday with parades, picnics, and fireworks as they proudly wave the red, white, and blue American flag.

   Fiction or nonfiction? _nonfiction_

159

Food Words

Directions: This puzzle contains the names of foods listed on the menu. Circle the words. Look across and down. Then, color the pictures.

Color the pictures.

160

Food Words

Directions: Write the correct food word from the Word Bank under each picture.

Word Bank			
bread	cheese	eggs	fruit
meat	milk	supermarket	vegetables

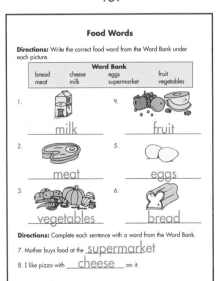

1. milk
4. fruit
2. meat
5. eggs
3. vegetables
6. bread

Directions: Complete each sentence with a word from the Word Bank.

7. Mother buys food at the _supermarket_

8. I like pizza with _cheese_ on it.

161

329

Food Words

Directions: Circle the names of vegetables in green. Circle the names of drinks in red. Circle the names of desserts in blue.

Directions: Write each food word on the correct line.

Drinks	Vegetables	Desserts
water	corn	cookie
juice	peas	pie
milk	carrot	cake

162

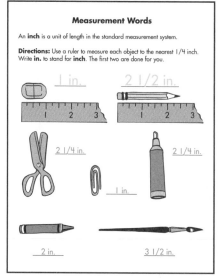

Measurement Words

An **inch** is a unit of length in the standard measurement system.

Directions: Use a ruler to measure each object to the nearest 1/4 inch. Write **in.** to stand for **inch**. The first two are done for you.

1 in.   2 1/2 in.
2 1/4 in.   2 1/4 in.
1 in.
2 in.   3 1/2 in.

163

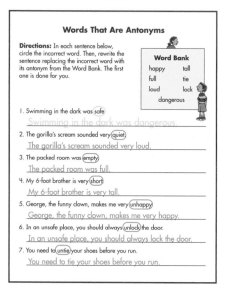

Words That Are Antonyms

Directions: In each sentence below, circle the incorrect word. Then, rewrite the sentence replacing the incorrect word with its antonym from the Word Bank. The first one is done for you.

Word Bank
happy   tall
full   tie
loud   lock
dangerous

1. Swimming in the dark was safe.
   Swimming in the dark was dangerous.
2. The gorilla's scream sounded very quiet.
   The gorilla's scream sounded very loud.
3. The packed room was empty.
   The packed room was full.
4. My 6-foot brother is very short.
   My 6-foot brother is very tall.
5. George, the funny clown, makes me very unhappy.
   George, the funny clown, makes me very happy.
6. In an unsafe place, you should always unlock the door.
   In an unsafe place, you should always lock the door.
7. You need to untie your shoes before you run.
   You need to tie your shoes before you run.

164

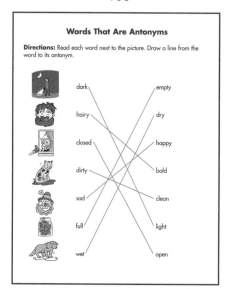

Words That Are Antonyms

Directions: Read each word next to the picture. Draw a line from the word to its antonym.

dark — open
hairy — bald
closed — happy
dirty — clean
sad — dry
full — empty
wet — light

165

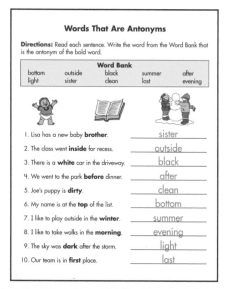

Words That Are Antonyms

Directions: Read each sentence. Write the word from the Word Bank that is the antonym of the bold word.

Word Bank
bottom   outside   black   summer   after
light   sister   clean   last   evening

1. Lisa has a new baby **brother**.   sister
2. The class went **inside** for recess.   outside
3. There is a **white** car in the driveway.   black
4. We went to the park **before** dinner.   after
5. Joe's puppy is **dirty**.   clean
6. My name is at the **top** of the list.   bottom
7. I like to play outside in the **winter**.   summer
8. I like to take walks in the **morning**.   evening
9. The sky was **dark** after the storm.   light
10. Our team is in **first** place.   last

166

Holiday Words

Valentine's Day	Fourth of July	Thanksgiving

Directions: Write the name of each holiday beside its picture. Remember that names of holidays begin with capital letters.

Valentine's Day

Thanksgiving

Fourth of July

167

330

Food Words

A **calorie** is a unit for measuring the amount of energy a food can produce when taken into the body.

Directions: Read the menu. Then, answer the questions.

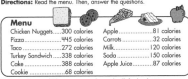

Menu

Chicken Nuggets.....300 calories	Apple...................81 calories
Pizza.......................445 calories	Carrots.................32 calories
Taco ....272 calories	Milk.....................120 calories
Turkey Sandwich.....338 calories	Soda...................150 calories
Cake ....388 calories	Apple Juice...........87 calories
Cookie ....68 calories	

1. Gavin chooses chicken nuggets, cake, and milk for lunch. How many calories does he eat? __808__

2. Ramona has milk and an apple for breakfast. She has pizza and apple juice for lunch. Then, she has a taco and soda for dinner. How many calories does she eat in all? __1155__

3. Doug eats a turkey sandwich, carrots, cake, and milk for lunch. Ruben eats chicken nuggets, an apple, a cookie, and apple juice. Who eats more calories? __Doug__ How much more? __342__

4. Write the three items from the menu that you would choose to eat for lunch.
   __Answers will vary.__

5. How many total calories are there in your lunch?
   __Answers will vary.__

168

Food Words

Directions: Read the story. Then, answer the questions. Try the recipe with the help of an adult.

Cows live on a farm. The farmer milks the cow to get milk. Many things are made from milk. We make ice cream, sour cream, cottage cheese, and butter from milk. Butter is fun to make! You can learn to make your own butter. First, you need cream. Put the cream in a jar and shake it. Then, you need to pour off the liquid. Next, you put the butter in a bowl and stir! Add a little salt and stir! Finally, spread it on crackers and eat!

1. What animal gives us milk? __cow__

2. What four things are made from milk? __cottage__
   __ice cream__ __sour cream__ __cheese__ __butter__

3. What did the story teach you to make? __butter__

4. Put the steps in order. Write the numbers 1, 2, 3, or 4 by the correct sentence.

   __4__ Spread the butter on crackers and eat!

   __2__ Shake the cream in a jar.

   __1__ Start with cream.

   __3__ Add salt to the butter.

169

Food Words

The Pyramid Food Chart shows how much to eat from each food group. Tim has a turkey, cheese, and lettuce sandwich with mayonnaise. He also has an apple and some orange juice.

Pyramid Food Chart

Fats, Oils, and Sweets— very few servings

Milk Group— 2 or 3 servings

Meat Group— 2 servings

Vegetable Group— 4 servings

Fruit Group— 3 servings

Bread Group— 9 servings

Directions: Color in the graph to show how many servings of each food group Tim ate for lunch. (Hint: A serving of bread is one slice.)

Tim's Lunch

Number of Servings	Bread	Vegetable	Fruit	Milk	Meat	Fats
8						
7						
6						
5						
4						
3						
2	■		■			
1	■	■	■	■	■	■

170

Measurement Words

Directions: Write **feet**, **yards**, or **miles** on each line to tell how you would measure each thing.

1 foot = 12 inches
1 yard = 36 inches or 3 feet
1 mile = 1,760 yards __Answers may vary.__

1. length of a river __miles__

2. height of a tree __feet__

3. width of a room __feet__

4. length of a football field __yards__

5. height of a door __feet__

6. length of a dress __yards__

7. length of a race __yards__ or __miles__

8. height of a basketball hoop __feet__

9. width of a window __feet__

10. distance a plane travels __miles__

Directions: Solve the problem.

Tara races Tom in the 100-yard dash. Tara finishes 10 yards in front of Tom. How many feet did Tara finish in front of Tom? __30__

171

Words That Are Antonyms

Directions: Complete each sentence with the correct antonym. Write it on the line. Use the clues in the picture and below each sentence. Then, color the picture.

Color the picture.

1. Spotty's suitcase is ___ . __open__
   (antonym for closed)

2. Spotty has a ___ on his face. __smile__
   (antonym for frown)

3. His pillow is ___ . __soft__
   (antonym for hard)

4. His coat is ___ . __big__
   (antonym for little)

5. Spotty packs his stuffed animal ___ . __last__
   (antonym for first)

172

Words That Are Antonyms

Anna and Luke like to do opposite things. Help them design their new white t-shirts using antonyms.

Directions: Think of a pair of antonyms. Write one on each shirt. Draw pictures on the shirts to match the antonyms.

Words and pictures will vary.

173

Words That Are Antonyms

Directions: Read each sentence. Rewrite the sentence by changing the underlined word to its antonym.

Answers may vary.

The clown is <u>happy</u>.

1. The clown is unhappy.

The boy swims <u>quickly</u>.

2. The boy swims slowly.

The bell rings <u>loudly</u>.

3. The bell rings quietly.

The popcorn is <u>hot</u>.

4. The popcorn is cold.

174

Words About Holidays

In China, the most celebrated holiday is the **New Year**. The **Lantern Festival** is part of the celebration. That is when the Chinese people welcome the first full moon of the year. The Chinese New Year is fixed according to the lunar calendar. It occurs somewhere between January 30 and February 20. Each Chinese year is represented by one of 12 animals.

Look at the chart below to see what animal represents the year you were born.

RAT	OX	TIGER	HARE (RABBIT)	DRAGON	SNAKE	HORSE	RAM	MONKEY	ROOSTER	DOG	PIG
1900	1901	1902	1903	1904	1905	1906	1907	1908	1909	1910	1911
1912	1913	1914	1915	1916	1917	1918	1919	1920	1921	1922	1923
1924	1925	1926	1927	1928	1929	1930	1931	1932	1933	1934	1935
1936	1937	1938	1939	1940	1941	1942	1943	1944	1945	1946	1947
1948	1949	1950	1951	1952	1953	1954	1955	1956	1957	1958	1959
1960	1961	1962	1963	1964	1965	1966	1967	1968	1969	1970	1971
1972	1973	1974	1975	1976	1977	1978	1979	1980	1981	1982	1983
1984	1985	1986	1987	1988	1989	1990	1991	1992	1993	1994	1995
1996	1997	1998	1999	2000	2001	2002	2003	2004	2005	2006	2007
2008	2009	2010	2011	2012	2013	2014	2015	2016	2017	2018	2019

Directions: The **Lantern Festival** is celebrated on the third day of the New Year. Make a colorful lantern to hang in your room.

1. Fold a brightly colored piece of construction paper vertically.

2. Cut strips from the folded side, stopping 2 inches from the open edge.

3. Open the paper. Bend the paper. Wrap it in a circle and staple it in place.

4. Cut out a long paper strip and staple it to the lantern to make a handle.

175

Food Words

Directions: Read each nutrition facts label. Use the labels to write the correct answers on the lines.

1. Serving size 1 cup

2. Number of servings per container About 3

3. Calories per serving 180

4. Number of calories per container 540 About

Nutrition Facts
Serving Size 1 cup (236g)
Servings Per Container About 3
Amount per serving
Calories 180 Calories from Fat 70
% Daily Value*
Total Fat 8g 12%
Saturated Fat 3.5 18%
Cholesterol 30mg 10%
Sodium 920mg 38%
Total Carbohydrate 18g 6%
Dietary Fiber 2g 8%
Sugar 3g
Protein 10g

Nutrition Facts
Serving Size 1 cup (215g)
Servings Per Container About 2
Amount per serving
Calories 380 Calories from Fat 200
% Daily Value*
Total Fat 22g 33%
Saturated Fat 13 66%
Cholesterol 60mg 20%
Sodium 1150mg 48%
Total Carbohydrate 28g 9%
Dietary Fiber 5g 18%
Sugar 1g
Protein 17g
Vitamin A 35% • Vitamin C 4%
Calcium 24% • Iron 20%

5. You eat 2 cups of this food. How many calories do you eat? 760

6. Shana wants to eat 500 calories for lunch. She has 1 serving of this food. How many more calories does she need to eat? 120

7. Roberto eats two servings. How much fat in grams does he consume? 44g

His daily intake of fat should be 30 g. Does he eat too little or too much? too much

By how little/much? 14g

176

Food Words

Directions: Look at the food items on the table. Then, answer the questions.

1. What food is sphere shaped? plum

2. What food has 4 sides and 4 corners that are all the same? crackers

3. What food has 6 sides that are all squares? cake

4. What food is an oval? eggs

5. What food is a rectangular prism? bread

6. What food is a cylinder? peanut butter

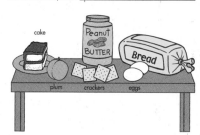

177

Food Words

Directions: Color each piece of fruit that is cut into two equal parts. Write the name of each fruit you colored.

1. apple
2. pear
3. strawberry
4. orange

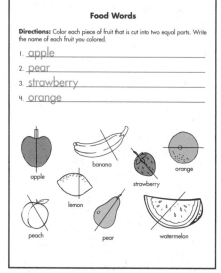

178

Unit 7 Review

Directions: Think about a holiday that you like to celebrate. Write it on the line.

Answers will vary.

Now, think about what you like to eat on this special day. Make up a menu that includes what you eat at breakfast, lunch, and dinner. Be sure to include items from each food group.

Breakfast	Lunch	Dinner

179

Compound Words

Some short words can be put together to make one new word. The new word is called a **compound word**.

Example:

nut + shell = nutshell

Directions: Choose a word from the Word Bank to make a compound word that completes each sentence.

Word Bank

board	bone	ground	prints	shake	house
brush	man	top	shell	ball	hive

Example:
The bird built its nest in the **treetop**.

1. We pitched our tent at the camp_ground_.
2. You would not be able to stand up without your back_bone_.
3. The police officer looked for finger_prints_.
4. She placed the hair_brush_ in her purse.
5. It is important to have a firm hand_shake_.
6. The teacher wrote on the chalk_board_.
7. The egg_shell_ is cracked.
8. Our whole family plays foot_ball_ together.
9. Be sure to put a top hat on the snow_man_.
10. Spot never sleeps in his dog_house_.
11. The beekeeper must check the bee_hive_ today.

181

Compound Words

Directions: Use the compound words in the Word Bank to answer the questions. The first one is done for you.

Word Bank

sailboat	blueberry	bookcase	tablecloth	beehive
dishpan	pigpen	classroom	playground	bedtime
broomstick	treetop	fireplace	newspaper	sunburn

Which compound word means . . .

1. a case for books? _bookcase_
2. a berry that is blue? _blueberry_
3. a hive for bees? _beehive_
4. a place for fires? _fireplace_
5. a pen for pigs? _pigpen_
6. a room for a class? _classroom_
7. a pan for dishes? _dishpan_
8. a boat to sail? _sailboat_
9. a paper for news? _newspaper_
10. a burn from the sun? _sunburn_
11. the top of a tree? _treetop_
12. a stick for a broom? _broomstick_
13. the time to go to bed? _bedtime_
14. a cloth for the table? _tablecloth_
15. ground to play on? _playground_

182

Compound Words

Directions: Find one word in the Word Bank that goes with each of the words below to make a compound word. Write the compound words on the lines.

Word Bank

board	room	thing	side	bag
writing	book	hopper	toe	ball
class	where	work	out	basket

1. coat_room_
2. snow_ball_
3. home_work_
4. waste_basket_
5. tip_toe_
6. chalk_board_
7. note_book_
8. grass_hopper_
9. school_bag_
10. with_out_

Look at the words in the Word Bank that you did not use. Use those words to make your own compound words.

Answers will vary.

1. _handwriting_
2. _classroom_
3. _everywhere_
4. _something_
5. _outside_

183

People Words

Directions: Find a word from the Word Bank to name each picture. Write it on the line below the picture.

Word Bank

baby	man	boy	woman	girl	men	family	children	people

1. _baby_   4. _girl_   7. _man_

2. _boy_   5. _woman_   8. _men_

3. _family_   6. _children_   9. _people_

184

Words About the Human Body

Directions: The letters in each word are mixed up. Unscramble the letters and write each word about the human body correctly. Use the Word Bank to help you.

Word Bank

stomach	ears	skin	heart
fingers	skeleton	ankle	bones

1. ntloesek _skeleton_
2. sringef _fingers_
3. sear _ears_
4. snobe _bones_
5. tareh _heart_
6. nisk _skin_
7. lenka _ankle_
8. homcsat _stomach_

185

Words About the Human Body

Directions: Draw a line to match each word about the human body to its description on the right.

1. bones — This tells your body what to do.
2. lungs — You speak with this.
3. heart — This holds your head up.
4. mouth — It carries oxygen to your body.
5. neck — This helps you bend your arm.
6. brain — You use these to breathe.
7. elbow — These support and shape your body.
8. blood — It pumps blood.

186

333

Words About the Human Body

Word Bank

arms	chin	ears	eyes	feet
hand	legs	mouth	neck	nose

Directions: Draw a picture of yourself. Use the words in the Word Bank to label the parts of your body.

Pictures will vary.

187

Words About Weight

Ounces and **pounds** are measurements of weight. An ounce is used to measure the weight of very light objects. A pound is used to measure the weight of heavier objects.

Example:

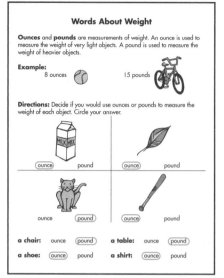

8 ounces   15 pounds

Directions: Decide if you would use ounces or pounds to measure the weight of each object. Circle your answer.

(ounce)   pound   (ounce)   pound

ounce   (pound)   (ounce)   pound

a chair: ounce   (pound)   **a table:**   ounce   (pound)

a shoe: (ounce)   pound   **a shirt:**   (ounce)   pound

188

Compound Words

Directions: Look at the words below the pictures. Put the words together to make compound words. Write the new words on the lines. The first one is done for you.

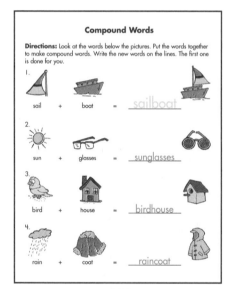

1. sail + boat = <u>sailboat</u>

2. sun + glasses = <u>sunglasses</u>

3. bird + house = <u>birdhouse</u>

4. rain + coat = <u>raincoat</u>

189

Compound Words

Directions: Use words from the Word Bank to write the compound word that matches each description.

Word Bank

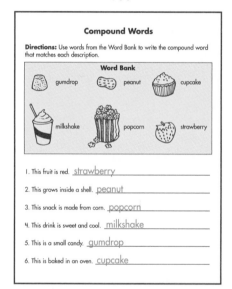

gumdrop   peanut   cupcake

milkshake   popcorn   strawberry

1. This fruit is red. <u>strawberry</u>

2. This grows inside a shell. <u>peanut</u>

3. This snack is made from corn. <u>popcorn</u>

4. This drink is sweet and cool. <u>milkshake</u>

5. This is a small candy. <u>gumdrop</u>

6. This is baked in an oven. <u>cupcake</u>

190

Compound Words

Directions: Find the two words that make up each animal's name. Write them on the lines.

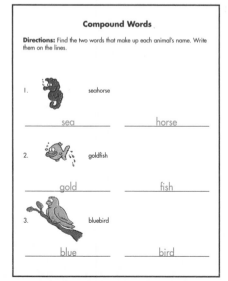

1. seahorse

<u>sea</u>   <u>horse</u>

2. goldfish

<u>gold</u>   <u>fish</u>

3. bluebird

<u>blue</u>   <u>bird</u>

191

People Words

Directions: Write a people word on the line to complete each sentence.

Suggested answers:

1. The <u>woman</u> rang up the girl's groceries.

2. The <u>boy</u> surprised his friend with a gift.

3. The <u>man</u> announced that dinner was ready.

4. The <u>woman</u> helped her son build a snowman.

192

Words About the Human Body

Directions: Draw a line to match the sense to the body part that works with it.

taste — tongue
smell — nose
sight — eyes
hearing — ears
touch — skin

Directions: List three of your favorites for each sense. An example is given.

Taste — _pretzel_ _Answers will vary._

Smell — _baking cookies_

Sight — _Mom_

Hearing — _barking dog_

Touch — _cold snow_

193

Words About the Human Body

Directions: Draw a line from each word to where it is on the body. Then, circle the words in the puzzle. Look across and down.

head   neck
chest   elbow
waist   knee
ankle   heel

```
T T E H E A D K
N A L N E C K H
F N B N R H R E
K O K N E E E E
Y L W A I S T L
Z E L D Y T Q F
```

194

Words About the Human Body

Directions: Find and circle seven words about the human body. Look across and down. Then, write the words on the lines.

```
a r m s y u h n
l g d r n m s b
e l b o w k l l
g a a k r e k s
z q c n e c k c
c e k e y e s a
p s d e b j p o
```

1. _arms_   5. _leg_
2. _elbow_   6. _back_
3. _neck_   7. _knee_
4. _eyes_

195

Words About Volume

Directions: Read about volume. Then, answer the questions.

Volume tells how much a container can hold. You can measure volume in many ways. One **cup** holds 8 ounces. One **pint** holds 2 cups. One **quart** holds 2 pints. One **gallon** holds 4 quarts.

8 ounces = 1 cup	2 pints = 1 quart
2 cups = 1 pint	4 quarts = 1 gallon

1. You should drink 8 cups of water a day. This keeps you healthy. How many quarts is this?
   a. 4 quarts
   b. 2 quarts
   c. 1 quart

2. Mary has had 2 pints of water today. How many more cups does she need to stay healthy? _4_

3. The school orders 10 gallons of milk a day. This is the same as _80_ pints.

4. A teacher buys 1 gallon of juice. The students drink 2 quarts. How many quarts are left? _2_

196

Compound Words

Directions: Draw a line to separate the compound words into two words. Then, write a sentence using the compound word. The first one is done for you.

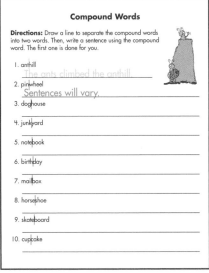

1. ant|hill
   The ants climbed the anthill.
2. pin|wheel
   Sentences will vary.
3. dog|house
4. junk|yard
5. note|book
6. birth|day
7. mail|box
8. horse|shoe
9. skate|board
10. cup|cake

197

Compound Words

Directions: Join words from the first column with words from the second column to make compound words. Then, write the new words on the lines.

grand — mother
snow — ball
eye — brows
down — stairs
rose — bud
shoe — string
note — book
moon — light

1. _grandmother_   5. _rosebud_
2. _snowball_   6. _shoestring_
3. _eyebrows_   7. _notebook_
4. _downstairs_   8. _moonlight_

198

Compound Words

Directions: Draw a line under the compound word in each sentence. Write the two words on the line that make up the compound word.

1. A firetruck came to help put out the fire.
   fire , truck

2. I will be nine years old on my next birthday.
   birth , day

3. We built a treehouse at the back.
   tree , house

4. Dad put a scarecrow in his garden.
   scare , crow

5. It is fun to make footprints in the snow.
   foot , prints

6. I like to read the comics in the newspaper.
   news , paper

7. Cowboys ride horses and use lassos.
   cow , boys

199

People Words

Directions: Write a sentence using each of the people words.

1. Sentences will vary.

   children

2. _____

   girl

3. _____

   boy

4. _____

   baby

200

Words About the Human Body

Directions: Use the Word Bank to write the name of each bone on the correct line.

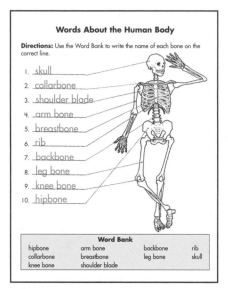

1. skull
2. collarbone
3. shoulder blade
4. arm bone
5. breastbone
6. rib
7. backbone
8. leg bone
9. knee bone
10. hipbone

Word Bank			
hipbone	arm bone	backbone	rib
collarbone	breastbone	leg bone	skull
knee bone	shoulder blade		

201

Words About the Human Body

Directions: Find and circle the words in the puzzle about the human body. Look across and down.

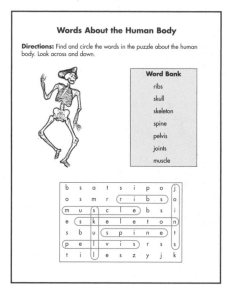

Word Bank
ribs
skull
skeleton
spine
pelvis
joints
muscle

b	s	a	t	s	i	p	o	j
o	s	m	r	r	i	b	s	o
m	u	s	c	l	e	b	s	i
e	s	k	e	l	e	t	o	n
s	b	u	s	p	i	n	e	s
p	e	l	v	i	s	r	s	s
t	i	l	e	s	z	y	j	k

202

Words About the Human Body

Directions: Read about some of the major bones in your body. Then, draw a line from each bone to the part of the body where it is found.

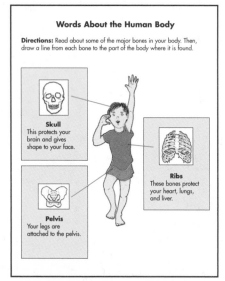

Skull
This protects your brain and gives shape to your face.

Ribs
These bones protect your heart, lungs, and liver.

Pelvis
Your legs are attached to the pelvis.

203

Unit 8 Review

Directions: Circle the compound word in each row.

1. collarbone   ribs   skull
2. jacket   mittens   snowman
3. pelvis   backbone   knee
4. bedtime   pillow   blanket
5. recess   eraser   chalkboard

Directions: Write a sentence for each of the people word pairs.

1. boy/man
   Sentences will vary.

2. girl/woman

3. family/children

204

Words That Are Homophones

Homophones are words that sound the same but have different spellings and meanings. **Toe** and **tow** are homophones. So are **ate** and **eight**.

Directions: Write the word from the Word Bank next to its picture.

Word Bank			
so	see	blew	pear

1. 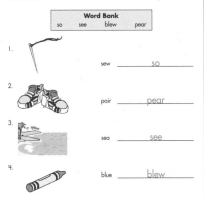 sew _____so_____

2. pair _____pear_____

3. sea _____see_____

4. blue _____blew_____

206

Words That Are Homophones

Directions: Read each word. Circle the picture that goes with the word.

1. sun

4. hi

2. ate

5. four

3. buy

6. hear

207

Words That Are Homophones

Directions: Read the sentences. The bold words are homophones. Follow the directions to decorate a special birthday cake.

1. The baker **read** a recipe to bake a doggy cake. Color the plate he put it on **red**.

2. Draw a **hole** in the middle of the doggy cake. Then, color the **whole** cake yellow.

3. Look **for** the top of the doggy cake. Draw **four** candles there.

4. In the hole, draw what you think the doggy would really like.

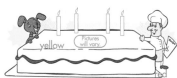
yellow   Pictures will vary.

5. Write a sentence using the words **hole** and **whole**.
   Sentences will vary.

6. Write a sentence using the words **read** and **red**.
   Sentences will vary.

208

Words About the Lincoln Memorial

Directions: Read about the Lincoln Memorial. Then, fill in the circle beside the answer that best completes each sentence.

The **Lincoln Memorial** honors Abraham Lincoln, our 16th president. Lincoln believed that all people were created equal. The memorial symbolizes this belief. Inside are two murals which represent freedom, brotherhood, unity, and charity. The building is surrounded by 36 columns. They represent the 36 states in the Union at the time of Lincoln's death. Many people visit this famous memorial in Washington, D.C.

1. The Lincoln Memorial honors
   - (A) Lincoln, Nebraska.
   - **(B)** Abraham Lincoln.
   - (C) freedom.

2. The columns represent
   - **(A)** states of the Union.
   - (B) justice.
   - (C) strength.

3. The Memorial is in
   - (A) Lincoln, Nebraska.
   - (B) Springfield, Illinois.
   - **(C)** Washington, D.C.

4. Abraham Lincoln was our
   - (A) king.
   - **(B)** president.
   - (C) brother.

209

Words About Senses

hear   smell   taste   see   feel

Directions: Read each sentence. Then, write which sense would be used for each one.

1. Andrew reads his book.   see
2. Juicy red apples are delicious.   taste
3. We knew a skunk was nearby.   smell
4. I couldn't find my backpack.   see
5. The dog's bark kept us awake.   hear
6. We ate brownies for dessert.   taste
7. I like to listen to music.   hear
8. Jon built a model airplane.   feel
9. The odor from his sneakers was strong.   smell
10. She tapped her friend on the shoulder.   feel

210

Words About Senses

Directions: Color the pictures. Then, cut out the flowers at the bottom of the page. Pick one flower and look at the object word on it. Glue the flower on the vase that tells which sense you would mainly use with the object on that flower.

Color the pictures.

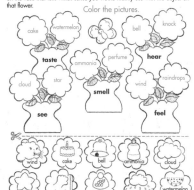

cake   watermelon   bell   knock
taste   ammonia   perfume   **hear**
cloud   star   wind   raindrops
smell
see   **feel**

wind   cake   bell   ammonia   cloud
star   knock   perfume   raindrops   watermelon

211

Shape Words

Directions: Use the words in the Word Bank to complete the puzzle about shapes.

Word Bank			
rectangle	circle	cube	diamond
sphere	triangle	cone	prism
cylinder	oval	square	

Across
1. A ball is this shape.
2. A three-dimensional shape with 6 sides that are all square.
4. A shape with no corners.
6. A party hat is this shape.
7. A shape with 3 sides and 3 corners.
8. A kite is this shape.
9. A rectangle box shape.

Down
1. A shape with 4 sides and 4 corners that are all the same.
3. A shape with 4 sides and 4 corners, 2 sides are long and 2 sides are short.
5. A round shape that is stretched out in the middle.
6. A soup can is this shape.

Crossword answers: sphere, cube, circle, cone, triangle, diamond, prism

213

Words That Are Homophones

Homophones are words that sound the same but have different spellings and meanings.

Examples: Pear and **pair** are homophones.
To, **too**, and **two** are three homophones.

Directions: Draw a line from each word on the left to its homophone on the right.

blue	knight
night	too
beet	blew
write	see
hi	meet
two	son
meat	bee
sea	high
be	right
sun	beat

214

Words That Are Homophones

Directions: Read each sentence. Then, write the correct word on the line. The first one is done for you.

1. **blue blew**   She has ___blue___ eyes.
   The wind ___blew___ the barn down.

2. **eye I**   He hurt his left ___eye___ playing ball.
   ___I___ like to learn new things.

3. **see sea**   Can you ___see___ the winner from here?
   He goes diving for pearls under the ___sea___ .

4. **eight ate**   The baby ___ate___ the banana.
   Jane was ___eight___ years old last year.

5. **one won**   Jill ___won___ first prize at the science fair.
   I am the only ___one___ in my family with red hair.

6. **be bee**   Jenny cried when a ___bee___ stung her.
   I have to ___be___ in bed every night at eight o'clock.

7. **two to too**   My father likes ___to___ play tennis.
   I like to play, ___too___ .
   It takes at least ___two___ people to play.

215

Words That Are Homophones

Directions: Fill in the circle beside the word that names each picture.

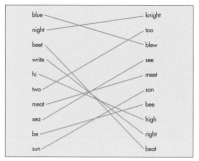

1. ○ son ● sun
2. ● flower ○ flour
3. ○ too ● two
4. ● road ○ rode
5. ○ bare ● bear
6. ● wheel ○ we'll
7. ○ knows ● nose
8. ○ pale ● pail
9. ○ rose ○ rows

216

Words About the Statue of Liberty

Directions: Read about the Statue of Liberty. Then, read each sentence below. If the sentence is true, put a **T** on the line. If it is false, put an **F** on the line.

The **Statue of Liberty** is a symbol of the United States. It stands for freedom. The Statue of Liberty is located on an island in New York Harbor. It is the tallest statue in the United States.

The statue is of a woman wearing a robe. She is holding a torch in her right hand. She is holding a book in her left hand. She is wearing a crown. The Statue of Liberty was a gift from the country of France.

Each year, people come from all over the world to visit the statue. Not only do they look at it, they can also go inside the statue. At one time, visitors could go all the way up into the arm. In 1916, the arm was closed to visitors because it was too dangerous.

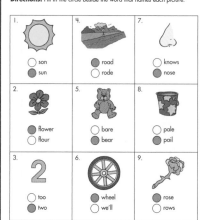

__T__ 1. The Statue of Liberty is a symbol of the United States.

__F__ 2. People cannot go inside the statue.

__F__ 3. The statue was a gift from Mexico.

__T__ 4. People used to be able to climb up into the statue's arm.

__F__ 5. It is a very short statue.

__T__ 6. The woman statue has a torch in her right hand.

__T__ 7. People come from all over to see the statue.

217

Feeling Words

Directions: Use the Word Bank to find and circle the feeling words in the puzzle. Look across and down.

Word Bank						
angry	happy	sick	friendly	mad	silly	tired
funny	sad	sleepy	worried	glad	safe	smart

218

Feeling Words

Directions: Read the feeling words next to each picture. Choose the one that best describes how each person might be feeling. Write a sentence for each picture.

Example:

sick / tired / happy — The girl _is happy._

content / angry / sleepy — 1. The lady _is content._

funny / tired / glad — 2. The man _is tired._

hungry / sleepy / sad — 3. The boy _is hungry._

219

Feeling Words

Directions: Write a sentence for each feeling word in the Word Bank.

Word Bank			
surprised	happy	sad	angry
excited	shy	scared	sorry

Sentences will vary.

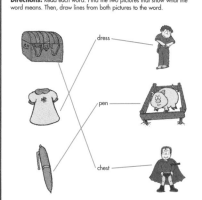

220

Shape Words

Directions: Find the shapes that are in the picture. Use the clues to find the shapes that are described.

1. Color the shapes blue that have 4 sides and 4 corners that are all the same.
2. Color the shapes red that have no corners and are ball-shaped.
3. Color the shapes yellow that have 4 sides and 4 corners, but the angles are not the same.
4. Color the shapes green that have 4 sides. Two of the sides are long and 2 are short.
5. Color the three-dimensional shapes orange that have 6 sides and each side is a square.
6. Color the shapes purple that are round and the middles are stretched out.

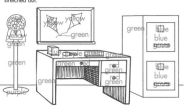

221

Words That Are Homonyms

Homonyms are words that are spelled and pronounced the same but have different meanings.

Directions: Read each word. Find the two pictures that show what the word means. Then, draw lines from both pictures to the word.

dress

pen

chest

222

Words That Are Homophones

Directions: Use the words in the Word Bank to complete the puzzle about homophones.

Word Bank	
see	knew
sea	right
one	write
won	meet
new	meat

Across
2. _____, two, three
5. We _____ the game!
6. You do this with your eyes.
7. You do this with your pencil.
10. People eat this.

Down
1. Not old
3. I _____ you would like this.
4. We will _____ at 8:00.
8. Not left
9. Smaller than an ocean

223

Words That Are Homophones

Directions: Use the words in the Word Bank to complete the puzzle about homophones.

Word Bank	
blew	right
blue	write
too	be
two	bee
to	
sun	
son	

Across
1. Julia _____ out the candles.
4. Three days ago, she was stung by a _____ .
5. After _____ days she felt better.
Down
1. She has on _____ shoes for her party.
2. She will _____ a letter to her grandma.
3. Julia is a girl, so she is not her mother's _____ .

224

Words About Landmarks

The United States has many historical landmarks. One of these landmarks is the **Golden Gate Bridge**, built in 1937. Stretching 1.7 miles, it is a symbol of San Francisco. Beneath the bridge, the San Francisco Bay and Pacific Ocean connect. People can cross the bridge by car, bicycle, or foot. It is painted bright orange so it can be seen in the fog.

Directions: Pretend you just visited the Golden Gate Bridge. Write a note telling your friend about it. Write your message on the left side. Write your friend's name and address on the right side.

VISIT
San Francisco

Answers will vary

Golden Gate Bridge • San Francisco, California

225

Feeling Words

Directions: Read the story. Then, fill in the circle beside the phrase that completes each sentence.

It is a rainy day. Mom tells Tosh to stay inside until the weather clears up. Tosh lies on his bed and pouts. Now and then, he checks to see if the rain has stopped.

1. Tosh probably wants to
   - ● go outside and play.
   - ○ lie in bed all day.

2. Tosh probably feels
   - ○ happy.
   - ● bored and grumpy.

3. When it stops raining, Tosh will probably feel
   - ○ angry.
   - ● glad.

226

Feeling Words

Word Bank

annoyed	angry	proud
sleepy	bored	confused

Directions: Complete each sentence with a word from the Word Bank.

1. The alarm went off too early. I am still __sleepy__ .

2. I am so __proud__ of winning the spelling bee.

3. I am __confused__ . What did you say your name was?

4. I am __annoyed__ that you tore up the newspaper, Rex!

5. I can't play outside, so I am __bored__ .

6. I am __angry__ that a gopher ate all my plants!

227

Feeling Words

Directions: Use feeling words to complete each sentence.

1. When I spend time with my friends, I feel __Words will__ .
2. When I don't do something well, I feel __vary.__ .
3. When I get a good grade, I feel _____ .
4. When my friend and I fight, I feel _____ .

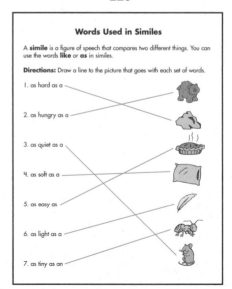

228

Unit 9 Review

Directions: Draw a picture of a robot using the shapes in the Word Bank. Label the parts of your robot.

Word Bank

rectangle	triangle	square	oval	circle	diamond

Pictures will vary.

Directions: Circle the correct word that completes each sentence. Then, write it on the line.

1. I __ate__ spaghetti for dinner.
   eight (ate)
2. I __hear__ my mom calling me.
   here (hear)
3. The monkey climbs __high__ up in the tree.
   (high) hi
4. She likes to __sew__ her own clothes.
   so (sew)

229

Words Used in Similes

A **simile** is a figure of speech that compares two different things. You can use the words **like** or **as** in similes.

Directions: Draw a line to the picture that goes with each set of words.

1. as hard as a
2. as hungry as a
3. as quiet as a
4. as soft as a
5. as easy as
6. as light as a
7. as tiny as an

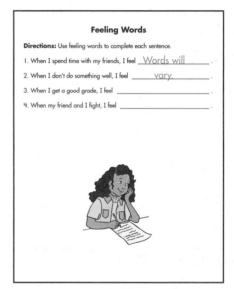

231

Words That Compare

Words that end in **-er** compare two things. Words that end in **-est** compare more than two things.

Directions: Read each sentence. Circle the correct word that describes how each plant has grown.

1. A sunflower grew 3 inches. A daisy grew 2 inches. The sunflower is _____ than the daisy.
   a. shorter   (b. taller)

2. Tomato plant A grew up 2 inches. Tomato plant B grew up 1 inch. Tomato plant A is _____ than tomato plant B.
   a. smaller   (b. taller)

3. The students cut the grass around the garden. They let the grass behind the school and in the playground grow. The grass around the garden is the _____.
   (a. shortest)   b. tallest

4. A student weighed a carrot from the garden. It weighs 3 pounds. A cucumber from the same garden weighs 2 pounds. The carrot is _____ than the cucumber.
   a. lighter   (b. heavier)

232

Words That Compare

Directions: Write the correct words on the lines to complete the chart.

	Word	-er compares two	-est compares more than two
1.	tall	taller	tallest
2.	fast	faster	fastest
3.	light	lighter	lightest
4.	strong	stronger	strongest
5.	big	bigger	biggest

Directions: Using the chart, write the correct comparison word on the line to complete each sentence.
Suggested answers:
6. That tree is __taller__ than the bush.

   The tree is the __tallest__ one in the forest.

7. His car is the __fastest__ in the race.

   Dad's car is __faster__ than my bike.

8. The feather is the __lightest__ item in the box.

   A feather is __lighter__ than a pencil.

233

Transportation Words

Directions: Look at the numbered pictures. Write the numbers of the pictures beside each question. There may be more than one correct answer for each question.

What can carry more than one person?	1, 2, 3, 4, 5, 6, 7, 8, 11
What moves on wheels?	2, 3, 4, 6, 7, 9, 10, 12
What moves on just two wheels?	3, 9
What makes a very loud noise?	1, 2, 3, 4, 7, 8, 12
What moves through water?	1, 11
What has a motor to make it run?	1, 2, 3, 4, 5, 7, 8, 12
What can hold large, heavy objects?	1, 2, 4, 5
What can travel very fast?	2, 3, 4, 5, 7, 8
What has to be pushed or pulled?	6, 9, 10, 11

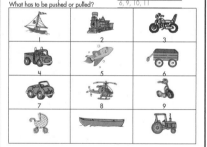

234

Words About Matter

All things are made of matter. Matter takes up space. It can take three forms: solid, liquid, or gas.

Solids have shape and volume. They do not change shape easily.

Liquids have volume, but they have no shape of their own. They take the shape of the container they are in.

Gases have no shape or volume. Most gases are invisible.

Directions: Find and circle the words in each word search that are examples of each kind of matter. Look across, down, and diagonally. Then, write the words on the lines.

SOLIDS
table
rat
bee
leaf
rope
tie
trees

LIQUIDS
pop
cola
juice
water
oil
milk

GASES
oxygen
helium
air
ether

235

Words About Matter

Directions: Water is a type of matter. Water turns into a solid at a temperature of 32°F. This is called the freezing point. Does all water freeze at 32°F? Do the experiment to find out.

You will need:
   2 small paper cups
   4 teaspoons salt
   water
   marking pen
   freezer

1. Fill both cups with water.

2. Mix 4 teaspoons of salt in one of the cups. Write **salt** on that cup.

3. Put both cups in the freezer. Check on them every hour for four hours.

I found out . . .
the cup of plain water __Answers will vary.__

the cup of salt water _____

What happened?

When the temperature of water gets very cold, the particles of water hook together to make ice crystals. Salt gets in the way of this process, and an even lower temperature is needed before ice crystals will form.

236

Words About Matter

Directions: Follow the instructions to mix a solid and a liquid to make clay.

Ingredients:
   1 cup salt
   2 cups flour
   3/4 cup water

Mix the salt and flour. Then, add the water. DO NOT eat the clay. Use your hands to mix the clay. Now, roll it out. What can you make with your clay?

1. Circle the main idea:
   Do not eat the clay.
   (Mix a solid and a liquid to make clay.)

2. What is the liquid ingredient in the clay? __water__

3. Is the clay a solid or a liquid? __solid__

237

Map Words

Directions: Look at the map. Pretend you are standing in the town square. Circle the correct letter to answer each question.

1. What direction is the library from you?
   a. North
   b. West
   c. South

2. What direction must you go to reach the post office?
   a. East
   b. North
   c. West

3. Which direction must you go to get to the park?
   a. North
   b. West
   c. East

4. You are standing at the school facing the post office. Which direction must you turn to get to the lake?
   a. right
   b. left

5. Draw a bus in the street south of the school.

6. Draw a tree in the middle of the park.

238

Words Used in Similes

Directions: Look at each picture. Write a sentence that uses a simile. Use the word under the picture.

Example:

cold — My hands are as cold as ice.

1. hard — _Sentences will vary._

2. slow

3. soft

4. happy

239

Words That Compare

The suffixes **-er** and **-est** can be used to compare. Use **-er** when you compare two things. Use **-est** when you compare more than two things.

Examples: The puppy is **smaller** than its mom.
This puppy is the **smallest** puppy in the litter.

Directions: Complete each sentence using a word that compares. Add **-er** or **-est** to the base word under each line.

Base Word

1. The dog is _louder_ than the puppy.
   loud

2. The tan puppy is the _oldest_ in the litter.
   old

3. I think cats are _neater_ than dogs.
   neat

4. You can run _faster_ than my dog.
   fast

5. Those are the _kindest_ words I have ever heard.
   kind

6. You are _taller_ than your brother.
   tall

240

Words That Compare

Directions: Read each sentence. Choose the correct word. Then, write it on the line.

big
bigger
biggest

1. The town made the _biggest_ snowman on record.
2. Emmett made a _big_ snowman.
3. Sara helped him make it even _bigger_.

fast
faster
fastest

1. The snowman's head fell off and started to roll very _fast_.
2. It was the _fastest_ rolling snowball anyone had ever seen.
3. It rolled _faster_ than they could run.

white
whiter
whitest

1. As the snowball rolled closer, Mr. Wetzel's face became even _whiter_.
2. After it snowed all night, the town was the _whitest_ it had ever been.
3. Mr. Wetzel's face turned _white_ when he saw the snowball rolling toward his candy store.

241

Transportation Words

Directions: Read the descriptions in Column A. Choose a transportation word from Column B that matches each description. Then, write the number of the answer in the correct square. The first one is done for you.

Column A

A. Filled with helium
B. Runs on gasoline
C. Powered by wind
D. Burns coal or wood
E. Runs on nuclear energy
F. Moves on snow or ice
G. Moves by pedals
H. Powered by oars
I. Pulled by horses or oxen

Column B

1. rowboat
2. sailboat
3. steam locomotive
4. blimp
5. submarine
6. wagon
7. sled
8. bicycle
9. car

A	B	C
5	10	3
D	E	F
4	6	8
G	H	I
9	2	7

Add the numbers across, down, and diagonally. What answer do you get? _18_

242

342

Words About Matter

Directions: Read about rain. Then, follow the instructions.

Clouds are made up of little drops of ice and water. They push and bang into each other. Then, they join together to make bigger drops. More raindrops cling to them. They become heavy and fall quickly to the ground.

Write **first**, **second**, **third**, **fourth**, and **fifth** on the lines to put the events in order.

fourth — More raindrops cling to them.

first — Clouds are made up of little drops of ice and water.

third — They join together and make bigger drops that begin to fall.

second — The drops of ice and water bang into each other.

fifth — The drops become heavy and fall quickly to the ground.

243

Words About Matter

Directions: Water exists in three different forms: solid, liquid, and gas. Read the story. Then, find and circle the bold words in the puzzle. Look across, down, and diagonally.

Have you ever felt **grass** early in the **morning**? It feels very **wet**. The water is not rain. It is **dew**! When the sun rises in the morning, it warms the **air**. Some of the **water** in the **warm** air **evaporates**. It changes into a gas. These "floating" water **molecules** fall to the **cool** grass. The warm molecules land on the grass and become a **liquid** again. This is called **condensation**.

```
R  S  A  C  O  N  W  M  O  L  G  T  M
C  O  N  D  E  N  S  A  T  I  O  N  O
A  W  L  E  S  B  O  G  R  T  G  S  L
L  A  D  W  G  A  I  R  R  M  R  W  E
I  T  R  T  C  X  W  E  T  B  A  A  C
Q  E  V  A  P  O  R  A  T  E  S  L  U
U  R  M  O  R  S  O  D  X  R  S  B  L
I  U  L  J  G  C  H  L  D  C  F  N  E
D  S  M  O  R  N  I  N  G  E  S  R  S
```

244

Words About Matter

Directions: Answer the questions about these three modes of transportation.

blimp   **boat**   **bulldozer**

1. Which is filled with gas? <u>blimp</u>

2. Which floats on water? <u>boat</u>

3. Which moves solid matter from one place to another? <u>bulldozer</u>

4. Which floats in the air? <u>blimp</u>

5. Which moves on land? <u>bulldozer</u>

245

Words About Graphs

A **graph** has rows. A **row** goes across.

←———— **across** ————→

A **graph** also has columns. A **column** goes up and down.

up and down

This graph shows how many fish are at the pet store each week.

First Saturday	🐟	🐟	🐟			
Second Saturday	🐟	🐟	🐟	🐟	🐟	🐟
Third Saturday	🐟	🐟	🐟	🐟		
Fourth Saturday	🐟	🐟				

Directions: Color the fish at the store on the third Saturday **red**. Color the fish at the store on the first Saturday **blue**, the second Saturday **yellow**, and the fourth Saturday **green**. How many fish did the store have on the first Saturday? <u>3</u> second Saturday? <u>6</u> third Saturday? <u>4</u> fourth Saturday? <u>2</u>

246

Commonly Misused Words

The word **their** is the possessive form of **they**. In other words, it refers to something that belongs to **them**.

The word **there** means "at or in that place."

The word **they're** means "they are."

Examples: The kids hold **their** basketballs. Tim is looking over **there**. **They're** about to start playing.

Directions: Write **their**, **there**, or **they're** on each line to finish the sentence correctly.

1. Look over <u>there</u> !

2. The Smiths are having <u>their</u> yard sale.

3. <u>They're</u> selling a good bike.

4. I will ask my mom to go <u>there</u> .

247

Commonly Misused Words

Its is a pronoun. It means "belonging to it." It does not have an apostrophe.

Example: The elephant lifted **its** trunk.

It's is a contraction. It means "it is." It does have an apostrophe.

Example: **It's** fun to see the animals.

Directions: Write **its** or **it's** on each line to finish the sentence correctly.

1. The elephant did <u>its</u> best trick.

2. <u>It's</u> difficult to stand on that small box.

3. The lion swished <u>its</u> tail.

4. Don't worry. <u>It's</u> not a dangerous lion.

248

Commonly Misused Words

Your means "belonging to you." It does not have an apostrophe.

Example: I am **your** friend.

You're is a contraction. It means "you are." It does have an apostrophe.

Example: **You're** my best friend.

Directions: Write **your** or **you're** on each line to finish the sentence correctly.

1. We can sell lemonade at <u>your</u> house.

2. We'll use lemons from <u>your</u> tree.

3. It looks like <u>you're</u> having fun.

4. If <u>you're</u> thirsty, have some lemonade!

5. Let me fill <u>your</u> glass for you.

249

Transportation Words

Directions: Circle the correct answer that completes each sentence.

1. A large truck used for moving furniture is called a
   a. dump truck.
   b. van.
   c. pickup truck.

2. A large vehicle for transporting children to school is called a
   a. bus.
   b. yacht.
   c. jet.

3. A long line of boxcars that runs on a track is called a
   a. submarine.
   b. train.
   c. bicycle.

4. A vehicle that moves through water is called a
   a. ship.
   b. tank.
   c. sled.

5. A vehicle pulled by horses or oxen is called a
   a. hot air balloon.
   b. tricycle.
   c. wagon.

250

Words About Magnets

Every magnet has a north and a south **pole**. The north pole of one magnet attracts and pulls the south pole of another magnet. Two poles that are the same (two north poles or two south poles) do not attract each other. Instead, they push away from each other.

Directions: Using the information above, continue labeling the horseshoe and bar magnets below with **N** (for north) and **S** (for south). Then, color the magnets that are attracted to each other.

251

Words About Energy

Directions: Use the words in the Word Bank to write the sources of energy above the correct cauldron. Then, color the pictures.

Word Bank		
lamp	alarm	camp stove
candle	furnace	curling iron
trumpet	buzzer	flashlight

camp stove
furnace
curling iron

heat

Color the pictures.

trumpet
alarm
buzzer

sound

lamp
candle
flashlight

light

252

Words About Energy

Directions: Read about energy. Then, find and circle the bold words in the puzzle. Look across, down, and diagonally.

When **rays** of **sun** hit the earth, the earth absorbs or reflects the heat. Darker surfaces absorb the **radiation**. Lighter surfaces **reflect** the radiation. That is why you feel cooler when you wear light-colored clothing in the **summer**.

r	r	u	a	p	t	n	d	s	s
s	h	i	j	w	s	d	s	u	c
r	a	d	i	a	t	i	o	n	d
e	a	e	r	b	k	d	h	o	l
f	s	y	e	s	u	m	m	e	r
l	c	n	s	o	l	g	j	e	e
e	y	b	s	r	e	k	e	r	a
c	u	t	m	b	a	w	n	s	d
t	i	a	p	b	q	l	o	h	s

253

Unit 10 Review

Directions: Fill in the graph to show how many times during the week you used each mode of transportation.

	Sunday	Monday	Tuesday	Wednesday	Thursday	Friday	Saturday
bicycle	Graphs will vary.						
car							
bus							
scooter							
other?							

Directions: Write sentences using the words from the Word Bank.

Word Bank				
gas	its	lightest	magnets	north

Sentences will vary.

254

Words That Are Plural

Some words name only one person or thing, such as the word **ball**. Other words name more than one thing, such as the word **balls**.

Words that name more than one thing are called **plurals**. Plurals often are made by adding **-s** to the end of a word.

Directions: Write the plurals of each word. Then, draw a second item to make each picture plural.

1. jet _____ **jets**

2. doll _____ **dolls**

3. car _____ **cars**

4. game _____ **games**

5. duck _____ **ducks**

6. drum _____ **drums**

7. top _____ **tops**

8. horn _____ **horns**

256

Words That Are Plural

Directions: Write the words on the fish in the correct tank. Then, color the fish.

| kites | mitten | star | cats | bird | rocks | girls | lunch |

One   Color the fish.

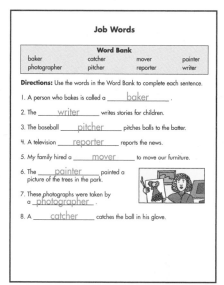

mitten   bird

star   lunch

More Than One (Plural)

kites   rocks

cats   girls

257

Words That Are Plural

Directions: Read the words in the Word Bank. If the word means **one**, write it on the paint jar. If the word means **more than one**, write it on the paintbrushes.

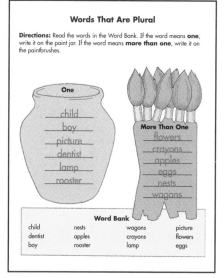

One

child
boy
picture
dentist
lamp
rooster

More Than One

flowers
crayons
apples
eggs
nests
wagons

Word Bank

child	nests	wagons	picture
dentist	apples	crayons	flowers
boy	rooster	lamp	eggs

258

Job Words

Word Bank

| baker | catcher | mover | painter |
| photographer | pitcher | reporter | writer |

Directions: Use the words in the Word Bank to complete each sentence.

1. A person who bakes is called a ____baker____ .

2. The ____writer____ writes stories for children.

3. The baseball ____pitcher____ pitches balls to the batter.

4. A television ____reporter____ reports the news.

5. My family hired a ____mover____ to move our furniture.

6. The ____painter____ painted a picture of the trees in the park.

7. These photographs were taken by a ____photographer____ .

8. A ____catcher____ catches the ball in his glove.

259

Words About Simple Machines

Simple machines are tools that make work easier. Simple machines help us lift, pull, split, fasten, and cut things. These machines use energy to work and have few or no moving parts. We use simple machines every day, such as when we open a door, turn on the water faucet, or open a can of soup.

Directions: Read the descriptions of the simple machines. Then, draw a line to match each description to the correct picture.

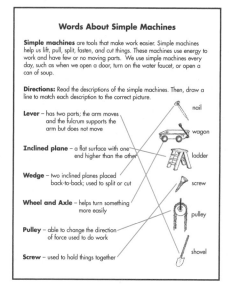

Lever – has two parts; the arm moves and the fulcrum supports the arm but does not move

Inclined plane – a flat surface with one end higher than the other

Wedge – two inclined planes placed back-to-back; used to split or cut

Wheel and Axle – helps turn something more easily

Pulley – able to change the direction of force used to do work

Screw – used to hold things together

nail
wagon
ladder
screw
pulley
shovel

260

Words About Simple Machines

Directions: Use the words in the Word Bank to complete each sentence.

Word Bank

| inclined plane | wedge | lever |
| screw | wheel and axle | pulley |

1. A ramp is an _inclined plane_ .

2. A seesaw is an example of a ____lever____ .

3. A knife is a ____wedge____ .

4. The bottom of a light bulb is a ____screw____ .

5. A skateboard is an example of a _wheel and axle_.

6. A ____pulley____ is used to raise and lower a flag.

261

Words About Simple Machines

A **wedge** is a type of inclined plane. It is made up of two inclined planes joined together to make a sharp edge. A wedge can be used to cut things. Some wedges are pointed.

Directions: Color only the pictures of wedges.

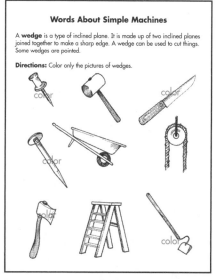

color   color

color

color

262

345

Words About Tangrams

Directions: Read about tangrams. Then, answer the questions.

A **tangram** is a set of seven shapes. The shapes can be put together to make a square. A tangram set has five triangles, one square, and one parallelogram. Each piece is called a **tan**.

This game is from China. People use the shapes to make pictures of animals. They make the animals while they tell stories. You can make a rabbit, a goose, a wolf, and even an alligator.

1. How many shapes are in a tangram set? __seven__

2. How many of the shapes are triangles? __five__

3. What other two shapes are in a tangram set?
   __square, parallelogram__

4. What is each piece of a tangram set called? __tan__

5. What country do tangrams come from? __China__

6. What are tangrams used to tell? __stories__

263

Words That Are Plural

A **plural** is a word that means more than one person or thing. Add **-s** or **-es** to the end of a word to make it plural.

Add **s** to these words.	Add **es** to words that end in **s**, **x**, **sh** or **ch**.
cup — cups	glass — glasses
sink — sinks	box — boxes
stove — stoves	dish — dishes
table — tables	bench — benches

Directions: Write a sentence using the plural of each word.
Sentences will vary but should include the words:

1. house __houses__

2. bush __bushes__

3. dress __dresses__

4. lamp __lamps__

264

Words That Are Plural

Directions: Read the story. Then, circle the correct word that completes each sentence.

Angela learned a lot about sharks when her class visited the city aquarium. She learned that sharks are fish. Some sharks are as big as an elephant, and some can fit into a small paper bag. Sharks have no bones. They have hundreds of teeth, and when they lose them, they grow new ones. They eat animals of any kind. Whale sharks are the largest of all fish.

1. Shark / (Sharks) are fish.

2. Sharks have no (bones) / bone.

3. They have hundreds of tooth / (teeth).

4. They eat animal / (animals) of any kind.

5. Sharks can be as big as an elephants / (elephant).

6. Others can fit into a paper bags / (bag).

265

Words That Are Plural

Some words have special plural forms.

Example: leaf — leaves

Directions: Read the words in the Word Bank. The words on the right are special plurals. Complete each sentence with one of these plurals.

Word Bank
tooth — teeth
child — children
foot — feet
mouse — mice
woman — women
man — men

1. I lost my two front __t e e t h__ !

2. My sister has two pet __m i c e__ .

3. My mother and her sister are nice __w o m e n__ .

4. The circus clown had big __f e e t__ .

5. The teacher played a game with the
   __c h i l d r e n__ .

6. Little boys grow up to be __m e n__ .

266

Job Words

Directions: Draw a line from each job in the circle to the person it names.

nurse
police officer
clerk
doctor
teacher
barber

267

Words About Simple Machines

A **lever** is a simple machine used to lift or move things. It has two parts. The **arm** is the part that moves. The **fulcrum** supports the arm but does not move.

Directions: Label the parts of this lever.

__arm__

__fulcrum__

Directions: The letters in each word are mixed up. Unscramble the letters to write the names of these kinds of levers.

rbowcra
__crowbar__

serlip
__pliers__

emrahm
__hammer__

ssorciss
__scissors__

268

346

Words About Simple Machines

Directions: Levers help make our work easier. Color all the levers. Then, find and circle their names in the puzzle. Look across and down.

color

color

color

c	a	n	o	p	e	n	e	r	a
r	s	d	d	l	j	k	l	m	n
o	h	s	c	i	s	s	o	r	s
w	v	h	b	e	z	x	c	a	w
b	t	o	b	r	o	o	m	k	l
a	d	v	n	s	u	k	f	s	w
r	u	e	h	a	m	m	e	r	g
w	f	l	h	g	f	a	d	s	v

color

color

color

color

269

Words About Simple Machines

An **inclined plane** has a slanted surface. It is used to move things from a low place to a high place. Some inclined planes are smooth. Others have steps.

Directions: Color the inclined planes in the picture.

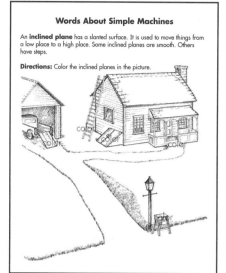

color

color

color

270

Shape Words

Directions: The objects on the left are CDs. Color the CDs. Then, draw a line from each CD to the case on the right that matches it. The shapes may be **tilted**, **flipped**, or **turned**.

Color the CDs.

1.
2.
3.
4.
5.

A.
B.
C.
D.
E.

271

Words That Are Plural

Directions: Read the sentences. Write the noun you find in each sentence. If it is a plural noun, circle it.

Example: _(socks)_ My socks do not match.

1. _(birds)_ The birds could not fly.
2. _(apples)_ Some apples are tart.
3. _mother_ My mother likes to cook.
4. _lake_ Swimming in the lake is fun.
5. _(flowers)_ The flowers grow quickly.
6. _(eggs)_ The eggs are colorfully decorated.
7. _bicycle_ It is easy to ride a bicycle.
8. _cousin_ My cousin is very tall.
9. _boy_ The boy went fishing.
10. _(parents)_ My parents went out to eat.
11. _ankle_ Her ankle is swollen.
12. _brother_ My brother was born today.
13. _slide_ The slide is steep.
14. _doctor_ The doctor was late.

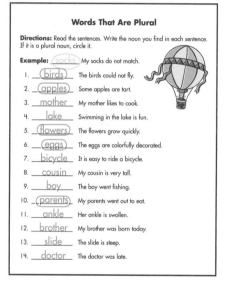

272

Words That Are Plural

To show more than one of something, add **-s** to most words.
Examples: one dog **two dogs**   one book **two books**

Some words are different. For words that end in **x**, use **-es** to show more than one.
Examples: one fox **two foxes**   one box **two boxes**

Some words become different words when they show more than one.
Example: one mouse **two mice**

Some words stay the same when they show more than one.
Examples: one deer **two deer**   one fish **two fish**

Directions: Write the word that names each picture to complete the sentences.

1. The ___ run fast.   _rabbits_

2. The ___ are eating.   _deer_

3. Have you seen any ___ today?   _bears_

4. Where do the ___ live?   _foxes_

5. Did you ever have ___ for pets?   _mice_

273

Words That Are Plural

Directions: Complete each line of the poem with plural words. Make sure each line of the poem rhymes!

Two little ___ _mice_
Ran around twice.

Then, two red ___ _foxes_
Jumped out of some boxes.

Last came two ___ _deer_ ,
What were they doing here?

The animals come until the day ends.
I welcome them, for they are my friends.

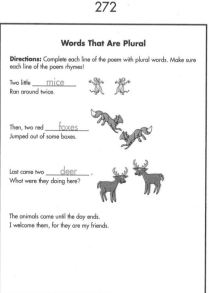

274

Job Words

Directions: What do you want to do when you grow up? Write about the job. Then, draw a picture of yourself doing the job.

Sentences will vary.

Pictures will vary.

275

Words About Simple Machines

Directions: Use the words in the Word Bank to write the name of the simple machine under each picture.

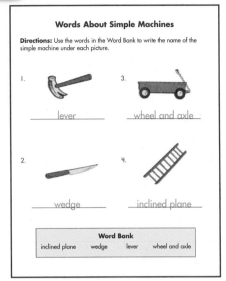

1. lever

3. wheel and axle

2. wedge

4. inclined plane

Word Bank

inclined plane   wedge   lever   wheel and axle

276

Words About Simple Machines

Directions: Read the sentences. Fill in the circle below the name of the simple machine that matches each description.

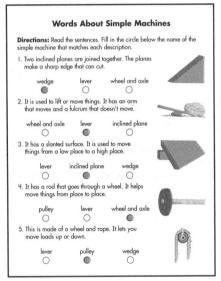

1. Two inclined planes are joined together. The planes make a sharp edge that can cut.

wedge ●   lever ○   wheel and axle ○

2. It is used to lift or move things. It has an arm that moves and a fulcrum that doesn't move.

wheel and axle ○   lever ●   inclined plane ○

3. It has a slanted surface. It is used to move things from a low place to a high place.

lever ○   inclined plane ●   wedge ○

4. It has a rod that goes through a wheel. It helps move things from place to place.

pulley ○   lever ○   wheel and axle ●

5. This is made of a wheel and rope. It lets you move loads up or down.

lever ○   pulley ●   wedge ○

277

Words About Simple Machines

Directions: This crossword puzzle has words for simple machines. Use the picture clues to help you fill in the squares.

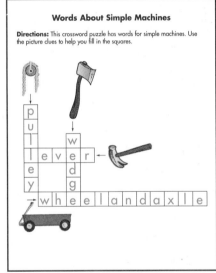

p
u
l   w
l e v e r ←
e   d
y   g
→ w h e e l a n d a x l e

278

Unit 11 Review

Directions: Write the plural of each word. Then, write a sentence using each plural.

1. drum _____ drums _____
   Sentences will vary.

2. box _____ boxes _____

3. machine _____ machines _____

4. house _____ houses _____

5. teacher _____ teachers _____

6. tooth _____ teeth _____

7. lever _____ levers _____

8. square _____ squares _____

279

Story Words

Fiction is a made-up story. **Nonfiction** is a true story.

Directions: Read the stories about two famous baseball players. Write **fiction** or **nonfiction** in the baseball bats.

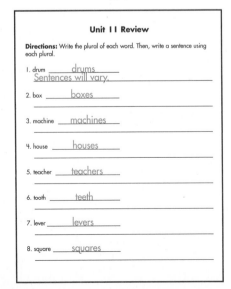

1. In 1998, Mark McGwire played for the St. Louis Cardinals. He liked to hit homeruns. On September 27, 1998, he hit home run number 70, to set a new record for the most home runs hit in one season. The old record was set in 1961 by Roger Maris, who later played for the St. Louis Cardinals (1967 to 1968), when he hit 61 home runs.

nonfiction

2. The Mighty Casey played baseball for the Mudville Nine and was the greatest of all baseball players. He could hit the cover off the ball with the power of a hurricane. But, when the Mudville Nine was behind 4 to 2 in the championship game, Mighty Casey struck out with the bases loaded. There was no joy in Mudville that day because the Mudville Nine had lost the game.

fiction

281